SITUATING
WRITING PROCESSES

PERSPECTIVES ON WRITING
Series Editors, Susan H. McLeod and Rich Rice

The Perspectives on Writing series addresses writing studies in a broad sense. Consistent with the wide ranging approaches characteristic of teaching and scholarship in writing across the curriculum, the series presents works that take divergent perspectives on working as a writer, teaching writing, administering writing programs, and studying writing in its various forms.

The WAC Clearinghouse, Colorado State University Open Press, and University Press of Colorado are collaborating so that these books will be widely available through free digital distribution and low-cost print editions. The publishers and the Series editors are committed to the principle that knowledge should freely circulate. We see the opportunities that new technologies have for further democratizing knowledge. And we see that to share the power of writing is to share the means for all to articulate their needs, interest, and learning into the great experiment of literacy.

Recent Books in the Series

Asao B. Inoue, *Labor-Based Grading Contracts: Building Equity and Inclusion in the Compassionate Writing Classroom* (2019)

Mark Sutton and Sally Chandler (Eds.), *The Writing Studio Sampler: Stories About Change* (2018)

Kristine L. Blair and Lee Nickoson (Eds.), *Composing Feminist Interventions: Activism, Engagement, Praxis* (2018)

Mya Poe, Asao B. Inoue, and Norbert Elliot (Eds.), *Writing Assessment, Social Justice, and the Advancement of Opportunity* (2018)

Patricia Portanova, J. Michael Rifenburg, and Duane Roen (Eds.), Contemporary Perspectives on Cognition and Writing (2017)

Douglas M. Walls and Stephanie Vie (Eds.), *Social Writing/Social Media: Publics, Presentations, and Pedagogies* (2017)

Laura R. Micciche, *Acknowledging Writing Partners* (2017)

Susan H. McLeod, Dave Stock, and Bradley T. Hughes (Eds.), *Two WPA Pioneers: Ednah Shepherd Thomas and Joyce Steward* (2017)

Seth Kahn, William B. Lalicker, and Amy Lynch-Biniek (Eds.), *Contingency, Exploitation, and Solidarity: Labor and Action in English Composition* (2017)

Barbara J. D'Angelo, Sandra Jamieson, Barry Maid, and Janice R. Walker (Eds.), *Information Literacy: Research and Collaboration across Disciplines* (2017)

SITUATING WRITING PROCESSES

By Hannah J. Rule

The WAC Clearinghouse
wac.colostate.edu
Fort Collins, Colorado

University Press of Colorado
upcolorado.com
Louisville, Colorado

The WAC Clearinghouse, Fort Collins, Colorado 80523

Printed for the WAC Clearinghouse by University Press of Colorado, Louisville, Colorado 80027

© 2019 by Hannah J. Rule. This work is licensed under a Creative Commons Attribution-Non-Commercial-NoDerivatives 4.0 International.

ISBN 978-1-64215-019-3 (PDF) | 978-1-64215-020-9 (ePub) | 978-1-60732-923-7 (pbk.)

Printed in the United States of America

Library of Congress Cataloging-in-Publication Data

Names: Rule, Hannah J., 1981– author.
Title: Situating writing processes / By Hannah J. Rule.
Description: Fort Collins, Colorado : The WAC Clearinghouse, [2019]
    | Series: Perspectives on writing | Includes bibliographical references.
Identifiers: LCCN 2019016589| ISBN 9781607329237 (pbk : alk. paper)
    | ISBN 9781642150209 (epub) | ISBN 9781642150193 (pdf)
Subjects: LCSH: English language—Composition and exercises—Study and
    teaching. | Composition (Language arts)—Study and teaching.
    | Authorship—Technique.
Classification: LCC LB1631 .R85 2019 | DDC 808/.0420712—dc23
LC record available at https://lccn.loc.gov/2019016589

Copyeditor: Don Donahue
Designer: Mike Palmquist
Series Editors: Susan H. McLeod and Rich Rice
Associate Editors: Heather MacNeill Falconer, Jonathan P. Hunt, and J. Michael Rifenburg
Cover Image: Justin Lincoln, "pseudoTrees-00342," modified by Hannah J. Rule and used under
a Creative Commons Attribution-ShareAlike 2.0 Generic (CC BY-SA 2.0) license.

This book is printed on acid-free paper.

The WAC Clearinghouse supports teachers of writing across the disciplines. Hosted by Colorado
State University, and supported by the Colorado State University Open Press, it brings together
scholarly journals and book series as well as resources for teachers who use writing in their courses.
This book is available in digital formats for free download at wac.colostate.edu.

Founded in 1965, the University Press of Colorado is a nonprofit cooperative publishing enterprise supported, in part, by Adams State University, Colorado State University, Fort Lewis College, Metropolitan State University of Denver, Regis University, University of Colorado, Universi-
ty of Northern Colorado, Utah State University, and Western State Colorado University. For more
information, visit upcolorado.com. The Press partners with the Clearinghouse to make its books
available in print.

CONTENTS

PREFACE

This book chases after writing processes—what they look like, where they live, how they elude us, what we assume about them. We're accustomed to thinking of them as a writer's own. But whose are they, really? The infinite processes and scenes and moments that coalesce in and around this book are not really mine alone. I know that for sure. It was never just me, but rather the many *wheres,* with *whats,* and with and for *whoms* that I've worked and studied and taught over the years that find their ways in to these pages.

Figure 1. Me, first thinking about situating writing processes,
May 22, 2011. Photo credit: Laura Micciche.

This project began in earnest in 2011. It began with a presentation in which I believe I asked some grad school friends to photograph their writing spaces and talk with me about them. Before that, I was inspired by Joe Harris, who while giving a talk at the University of Cincinnati on his great book, *Rewriting: How to do Things with Texts,* shared an image of his office. If my memory is right, he talked how that space—though it looked lonely, isolated, or disembodied—was actually teeming with *others,* populated by the partners that appear and do work with him in the form of sources. It started me thinking about the scale of process—about the local material environments in which processes unfold and also about those more amorphous process participants (sources, genres, rhetorical constraints, readers, discourse conventions, and so on) which both infiltrate and leap beyond the walls of any given writing room.

Before that, I credit my fascination with processes, especially as an avenue to composition histories, to Russel Durst, who helped me write about Janet Emig and wonder about postprocess. I thank Joyce Malek for all that she taught me about teaching and about honoring student writing. I am grateful to Julia Carlson, who worked with me to imagine my interests in Romanticism from a writing studies angle. I thank Jim Ridolfo for his tremendous knowledge of the field and invaluable and ongoing advice in navigating it. And to my dissertation director and friend, Laura Micciche, I extend infinite and ongoing gratitude for showing me how to teach, mentor, research, write, ask questions, and lead a balanced and rich academic life. Like many who know her, I want to be just like Laura when I grow up. She, and the rest of my doctoral committee—Russel, Jim, and Julia—ineluctably reflect in the writing, research, style, and aims of these pages. I was lucky to have had such stellar support in my graduate training, including from the Charles Phelps Taft Research Center, which supported my research with an enrichment grant and a 2012–2013 Dissertation Fellowship, and from the University of Cincinnati English department for the 2011 Pat Belanoff Summer Research Fellowship. I also thank the graduate student writers who participated in the multimodal case studies that formed the core of my dissertation. The details of that study may only pepper the periphery of this book, but what I took from peering into those writers' rooms and processes is very much at its core.

I wish also to warmly acknowledge my other teachers in the field, those who know me less or not really at all but nevertheless have gifted me their time, interest, and engagement that in different ways have helped shape this project: Andrea Lunsford, Nancy Sommers, Scott DeWitt, Kevin Roozen, Jody Shipka, Steve Parks, Jonathan Alexander, Amy Vidali, and many other anonymous reviewers. These connections, these interlocutors, have supported and challenged my thinking. I also want to thank my supportive department at the University of South Carolina, especially my chair, Nina Levine, for keeping me focused on the development of this project and my rhet/comp colleagues, Kevin Brock, Christy Friend, Chris Holcomb, Byron Hawk, and John Muckelbauer for their support, interest, and feedback. I also want to acknowledge the teachers and professors I've had through the years who ignited my interest in reading, words, writing processes, and working in academia: my third-grade teacher, Mrs. Waggoner, and her writer's workshop; Mrs. Francis, Mrs. Dunn, Mrs. Klein, Mrs. Dever; Bill Alberti, Allan Emery, Erin Labbie, and Steve Arch.

My thanks also go to Susan McLeod and Rich Rice, editors of the *Perspectives on Writing* Series, as well as my insightful reviewers. Their guidance has been invaluable in reshaping these pages into the form they are. Thanks too to Mike Palmquist of The WAC Clearinghouse and the editorial team there for their guidance in all production matters.

I want to also recognize the spaces through which this book, in its many versions, was forged—a graduate student computer lab, my dining table, a coffee shop that turned into a Starbucks, empty cubicles at the Langsford Center, Langsam Library, Thomas Cooper Library, Indah Coffee, Paneras, my orange arm chair, my first faculty office (one with my name on it), my current campus office, which I sometimes make into my writing "jail," and the constant accompaniment of background TV, especially those shows (cooking, remodeling, baking) where people successfully compose things in 60 minutes or less.

Huge gratitude and hugs go to OWG—my dear friends, my colleagues, my "open writing group." Allison Carr, Christina LaVecchia, Janine Morris, Katie Taylor: over the years, you've read many drafts, given me much feedback and support, and sat across from me for countless hours as we typed, sighed, laughed, and looked forward to knocking off our writing work and getting lunch. Though our sessions are fewer now and via video call (or in conference hotel rooms), you all are in this book. So too have other friends and now colleagues supported me in this project: Kelly Blewett, Carla Sarr (who supportively demanded that I make this work shine), Tessa Mellas, Ruth Williams.

I thank my family whose influence is here, too. My mother, Victoria, took me with her to college when I was a child, where I sat in her education classes and learned how cool a university campus was. When I was a bit older, her work as a children's librarian meant I spent tons of time on my own roaming the stacks. Without her and these scenes, I'm not sure I would have ended up a professor. I thank my Dad, Jan, who continues to believe so steadfastly in education and in teachers, but never became one himself. I thank him too for the electronic typewriter he bought me for a birthday. I'm grateful to my siblings, Ben and Elizabeth, who were among the first supporters of my writing. When they were at school and I was the youngest at home, I remember typing nonsense on an old typewriter in the living room. I made them "read" my work when they got home, and they laughed trying to sound-out the "words" and make meaning from my gibberish. They showed me clearly and early on how writing processes are never ours alone.

Finally, no writing is possible without my home, my family, my life—my husband Chris, Sammy, and all the guys. And our pup Del, who so far has been willing to demonstrate at least some modicum of patience for me to finish this book, waiting on my feet—just as he is right now—waiting for when I will close the laptop to take him on his walk. He's up and insisting now, pressing his head down on my keyboard. So, I better finish for now and go.

Figure 2. Me, with my electronic typewriter.

SITUATING
WRITING PROCESSES

INTRODUCTION
SEEING WRITING PROCESSES

"I have felt," Donald M. Murray writes in 1983, "writers should instead of public readings, give public workshops in which they write in public, allowing the search for meaning to be seen" (169). What Murray imagines here, it seems to me, is the virtues of writing in public, the value of freeing the writer from their cloisters. A writer's composing process, in other words, is a stage-worthy performance worth seeing.

Seeing writing processes unfold—this idea provokes. But rather than some kind of workshop, as Murray might imagine it, rather than a stage, a seated audience, a famous professional writer dramatizing their process and commenting upon what they're doing as they do it, I imagine something more candid. More than processes staged or dramatized, I want to see processes of all kinds, in the wild, *in situ*.

Maybe I could start with a big glass observation box, one that could enclose Murray and his writing space at home. We could peer through the glass to see him working, working the way Carol Berkenkotter remembers him in the summer of 1981 during the course of her 62-day study of his composing processes. "The clearest memory I have of Donald M. Murray," Berkenkotter recalls,

> is watching him writing at a long white wooden table in his
> study, which looks out on the New Hampshire woods. Beside
> his desk is a large framed poster of a small boy sitting on a bed
> staring at a huge dragon leaning over the railing glowering at
> him. The poster is captioned, "Donald imagined things." And
> so he did, as he addressed the problems writers face each time
> they confront a new assignment. (156)

But if we really wanted to make Murray's processes public in the way he muses about, if we aimed to make his search for meaning visible, my imagined glass looking box would have to be much bigger. It would have to fit much more than just Murray at his white wooden table. It would have to capture him, for one, in an unspecified room on Berkenkotter's campus engaged in a one-hour protocol where he was to write to a specified purpose, audience, and subject. As we peered through the glass, we might have seen Murray shift in his chair, sigh, stand, stretch, complain out loud, search the walls or out a window for a distraction. We might have seen the materials and ephemera he had before him, or the tools—pencil, paper, pen, notes, typewriter?—he was using. Or not using. Indeed, it is not clear if we would have seen Murray engaging in, as we conventionally picture it, a writing process in this room at all. As Murray reflects on his struggle to write on that day, during that hour, in that room, wherever it was and whatever it looked like: "The one-hour protocol was far worse than I had expected. . . . I have rarely felt so completely trapped and so inadequate. . . . That was nothing that the researcher did. It was a matter of the conditions" (Berkenkotter and Murray 169).

Under my giant imagined looking glass, I would want to see Murray everywhere he was—writing and not-writing and thinking and moving and capturing for Berkenkotter's study over 120 hours of audio recordings of himself describing his processes as he engaged them. I would want to see especially those matters of his environmental and material "conditions" and how they may have shaped and participated in the narratives Murray told about his writing during all those hours.

Making writing processes public—visible, really—in the way I am imagining, through an utterly sprawling observation glass, is obviously and utterly impossible. It would be impossible with these imaginary methods even to observe all the crannies and nooks of the processes of just *one* writer, like Donald Murray or any one of us. It would be impossible, in part, because writing processes move: processes range freely across spaces and times; they unfold in relation to things and places immediate, imagined, and recalled as they situate and resituate and meld with living. And making things more complicated still, I don't care to see just one single writer's processes. I want to see them all. I want to see the processes of the writer next to me at the café or the texter passing me on campus (I assume he was texting—but he well could have been emailing, tweeting, posting to discussion board, making a grocery list, or penning an essay for his composition or history course). I want to see the immeasurable *wheres* and *with whats* and *hows* that wind together to produce texts of all kinds. I want most to bring this glass looking box into my classrooms, to help writers wonder about, observe, describe, and consider processes across their and others' lives. And I don't want us to do this looking in order to come up with one final set of practices typical of processes or any one "big-T" Theory about how writing processes work. I want the looking instead to show us the all the many differences. I want us to see the details that demonstrate how writing processes are *always* and *differently* physically emplaced and context-contingent.

ANIMATING PURPOSE

As is surely now evident, I have an abiding fascination with composing processes, especially as lived experience. The tiny details of how writing gets made—how texts of all kinds come to be through pauses and in fits and starts, in coffee shops, on scrap paper, in email windows, through smart phones, by voice or through fingers, late at night, before or during a long shift at work, in one's car—for me is of unquenchable interest. But in the everyday, especially as writing teachers, we deal with writing almost exclusively in its noun form. While gestures to a "writing as noun/verb" binary is often associated with a research/ teaching split or a postprocess/process one (e.g., Shipka; Trimbur, "Changing"; Williams), it can be understood too to split process. Though the process movement supposedly liberated us from the flattened boundaries of the formalist page, we still engage process in classrooms today largely in artifactual, noun form: outlines, webs, freewriting, draft pages, track changes, portfolios, and so on. And as writing (n.) covers its tracks, the located physical labor of crafting texts—writing (v.)—recedes almost entirely from our view.

That is, what seems especially hidden is how writing processes *look*: how writing emerges through the cracks of living; how it is bodied and physical, populated and positional; how it is a matter always of its *conditions*—its places, tools, technologies, movements; how it is inhabited by bodies, by others present and by others who aren't yet there (those future readers in future contexts often unknown). These living dimensions—in short, that processes are *never not* physically, temporally, and materially located—recede further underground in the discourse and histories of processes in composition studies, as our field's stories have most emphasized processes as problem-solving, thinking, social inoculation or discourse approximation.

This book, in short, looks to fore that bodied underground of process. Countering the ways historically that process theories have seemed to overlook bodies and writing objects, I work in these pages toward *situating* writing processes. By situating, I first emphasize a baseline, though underconsidered, observation that writing processes can never be nowhere—processes only unfold through particular bodies; in specific locations, rooms, spaces, or places; with varying tools, objects, and ambient artifacts; and with others near and distant. Processes, in other words, are always already and chiefly *physical* (engaged by specific writers' specific bodies in specific times and places) and *material* (both entwined and made with physical objects). Processes too are *located*—not just staged in a place (though that observation too has been mostly sidelined in our process thinking) but of particular and infinite places, positions, rooms. This located physical *experience* of processes, I contend, has lived on the edges of process theories and practice. This book moves to shift those edges to the center.

Second, by situating, I mean to signal a shift in how we engage in process teaching with student writers. Rather than teaching process as drafts or *a priori* strategies, I argue for teaching process as a habit of locating the physical dynamics of students' own and others' specific writing acts. Writers benefit, I suggest, from developing curious inquiry toward the unique *wheres* and *with whats* of processes, those forces like time, affect, movement, technology, others, interruptions, objects, digital tools, and other local intimacies. Such detailed looking lays bare the susceptibilities of writing and, as a result, how much more than just writers alone participate in and shape processes in the world. This looking shows too how radically *different*, rather than reliably the same, processes are. As such, I argue, physically situating processes serves as a dynamic inroad toward responding to writing's differences on bigger, more conceptual scales—differences in discourse, community, culture, kairos, genre, audience, exigence, and many other expansive and local situated forces that constrain writing activity. By situating processes then, I shift what processes signal in writing pedagogies. Broadly, I prod process teaching from loose prescriptivism to detailed descriptivism. If traditional teaching process has been about writing routine, sameness, or strategy, situating processes instead emphasizes difference, responsivity, and improvisation.

From another angle, perhaps one more artful and certainly more imagistic, this book is an attempt to realize those glass looking boxes. It is about seeing located writing processes unfold (and about the partialities of that looking). It is about the disciplinary histories and theoretical stories we have told about writing processes and how those stories' assumptions leave their imprints on our classrooms today. It is about enacting processes in our teaching less as serial drafts alone and more as embodied *doing* in specific fluctuating spaces. It is about how we—writers and teachers of writing—*picture* writing processes and about the value of differentiating, emplacing, and particularizing those images. This book aims to discover, theorize, and teach *with* writing processes as physically situated, and thus, improvisational.

ANIMATING EXIGENCIES

To write about composing processes today—in a precarious political and social moment; amidst ever-cresting tides of misinformation and information overload; when our disciplinary attentions have rightly expanded beyond college writing instruction alone—could well strike as conservative, out of fashion, or perhaps beside the point. But still, and to some extent because of the tremendous challenges in contemporary literacy instruction, it strikes me as a ripe moment for rethinking process. I see my project as driven by at least four related exigencies. First, I respond to the ways our research, pedagogical, and theoretical discourses can depict processes as disembodied and placeless, an anchorlessness I seek to shift. Second, I investigate the positioning of process in our pedagogical thinking today as somehow at once backgrounded, prominent, and dismissed. Third, I reckon with what it means for pedagogy and process to be now twenty or thirty years "postprocess." And lastly, I engage a broader pedagogical conundrum: the productively disruptive deconstruction of general writing skills instruction that resulted from acknowledgment that all writing acts are profoundly and differently situated. Overall, pedagogical questions of process, postprocess, and contemporary anxiety about what writing instruction can achieve come together to drive my work in this book. To establish the ground and contexts of these exigencies, I explore each in some detail below.

PROCESS AS DISEMBODIED AND PLACELESS

A central motivation for this book comes from the ways process has been constructed across composition's history and discourses. Processes have been many things in our disciplinary thinking—widely framed, reframed, and questioned. But rarely have they been considered in terms of corporeality and materiality. For some time and especially through discourses of disability studies, gender and sexuality studies, feminisms, embodied pedagogies, and affect theories, compositionists have in various ways made positionality, embodiment, and materiality a significant lens for understanding the work, impact, and experience of writing (e.g., Alexander; Aronson; Banks; Bleich; Butler; Ehret and Hollett; Fleckenstein; Kirsch and Ritchie; McLeod; Micciche, *Doing*, "Writing"; Royster; Van Ittersum and Owens; Wallace; Wilson and Lewiecki-Wilson). From these varied perspectives, writing is ineluctably located, inseparable from bodies and spaces at once lived, enfleshed, and socio-culturally constructed. More recently as well, across work that can be loosely gathered under umbrella terms "sociomaterial" (Miller; Vieira) or the "material turn" (Barnett, "Toward"), compositionists have explored the environmental and object-oriented contingencies of writing. Drawing upon new materialist, actor-network theory, and object-oriented frameworks among others, this work constructs suasive and compositional acts as decentered and emergent events (e.g., Barnett, "Chiasms"; Barnett and Boyle; Rickert). Under the influence of these more recent and longstanding sociomaterialisms, writing is always already an ensemble production as it distributes across and through participatory objects and environments and others. But in spite of the many ways the field has grounded writing in lived experience, writing from the perspective of *process* remains still somehow stubbornly disembodied and placeless.

This gap provokes me to prioritize the *physicalities* of processes: composing processes as matters of situated physical action, bodily difference, environmental particularities, place, affective movement, material objects, writing technologies, and so on. I most often use the terms physical or physically situated (rather than embodied or embodiment) to signal first baseline recognition that (varied) bodies and (manifold) things and (infinite) places coproduce writing. It is not that I don't engage with embodiment, but I do find physicality a more accessible term for the majority of the field—our student writers—who especially benefit from a situated processes perspective (I'll say more about why I favor this term, physicality, in Chapter 3). Constructing processes as situated, physical, and material disrupts writers' pictures of processes, which often still today propagate as a defined set of methods, steps, or plans to rationally approach developing a school text, the process "wheel," or the transcendent "fantasy of instant text production" (Bizzell 175). Our process discourses continue to shimmer with a modernist aura of writing as transcendent mind work that is (somehow) irrespective of particular bodies, actions, objects, and spaces.

Stretching process pedagogy beyond textual strategies learned and repeated, I argue for teaching processes through emphasizing the innumerable *differences* about them as they iterate across domains. Toward helping student writers perceive these particularities, I outline practices that see and conceptualize processes as *emplaced physical activity*, a view that accesses "the rich texture of everyday writing processes" (Prior and Shipka 230). In a manner more metaphorical: at the center of my work in this book are those imagined glass observation boxes though which we might perceive some of the particular material and embodied "conditions" of particular writing scenes. As such, I consider writing processes both as three-dimensional bodily experience unfolding in time and as a descriptive, capacious concept that can help our instruction better nurture context-sensitivity, on-the-spot learning, and practicing writing as relational, contingent and improvisational, a view which complements and sees differently the more familiar process terrain of cognition or sociality.

PROCESS TEACHING TODAY

That writing is a process is a bedrock assumption in composition studies. Students who have practiced writing in schools in the last forty years will likely have some clear ideas about processes. Many or most have likely internalized particular strategies for brainstorming, revision, drafting, inventing, and so on. Process seems to be among the things that we teach to our students that sticks, as "For several decades, we have been teaching process, and according to our students, they transfer process" (Yancey et al. 28). This familiarity reflects too in our disciplinary thinking: Victor Villanueva names process "the 'Given' in our Conversations" (1) about writing and its teaching. Geoffrey Sirc spiritedly calls process "that huge, brilliant, longest-running cocktail party ever in composition" (196). And Helen Foster sees process as a matter of our primary disciplinary identity, writing, "All of us undoubtedly believe ourselves well versed in process theory and practice. With only a little exaggeration, it might be said that process constitutes the conceptual fabric of our disciplinary hegemony" (3). Given this wide-reaching familiarity, it might be said that process is so known it needs no intervention, let alone a book-length one.

But while writing as a process still to some extent defines or makes us, what it means to claim and to enact this commonplace today is, from my perspective, unstable. Especially now in this postprocess (or even post-postprocess) terrain or moment, what it means to say and to teach "writing as a process" is ever more unclear if still utterly familiar. Thus, one of my broad goals with this book is to awaken consideration of process practice and theory today, an effort that I understand as part of a tradition of periodically "taking stock" of process (Anson; DeJoy; Delpit; Faigley; Harris; Perl, *Landmark*; Tobin and Newkirk).

And when I look around to "take stock" of process in this moment, I see it in a contradictory position: one of vague disinterest *and* steady persistence. On one hand, process is a backseat pedagogical familiar. It is a part of our teaching we maybe take for granted, one that seems to march along in the background without much need for comment. Processes still sometimes show up to animate research studies (e.g., Ehret and Holland; Fraiberg; Pigg; Prior and Shipka; Shipka; Roozen; Van Ittersum and Ching), though sometimes accompanied by an argument or defense for doing so, as Pamela Takayoshi does in a 2018 issue of *CCC*. But there is little scholarly attention focused on process *teaching* today. On the other, teaching process knowledge prominently remains a central tenet of several recent documents that outline foundations for writing instruction (e.g., NCTE's "Professional Knowledge for the Teaching of Writing"). On another hand still, postprocess scholars claim that, far from central, writing processes are so unpredictable as to make appeal to or discussion of them plainly impossible or nonsensical. Writing acts are not and have never been codifiable (Dobrin, "Paralogic" 133; Dobrin et al. 17) and thus are not amenable to being taught as a process or as skills or knowledge. "If writing cannot be reduced to a process or system because of its open-ended and contingent nature," Thomas Kent writes in 2002, then writing is not only not a process but "nothing exists to teach as a body-of-knowledge" ("Paralogic" 149). In short, process today is at once embedded, prominent, and undermined. Given this contradictory positioning—settled in the background of our thinking, pronounced in our pedagogical schemes, undermined on the basis of complexity and situatedness—what might our work with process signify (differently) today? And how might these conflicting assumptions work together?

Writing processes, on that first hand, still shape our teaching. In his 2014 assessment, Chris Anson observes how process makes up much of composition's instructional landscape today even while we approach writing and literacy more principally in its political, civic, public, and cultural dimensions (225). Anson sums up the position of process as such:

> At base, process pedagogy is designed to help students engage in their writing, to develop self-efficacy, confidence, and strategies for meeting the challenges of multiple writing situations. These goals, like the methods that help to achieve them, are now deep in the discipline's bones, and are the lifeblood of its praxis. (226)

I agree with Anson's characterization of what process teaching continues to offer contemporary instruction. I wonder though the extent to which students experience efficacy and independence as they write across drafts that we, their writing instructors, closely monitor. I wonder if they experience or think about composing in everyday, mundane settings ever or at all in terms of processes. I wonder if they see how their writing processes in our classes might both relate to and differ greatly from writing situations outside of our classes. I am concerned that my students, our students, see processes narrowly—as only formal or specialized teacher-led steps to developing a school-based genre. And these worries for me are amplified by Anson's ringing phrase that process is "now deep in the discipline's bones" (226). This phrase reflects my sense that writing as a process feels so familiar to us today that it has frozen into under-interrogated assumptions or staid practices. Process may feel to us now like a given, an unthinking known, a commonplace that we don't have to expressly define or question because we already know what we mean by it.

Like Anson, Lad Tobin (with Thomas Newkirk) too assessed the state of process and its teaching, but in the mid-1990s. Tobin and Newkirk seized a moment to "take stock" of the process movement after years of critique and the stirrings of "postprocess" thinking. Tobin identified then a range of ongoing challenges to process approaches from both conservative stakeholders "who never liked the movement in the first place" and from critical compositionists who were eager to "move beyond it" (7). In his moment, Tobin sees as does Anson that process assumptions endure through criticism, as many process beliefs and practices continued then "to hold power" (7) for writers, students, and writing instructors. One difference though between Tobin's and Anson's reflective moment is that Tobin can identify active and "current criticisms [that] are fair, valid, and useful" (7). Those active criticisms worked in Tobin's moment to make process teaching more responsive and inclusive by attending to difference in terms of class, race, and gender; to technological change; and to the constructed, shaping roles of the writing instructor (10–11). I am not sure we enjoy the same range of "current criticisms" of process teaching today. Process just doesn't appear much as the central or interrogated term in recent scholarship, especially pedagogically-focused work.

At the same time though, process remains a declared center of various guides to contemporary pedagogical practice. Prominent position statements that set goals for secondary and postsecondary instruction—including the 2011 CWPA, NCTE, and NWP "Framework for Success in Postsecondary Writing" or NCTE's 2016 position statement "Professional Knowledge for the Teaching of Writing"—each include "writing processes" in their small sets of recommended outcomes and assumptions. Process is prominently valued in all these documents right alongside rhetorical knowledge and critical thinking. Thus, far from being an expired concept or one we are "beyond," process endures today as a philosophical basis of our pedagogies. In these documents (discussed in detail in Chapter 3), processes are defined familiarly as *strategies*—for example, the "multiple strategies, or *composing processes*" which are not linear, but are flexible and adaptable ("WPA Outcomes"). Process strategies: we know well how to teach those. This is a familiar idea about process teaching, one so familiar that it becomes a target for critique on grounds of oversimplification. Joseph Petraglia, for example, has undermined the oversaturated process notion that "writing is the outcome of a variety of steps and stages" (63). But I do not think that these documents' focus on "strategies" is reductive in the ways Petraglia means exactly. More so, I see in the repetition of processes as "strategies" a focus on that which is *teachable*, repeatable, and knowable-in-advance. And we are practiced at teaching writing process "knowledge," to borrow Anne Beaufort's terms—as "the ways in which one proceeds through the writing task in its various phases" (20). We have countless classroom methods for doing so—outlining, drafting, peer review, webbing, freewriting, reflection, track changes, zero-drafts, says-does, portfolios, graphic organizers, and many more.

But I wonder what such steady focus on process strategy or procedure has made us miss. I wonder about the edges, the phenomenology, the *experience* of processes—what is more unstable, what is situational and essential to writing processes but not expressly codifiable or repeatable across writing situations. Writing processes as "strategies," after all, are never really stable. Processes change based on innumerable factors, on how they are situated and "affected by the material, socially specific particulars of a given writing situation or 'community of practice'" (Beaufort 20). But we have prioritized much less in our teaching the infinite ways in which processes differ across infinite contexts and contingencies. As Peter Vandenberg, Sue Hum, and Jennifer Clary-Lemon emphasize in their 2006 volume, "The most obvious commonality among scenes of writing may be, most significantly, difference" (5). The editors emphasize the stakes of failing to open process and writing pedagogies more broadly to difference and positionalities, writing, "As student populations are increasingly characterized by variety and difference, pedagogies that avoid attention to context become increasingly less relevant" (7). Unless process teaching can open itself to particularities, we risk homogenization, generalization, and ultimately, irrelevance (Vandenberg et al. 6). So how can we teach processes in ways that are less focused on repeatable strategy and more sensitive to differences? How do we expand process teaching to account for contingent factors, including those alluded to in these pedagogical position statements—the shaping impact of changing technologies, different environments, varying purposes and audiences? How can we emphasize, again as these documents do, processes as not learned once and for all, processes as multiple, processes as adaptable and practiced to become rhetorically flexible and versatile? Developed across the chapters of this volume, my core answer to these questions is to work in our teaching to physically and materially situate writing processes.

It is important for me to underline at the outset too that my call to see writing processes in our teaching through those observation boxes, up-close and *in situ*, is not to ignore the ways that writing is simultaneously situated in more ephemeral and expansive contexts. Quite the opposite. When closely observed, processes become clearly differentiated in their immediate physical particulars like physical movement, duration, tools, interruptions, and so on. Drawing out those differences, I will argue, helps writers attune and respond to more distant social, rhetorical, genre, and many other constraints of writing situations across life domains. Writers can come to see theirs and others' writing processes as movement in partnership with, for just a few examples, immediate material writing environments, social contexts, cultural conventions, positionalities, and privilege. In other words, approaching processes as physical and material is an available in-road toward helping writers see and enact writing as situated, differentiated, and responsive. And from this physically grounded view, teaching and learning with process shifts as well. Rather than strategies, process teaching is descriptive, constructivist, discovery-oriented, and writer-led. More than *learning* writing processes, physically situating processes is to *learn how to learn* to respond to the changing conditions in which writing finds itself. It is putting in the hands of writer's themselves not the yields of our process inquiry, but its questions and observational methods.

THE QUESTION OF POSTPROCESS (OR, HOW THIS BOOK IS AND ISN'T POSTPROCESS)

Next, this project is motivated by need I see for reckoning with postprocess. As someone long interested in the tradition of process—its research, histories, theories, and especially its teaching—I've felt for some time uneasy about what we're supposed to make of or make with postprocess thinking. What is this varied work trying to push us toward? What happens to process teaching under its ranging influence? What threads or moments in postprocess discourse might be transformative for composition pedagogy specifically?

Certainly, a book like this—focused as it is on physicalizing and thus differentiating processes—cannot and should not avoid engagement with postprocess discussions. But what this engagement yields is complicated. Some of my claims about process teaching, including questioning the repeatability and stability of processes as strategies and emphasizing the context-contingent differences of all writing acts, are already familiar. These notions are hallmark gestures of postprocess theory. I will also rely on in these pages Thomas Kent's postprocess paralogics. So, to some extent, my inquiry could be called a postprocess one. At the same time, though, I recognize that postprocess intentionally declares itself a disunified discourse. Divergent and "ambiguous" (Whicker 498), postprocess represents not one coherent theory but a looser "mindset" (Kent, "Preface" xviii). As such, I want to establish how my concerns in this book both are and are not postprocess. The following may feel like a detour into an argument where otherwise I am previewing. But it is important for me to set a climate in which, across these pages, I can turn to specific postprocess claims and provocations that invigorate contemporary process praxis.

As I will echo in Chapter 2, often postprocess claims are fashioned as a wholesale *break*—a "break-free-and-don't-look-back" shift away from the era or tenets of the "process movement" and a wholly new direction for the field. As Petraglia asserted the impulse of postprocess in 1999, "we now have the theoretical and empirical sophistication to consider the mantra 'writing is a process' as the right answer to a really boring question. We have better questions now, and the notion of process no longer counts as much of an insight" ("Is There" 53). Most visibly, postprocess has broken free by plainly, staunchly, and repeatedly deconstructing process; or in Thomas Kent's prominent articulation, by asserting simply, "the fundamental idea that no codifiable or *generalizable* writing process exists or could exist" (*Post-Process* 1). And this gesture of undermining process can sometimes be attached to a wrecking ball for writing pedagogy's entire enterprise, because if "there are no codifiable processes by which we can characterize, identify, solidify, grasp discourse . . . there is no way to teach discourse, discourse interpretation, or discourse disruption" (Dobrin, "Paralogic" 133). Boring or radically impossible, process from this perspective would seem to be an unequivocal nonstarter. But at the same time, this blanket "break free" rhetoric is deployed toward varied aims, and it may actually not be a blanket at all. The accumulated postprocess sense that process is untenable, after all, has not erased our classroom traffic in this concept (and, actually, I do not think that is the intention of this claim, anyway). The repetition of this impossibility has perhaps to some extent, though, chilled our disciplinary discourse around process, helping to leave processes in our teaching today largely *unsituated*—out of time and place and considered still as all-purpose skills or strategies. The situated writing processes I seek in this book are then "postprocess" to the extent that they are not codifiable, that they always already unfold in excess of any models we might hazard about them, and that they entail impossibilities and uncertainties of various kinds. This is to say, I too undermine process along these familiar postprocess lines.

At the same time, I diminish the postprocess call to "abandon" (Jensen 11) process, a message often implicit in postprocess "break-free" rhetoric. One way I work to muddy the narratives around the process/post- "break" is by highlighting the ways some postprocess thinking can be conceptualized more as a *shift* than a break—a shift in the focus and scope of composing theories. In Chapter 2, I show how the postprocess moniker is linked to theories that understand writing on sweepingly huge, *macro*-scales: networks, communities, ecologies, complex systems, and so on. Indeed, John Trimbur, credited with the first using the term "post-process" (Matsuda 65), meant for it to embody his observation that compositionists were to turning focus away from individuals' processes and toward larger political and social contexts for literacies. I see *expansion,* or the scale and situatedness, of composition theories after the social turn as an alternative disciplinary storyline, a shift from process to *situated processes*, rather than an absolute break or rupture between process and post-. My focus on situatedness and scale does not aim to unify process and postprocess. But by focusing on situatedness at modulating scales, I expose how we've glossed over meaningful ways that writing is not just constrained by expansive, distant, ephemeral, or systemic forces, but equally by immediate physical dynamics.

Postprocess too often invokes expansion, and not just in terms of the scale of writing theory or the idea that writing cannot be contained in individuals alone. Postprocess expansion arguments are also forged in terms of the focus of the discipline. That is, appeals to postprocess often signal a drive to explore different questions, aims, and methods that exceed or avoid totally those of college writing instruction. I take no issue with this brand of postprocess break as disciplinary expansion. For many reasons that include, and well exceed, the influence of postprocess thinking, including for instance, ongoing focus on global Englishes, community writing, public writing, writing across the lifespan, workplace writing, nonwestern and cultural rhetorics, and many other burgeoning areas of scholarly focus—our field's considerations of writing now undoubtedly exceed college instructional concerns alone. As Vandenberg et al.

have it, the "dominant consensual belief" (7) in place twenty years ago that college writing is the "primary concern" in composition studies is now neither primary nor consensus. However, some still dissent to what they perceive as unrelenting pedagogical demand. Postprocess discourse, in other words, is often entwined with resistance to the so-called "pedagogical imperative." For example, Sidney I. Dobrin, J. A. Rice, and Michael Vastola claim in their 2011 collection an "unapologetic resistance to simple pedagogical application" (3) and declare interest instead in "questions and theories of writing not trapped by disciplinary expectations of the pedagogical" (14). This resistance, also invoked elsewhere (i.e., Dobrin, *Postcomposition*; Olson), claims that composition should let go of college writing instruction as its disciplinary center and with it, any concerns at all about "application." Indeed, I agree. Writing theory or research should not be beholden automatically to classroom "application" (though, at the same time, I do think invocations of the "pedagogical imperative" tend to oversimplify the complexities of pedagogy and praxis).

Pedagogy is not, if it ever was, the gravitational center of the field. The pedagogical should not be understood as an implicit demand. But it may not surprise that I do take issue with what I see as a central side effect of this kind of postprocess resistance: the ways it has led to cautiousness—even a moratorium—on rethinking pedagogical and process assumptions through certain postprocess and other postmodern claims. "Moratorium" as a fitting term came to my mind before I knew that this is too the way Victor J. Vitanza in 1991 described a broader relation among theory and practice in the field. In short, Vitanza "declare[s] a moratorium on attempting to turn theory into praxis/pedagogy. The field of composition demonstrates a resistance to theory by rushing to apply theory to praxis without ever realizing the resistance of theory itself to be theorized and applied" (160). Though I raise Vitanza's gesture to ultimately quibble with it, at the same time and as above, I agree with it. Not only should we not, we cannot just "turn" theory into classroom practice. Doing theoretical or "intellectual" work—to invoke Lynn Worsham's conception—always exceeds the inherently conservative, "narrow and policed" (101) terrain of disciplines or institutions or classrooms. Intellectual work is instead "relentlessly critical, self-critical, and potentially revolutionary, for it aims to critique, change, and even destroy institutions, disciplines, and professions that rationalize exploitation, inequality, and injustice" (101). Attempting to totalize or encapsulate theory and "apply" it is not only misguided and undesirable, but also essentially impossible.

Yet, I still question the reach and direction of this moratorium. Compositionists, like me, working in the subfield of composition pedagogy and engaging with the preconceptions and ideologies underlying process teaching, seem to be equally shooed away from engaging with postprocess claims. Of course, postprocess theorists themselves need not account for pedagogy. Of course, no theory can be somehow "translated" to practice. I do think, though, that this moratorium has had unfortunate consequences for contemporary (process) pedagogies. This interference can be illustrated in how Dobrin, Rice, and Vastola position "postprocess theories." They make clear that postprocess—however they ultimately imagine its bounds or boundlessness—shall not mingle with writing pedagogy. They state, "The potential of postprocess theories lies not in their reconfiguration of how disciplines like composition studies might rethink the teaching of writing" (17). In their efforts to wield postprocess as a kind of revolutionary cudgel poised to dismantle the discipline and remake us somehow instead "postpedagogy, postcomposition, and postdiscipline" (16), pedagogical engagement of any kind, as familiar disciplinary ground, is always already suspect. The editors worry about and resist the "normalizing" or "disciplinary affirmation" (7) of postprocess, calling into question how compositionists like Helen Foster and Matthew Heard have used postprocess ideas in relation to process theories or service learning. From my point of view, however, the editors' critiques seem leveled not at Foster's or Heard's specific methods or claims, but at the very notion that one can or should "do" anything praxis-oriented with postprocess at all.

And so, such a moratorium has cast the sense that any postprocess engagement with process, at least that which is not an outright cancellation or a refusal to "apply" it, is suspicious from the jump. Such suspicion is evident in Debra Jacobs' argument for process as a frame for reimagining the dynamics of liberatory pedagogies (663). Dispensing with the notion that process must mean predetermined maps or outcomes, Jacobs uses process to represent "interventions over time that disrupt the quotidian stream of consciousness—processural interventions that include critical inquiry into ways of reading processes and products (and their means of production)" (670). Jacobs clearly does not associate with any of the thoroughly critiqued trappings of the process paradigm—generalizability, repetition, acontextuality, and so on. But Jacobs confesses that she has "sought other ways to respond," beside process "since I am not entirely comfortable with the risk I take in advancing allegiance to what has been so thoroughly critiqued" (663). Jacobs' cautiousness speaks to the strength of the moratorium as she anticipates rebuff for simply saying process, for attempting to recast it productively, contingently, and in more postprocess-oriented ways for specific critical and liberatory ends.

I understand the urge to preserve the revolutionary potentialities of thinking postprocess. But, as John Whicker's work on the impossibilities of meaningfully defining postprocess demonstrates, invocations of this term are much too varied for anyone to once and for all declare dominion over what postprocess categorically might do or not do. In the context of my work in this book—an intervention in the subfield of composition pedagogy and the history and potentials of process and its teaching specifically—I clearly read postprocess, and this moratorium rhetoric, in a particular way. I question any broad cancellation force associated with postprocess as it has at once failed to undo process in the discipline and in classrooms and, simultaneously, held it frozen in place. What's more, much postprocess discourse has not kicked process out of the classroom *by design* through express and categorical *disinterest* in pedagogical questions. Dobrin et al.'s concerns are simply not about process teaching at all. Thus, I see their concerns as diverging from, rather than conflicting with, my own.

In sum, when I connect to postprocess claims across these pages, I do not enforce a pedagogical imperative; I do not mean that everything compositionists and theorists alike do must have some connection to pedagogy; I do not think that postprocess must be "applied"; and I do not unify postprocess "theory" as one thing nor do I wish to unify process and post-. And I don't think what I'm talking about is best called "postprocess" exactly. I do claim, though, that there are many relatively untapped postprocess claims that can help those of us thinking critically about writing pedagogy today transform it. These claims, I think, are less realized because they can come prepackaged with moratoriums or get caught up in performative calls to break free. I work around and through some of these barriers in this book in order to inspire and enact continued, ongoing critique of "untenable assumptions" in our process theories and practices and to reconstruct processes as physically emplaced, contingent, conditional, unpredictable, public, relational, decentered, or in short, improvisational.

THERE ARE NO "GENERALIZABLE SKILLS"

A final provocation and context for my work in this book is a vexing, but not particularly recent, challenge to contemporary writing instruction. Situating processes is especially imperative in light of a broader pedagogical revelation, one sometimes swept under the postprocess umbrella: the deconstruction of "general writing skills instruction" (GWSI). Much of this discussion and its attendant acknowledgment that all writing acts are situated and context-contingent is captured in Petraglia's 1995 volume, *Reconceiving Writing, Rethinking Writing Instruction*. Emphasizing the collection's "polemic" (xi) potential, Petraglia and his contributors undermine composition courses guided by GWSI assumptions, those that presume that there are "skills that transcend any particular content and context" (xii) and "that writing is a set of [those] rhetorical skills that can be mastered through formal instruction" (xi). Most all writing courses we teach smuggle in GWSI assumptions (excepting perhaps, Petraglia underlines, those like writing-intensive courses in the disciplines or creative writing) (xii), consenting expressly or implicitly to the promise of delivering blanket, universally applicable skills. They roll on though, Petraglia observes, in spite of the many ways our research, theory, and "common sense" piles up to tell us that *so much depends* on where, with whom, and for what writing is (xii). If we *really* faced what we know about writing's profound situatedness, our operating GWSI presumptions suddenly make little sense. David Russell notably dramatizes this curious absurdity by analogy, claiming that GWSI "is something like trying to teach people to improve their ping-pong, jacks, volleyball, basketball, field hockey, and so on by attending a course in general ball using" (58). Such an imagined course would have obvious challenges; for one, could "ball using" even be taught without the selection and practice of specific ball-using games? If so, which would be selected and why? There might be something to gain from a course featuring practice in select games. Maybe those who dedicated themselves to it might find that they gain some increased facility in certain ball-related activity. But "this does not mean that person's 'ball-using skill' is autonomous and general in any meaningful sense. It is the accumulation of some specific ball-using skills (and not others) learned in some specific ball games that bear some similarities" (Russell 58). In other words, any appearance of a "general skill" in writing is one forged only through repetitive engagement in specific located contexts (contexts that may have some observable similarities but are distinct nonetheless). Russell and others who expose "GWSI's inadequacy" (Petraglia xii) remind us, in short and in sum, that "there is no autonomous, generalizable skill or set of skills called 'writing' that can be learned and then applied to all genres or activities" (Russell 59).

Russell's language rings of Kent and others' postprocess mantra: there is no generalizable or codifiable writing process. Viewed from a GWSI perch, if there are no generalizable writing *skills*, then obviously there are also no general writing processes. It makes little sense to talk about process skills or process knowledge or process strategies *in general*. Doing so—as we (self not discluded) routinely do—is to construct processes pre-fab, in advance, and outside of the myriad contexts of their performance. In postprocess articulations, the solution to trafficking in what we might call GPWI—general *process* writing instruction—is to simply stop pretending that there is anything out there we can call a writing process and perhaps to accept too in the end that "writing cannot be taught" (Kent, "Paralogic" 149) at all. But of course process teaching rolls on— it's in our bones; it's our familiar, it's foundational to the maps that guide writing pedagogies today. And process remains enlightening and central in what we do—over our field's history, some say, we've been "able to agree on process only; [though] agreement on approach and content continues to elude us" (Yancey et al. 148). But somehow still process has isolated itself from the broad situating instincts we've had as a field. Process remains strangely unsituated. My work in this book as such proceeds from my instinct and observation that we haven't much problematized "general *process* writing instruction," an omission I try to amend. How can we legitimately "teach" writing processes when so much about their operation and art is shaped in and by differing contexts? What can we teach our students if we're not teaching process as enduring or repeatable strategies?

The revelation that generalizable writing skills do not exist is not new. It is not exigent in terms of recency. But, as Petraglia puts it, even if we have in some measure accepted writing's context-contingencies, "our field's usual long-term response . . . is to politely pretend we did not notice" (xii). This is especially the case with our assumptions about process. We are still wondering how to teach writing, and processes more specifically, in light of our theoretical awareness of writing's susceptibility and differences. Writing pedagogues have tried different ways to accommodate context: they've argued to push instruction out of first-year courses and into the disciplines or workplace contexts (e.g., Brent; Kent, *Paralogic;* Petraglia, *Reconceiving;* Smit); they've nudged our content away from writing skills and toward the study of our own discipline (e.g., Downs and Wardle); they've "postpedagogically" dispensed with the idea that writing can be taught at all (e.g., Dobrin et al.; Lynch). I will consider this challenge in the context of the latter alongside recent and prominent field interest in teaching for transfer. While postpedagogies undermine our ability to meaningfully teach such an unstable art as writing at all, transfer doubles-down on fashioning writing know-how that can *move*, that can traverse across and reemerge in unforeseen contexts. If postpedagogical transfer visions are to be realized, I will argue, we need a much more nimble, located, and improvisational approach to teaching (with) processes.

OVERVIEW AND CHAPTER SUMMARIES

Because we are now postprocess or beyond, because process still founds our teaching, because we are still trying to disrupt and move beyond "general skills" mythologies, because processes in our discourses and imaginations remain rather disembodied and unsituated, it is a fitting time to reexamine process in our disciplinary thinking and our teaching. This book represents one effort to do so, as I join other recent calls to reanimate attention to process (Jensen; Shipka; Takayoshi, "Short-Form"; Takayoshi, "Writing") as well as efforts to take periodic stock of process and its teaching (e.g., Anson; Harris; Tobin and Newkirk).

I examine process in this book *because* of the teaching of writing. And while I will discuss some of my classroom practices, I also build a history and theory of situated processes. I draw upon ranging material to do so: postprocess discourses; process research, theories, and scholarship; historical critiques of process pedagogies; recent scholarship under the banner of the "material turn" or the sociomaterial; contemporary writing theories that imagine processes on huge scales; as well as affect, feminist, and disability scholarship that locates writing across bodies and material environments. With these influences, I approach the animating questions of this book: What does it mean to physically situate writing processes? And how can doing so help us teach processes differently? By differently, I mean first in terms of *disruption*: modifying the ways writing pedagogies, students, and writing teachers picture writing processes as acontextual, transcendent, disembodied, placeless, or as matters of thinking. I also mean for *differently* to signal contingency—writing processes as they unfold *differently* through the participation of innumerable forces, positionalities, physical locations, and materials.

Ultimately, I aim to add a bodily, situated dimension to process history, theory, and classroom practice. I want to shift our methods toward those which invite in more of the unruliness and ranging *lived experience* of processes. And in so doing, I lead us toward bigger questions of writing pedagogy: How can we (or can we?) make our process instruction cross into new unknown contexts? What roles should the writing teacher take in process teaching? What roles for the student writer? How can and how should we teach knowing that writing processes can never be fully mastered or strategized, that they are inseparable from their shaping contexts, that writing is so context-contingent that teaching writing as we traditionally imagine it might be "impossible" (Dobrin, "Paralogic" 134; Kent, "Paralogic" 149; Lynch xv)?

This book reflects my belief that examining and situating processes can help transform postsecondary (and perhaps secondary) writing instruction. Renovations to this core concept can help writers see the complexities and constraints that shape their writing; it can help them see that their writing is as much the domain of others and communities as it is theirs; it can help them understand that the standards of good writing depends fully on where that writing is. But physically situating processes is far from the only thing we need in our classrooms to meet the needs of diverse student populations across varied institutional locations. I see my rethinking of process as a necessary but far from sufficient modification to writing pedagogy in today's complex landscapes. I recognize too that taking up process again—especially as I focus on even less teacher control and more constructivist descriptivism—risks, as it has before, enabling some writers but disadvantaging others. As demonstrated by Lisa Delpit, Maria de la Luz Reyes, Nancy DeJoy and others, process approaches have long been assumed to be always already progressive, liberating, or agentive. But process approaches in practice have failed to embody these ideals. They have failed some language learners, minoritized, and non-middle-class students by, for example, not making codes of power explicit (Delpit, "The Silenced" 287). They have failed also by operating on axes of "teacher-identified discourse" (DeJoy, "I Was" 163) or "enthymemic logic, identification, and mastery" (169). And too, they have failed by tending to chase an errant belief in one-size-for-all, assuming process strategies and models might be universally relevant to situations and writers alike. As I work to renovate process through bodily movement, constructivist discovery, observation and inquiry, and ultimately improvisation, I do so from an assumption of difference and descriptivism (not universality or prescriptivism). I recognize too that there is a host of writing-related knowledge and experience that needs other methods. But all of our instructional methods and concepts, process included, should *only ever* proceed from a context-contingent or situated perspective. And, my central point is that our classroom work with process *especially* needs now to be grounded and situated.

However needs manifest in specific classrooms with specific writers, I believe that writing students need one writing process "strategy" over any other: that of *situating*, learning to read particular writing situations and improvise processes in response. This goal is more important than only learning one set of rules or strategies that may only be helpful in a limited set of writing situations. Seeing writing processes as physical and material, in the ways I imagine in these pages, is one method for doing so, for helping student writers *feel* how writing is contingent, situated, relational, and fundamentally different across ranging contexts.

Toward these questions and goals, I first work to create a history, context, and theory of physically situated processes. In Chapter 1, I create a disciplinary heritage for the physicalities of processes through close readings of the work of Janet Emig, Sondra Perl, and Christina Haas. I demonstrate in Emig's work—work conventionally positioned as a landmark study in cognitive process—interest in writing's material tools, environmental conditions, and physical biology. In the evolution of Sondra Perl's process thinking, from her early process study of "unskilled writers" to her 2004 book *Felt Sense,* I emphasize how Perl theorized processes as *movement*, with prominent roles for physical sensations, bodily action, gut feelings and affect. Finally, I uncover a less-prominent claim in Christina Haas' study of writing tools and technologies: that writing is an *embodied practice*. This perspective, under-developed in Haas's focus on the technology question, is critical to my project, especially as I situate it in the sociomaterial turn. Haas' embodied practice is a means to see writing processes on broad scales of social and cultural knowledge in reciprocal and simultaneous relation to individual, located, physical writing acts.

This question of situatedness and scale continues in Chapter 2, as I attempt to account for why the embodiment and materialities of process have largely remained marginal in our theories and imaginaries. I advance two claims: first, that writing's situatedness—a central premise claimed by contemporary theories including actor network, ecological, activity, and postprocess—can be understood as a *part of,* not in contradistinction to, the "process paradigm." I develop this claim through readings of Patricia Bizzell and Marilyn Cooper's social theories, arguing that they situate individual processes in their innumerable social, community, and language contexts. Second, I argue that while situatedness can be seen as a longstanding assumption of process theories, the massive *scales* on which that situatedness is imagined in postprocess-oriented perspectives generates concern about the partiality of process-scaled views. I show how Nedra Reynolds and Margaret Syverson, in their expansive spatial and ecological theories of writing, struggle with the challenge of scale. Each theorist attempts to linger upon the immediate physical-material situatedness of processes and argues for its shaping, and underexamined, significance.

Taken together, these first chapters create precedence and need for seeing processes as physically emplaced and, second, establish how we can see discrete processes enmeshed in, rather than isolated from, larger forces and contexts. With this ground set, in Chapter 3, I aim to dismantle pictures of abstracted and disembodied processes in our teaching. I begin by exploring how recent pedagogical documents, like the 2016 NCTE position statement "Professional Knowledge for the Teaching of Writing," centrally define processes as strategies. Though the documents too account for context, flexibility, adaptation, multiplicity, there remains a pervasive sense that processes are divorced or immune from their shaping contexts. Aiming to interrogate these tacit images for writers and writing teachers, I advance a set of propositions that focus on dimensions of writing experience deemphasized in previous process theories and teaching. Drawing upon work in embodiment, affect, postprocess, new materialism, and disability studies, I divide this exploration into three tangled dimensions: writing processes as *activity,* as *physical,* and as *materially emplaced.*

I then enact this trope of picturing processes in process pedagogy. In Chapter 4, building on work that questions the knowledge we can claim as writing instructors and the roles that writing teachers and writers take (DeJoy; Dobrin), I argue for repositioning student writers in relation to process—no longer (if ever) as receivers or replicators of process strategies but instead as curious *situated process researchers.* Positioning student writers as *in-situ* descriptive researchers can help them perceive the environmental contingencies, detours, objects, tools, and embodied habits that constitute writing processes. These observations can lead students to readily adopt a situated view of writing: to learn to respond to writing's differences as they unfold across life domains. To illustrate, I present activities, repurposed from visual composing research methods, from my own first-year and intermediate writing classrooms.

In the final chapter, I continue focus on process pedagogy in the broader context of the deconstruction of general writing skills instruction. I focus on two opposing responses: transfer and postpedagogy. Postpedagogy undermines our ability to predict and control (future) writing situations; transfer aims to secure writing know-how that can travel and reemerge in future contexts. I mingle these visions to emphasize the value of writing instruction focused on situation and uncertainty—focusing writers on the immediacies and instabilities of where they are writing now, in the moment, on-the-spot. Such recognition, though, of susceptibility and contextual guessing challenges our sense of what teaching might look like. How do we "teach" something like processes when so much of their operation and art is shaped in and by contexts that we don't know? For my answer, I turn to theatrical improvisation—its theory, practice and especially its pedagogy as imagined by Viola Spolin, pioneer of the American improv tradition—as a final visual figure to imagine teaching with situated processes. Process as improv casts writing as a situational, vulnerable art, one of figuring out how best to respond on-the-spot to unique rhetorical situations, conditions, and discoverable and unknown constraints.

Teaching writing processes has been productively questioned. As Kent lays it out: "If writing cannot be reduced to a process or system because of its open-ended and contingent nature, then nothing exists to teach as a body-of-knowledge" ("Paralogic" 149). Certainly, process teaching is ill-advised if it means we are just setting expectations for process behaviors and then measuring how writers perform them during writing tasks we fully control. But that doesn't mean process teaching is over. We can instead, I will argue, teach *with* the emplaced *experiences* of processes. We can embrace process descriptivism and loosen the control of process prescriptivism, skills, or strategies. In so doing, we might help budge students' constructs of writing and writing processes to better prepare them for the versatility, changeability, and inherent uncertainties of doing writing in the world. *Situating Writing Processes* is a robust tour through process histories, writing theories, postprocess claims, and contemporary assumptions guiding our ranging writing pedagogies today that provides writing teachers means to address one of the discipline's most essential questions—how to engage some of the vast complexities of writing in order to help writers become more effective. The departure here though is that effectiveness is not secured in advance by receiving enduring process knowledge or reliably applicable skills, but rather by sharpening student writers' abilities to keenly discern the dynamics of—and improvise in—any given differentiated and physically-located writing scene.

CHAPTER 1

"DEEP IN THE DISCIPLINE'S BONES"—LATENT HISTORIES OF SITUATED PROCESSES

Process is emblematic—a central figure, maybe *the* figure, of composition studies' modern history. "Writing is a process and not a product" is the simple phrase said to have launched one thousand ships of inquiry into writing practice, theory, and teaching. With its familiarity and status, the "writing process movement" can be quickly caricatured—revolutionary, student-centered, invention, talk-aloud, cognitive, recursive, revision, expressive, around 1971, after current-traditional rhetoric and before postprocess. And this capacity for thumbnailing the "process movement" can have the effect of cementing into a "grand narrative[] of composition history" (McComiskey, "Introduction" 8), and an attendant assumption that once upon a time a burgeoning field at once embraced one radically new way of conceptualizing, studying, and teaching writing. But looking back, writing as a process defies such coherence. Instead, stories of process in composition studies appear more a knot of capacious and often colliding potentials—a classroom commonplace, a long historical moment, a set of competing assumptions about writing, an idea familiar to nearly every writer, a site of critique, an engine of both innovation and tradition, liberation and standardization.

More than a paradigm or movement, process is more aptly seen as stories plural, ones told through the details. After all, process has done and meant quite different things across its uptake by researchers, scholars, historians, and pedagogues over time. For Maxine Hairston, the writing process movement was that seismic wave of a paradigm shift. For Sondra Perl, it was never revolutionary but instead a legitimizing force ("Writing" xi). For James Marshall, process did have a revolutionary edge, fueled by rebellion against traditional formalist teaching (51). For Joseph Harris, process teaching failed to deliver the revolution it promised, unable to release writing instruction from its traditional past (55). For Lisa Delpit, process teaching only claimed to be liberatory, but in practice, instead perpetuated disadvantage for minoritized students who were held accountable to, but never taught, discourse codes of privilege ("The Silenced" 287). For Patricia Bizzell, process ignored socially-situated knowledge (93). For Lester Faigley, writing in 1986 at a time when "nearly everyone seems to agree that writing as a process is good" (527), saw processes differently depending on the theorist, as expressive, cognitive, social, or "historically dynamic" (537). For Thomas Kent, writing was never and can never be a generalizable process (*Post-Process* 5). For Lad Tobin, writing in the 1990s amidst a call from some to separate from process, "many of the fundamental beliefs of the writing process movement . . . continue to hold power for most writing teachers and students" (7). Just these few compositionists' voices complicate any easy hindsight narrative about a unified "process movement" and its supposed yields. Stories of writing process more than simplified master narratives reveal that, if anything, the longstanding centrality of process has cohered around productive *incoherence*, questioning, challenge, and disunity.

Process remains—perhaps equally in spite of and because of this unifying incoherence—still foundational in composition studies, especially in the teaching of writing. As Chris Anson writes in his 2014 retrospective, persisting through both critique and the expansion of the discipline, "the core of process pedagogy remains. . . . deep in the discipline's bones" (226). Likely Anson means to suggest that process remains vital, to both the histories and current practices of composition. But his phrase—*in the bones*—echoes evocatively to me. In the bones implies hidden but ineluctably structural, yet unmoving or calcified. In the bones suggests centrality, literally deeply foundational, but so much so as to not arouse attention or pointed consideration. As Kyle Jensen recently put it, process may be to us now a "grounded concept," one that continues to direct how we think, research, and teach. But significantly, such familiarity also means that process "does not generally receive sustained historical, theoretical, or material scrutiny" (17). In the bones reflects Jensen's point back to me: process may be alive in our classrooms, but enjoys little critical tension or even much of a second thought. Process is a known known to us all. We have over forty years of work and thinking to guide and direct our process practice. Process is in our bones. What more could be needed?

But a base claim I aim to establish is that in today's landscape, process could benefit from a reanimating of that tension and critical questioning that has marked its stories over time. For one, after years of saying that we're now "postprocess" (e.g., Kent; Petraglia), our process teaching has neither ended nor undergone significant renovation (an outcome in part intentional as many who take up the postprocess mantle have resolutely non-pedagogical goals like expanding field concerns beyond student writers and teaching [i.e., Dobrin, *Postcomposition*]). At the same time, as Anson, Tobin, and others have underlined, process teaching persists. And, as I discuss in Chapter 3, process persists not just a background concept, but as one in a small set of foundational assumptions advanced to guide the teaching of writing today. And so, for these and other reasons which unfold in this book, *in the bones* is not where this enduring, varied, historically problematic, and currently underconsidered framework should comfortably retire. Said another way, one simple aim of this book is to move process into composition's muscles again, so to speak—to exercise process and train it in relation to a range of contemporary writing theories, assumptions, and challenges in our field today. Toward this broad goal, in these first two chapters, I rouse some of this productive tension, this critical "scrutiny" (Jensen 17), by troubling broad narratives of process history.

In his story of process stories, Anson reminds us that process history is much more complicated and ranging than he or anyone could ever possibly sketch. "A complete account," Anson observes, "would take at least a book-length journey, and even then it would have to bypass many interesting studies, debates, and other artifacts that more accurately show the complexities and nuances of the movement" (225). Indeed, nuance often, and even necessarily, lacks in our disciplinary narratives. Bruce McComiskey recently described this lack acutely as he tries to square "any of the best-known histories of the discipline" ("Introduction" 7) with an archive he discovers of his own first-year composition essays. This metaphorical dissonance leads McComiskey and his contributors to the practice of microhistory. A complement to revisionist and counterhistory efforts that work against "the discipline's early drive toward abstract narrative histories" (34), microhistory is interested in overlooked sites, moments, and actors that have shaped local histories of composition but remain invisible in larger field narratives. As he wonders about all the unnamed contributors to composition, McComiskey is clear about who he does not see as figures suited for the focus of microhistory. "I do not mean people like Ann E. Berthoff or Edward P. J. Corbett or Janet Emig or Fred Newton Scott or Sondra Perl," McComiskey clarifies. "Their names are produced (or, more likely reproduced) in every narrative" (8). But as McComiskey himself might agree, just because we know their names well does not mean their contributions aren't too subject to glossing. There is always more to any compositionist's contributions than any grand narrative will capture. Indeed, even in the work of the most oversaturated familiar figures can emerge smaller, quieter histories and potentials.

In the spirit of microhistory of a different sort, in this chapter I turn first to two prominent figures in writing process narratives, Janet Emig and Sondra Perl, to argue that they construct writing processes as physically and materially situated. Emig and Perl's work both asserts and counters many familiar assumptions, and often indictments, of early writing process discourse and methods. Emig—ground-breaking process researcher with her contrived writing prompts, talk-aloud protocols, and laboratory-like observation methods—also asked us to consider processes with "at least a small obeisance in the direction of the untidy, of the convoluted, of the not-wholly-known" ("Uses" 48) and with an interest in writing tools, environments, and physical biology. Perl, cited most in process narratives for her pioneering scientistic study of "unskilled" writers and her composing style sheet methods, shifts over time to a stance that theorizes processes as *movement*—bodily, inarticulable, affective, and nonsystematic. Both Emig and Perl come to see writing processes as emplaced, material, and embodied. They question the coherence and transparency of processes while emphasizing physical rhythms and material choreography. But these perspectives have largely failed to rise and adjust the reigning storylines of the process paradigm as cognitive and social action, a shift I aim to make.

I conclude this chapter with a third process figure, Christina Haas. Haas' work is rarely, if ever, considered a part of process discourse as her book, *Writing Technology: Studies on the Materiality of Literacy*, makes its most obvious contributions to technology studies or computers and writing conversations. But in working to bridge the gap between social and cognitive paradigms with a focus on composing's material tools, Haas contributes a claim less emphasized in her work but significant for my own: that writing (process) is *embodied practice*. In my read, embodied practice is the lynchpin of Haas' intervention, containing and connecting broad cultural, community, and historical knowledge to the tiniest of individual embodied actions. In other words, embodied practice shows how writing can never be just an individual or social event but always both in dynamic interrelation.

With this focus on embodied practice, I conclude by situating Haas' work in the recent "material turn" in composition and rhetoric. This "turn," I argue, tends to view writing activity on expansive *macro-scales*, turning attention to giant contexts and systems involved in writing acts more than discrete writers alone. As such, process discourse and pedagogy has not much reflected the constitutive force of immediate and located physical-material interactions that Haas, Perl, Emig, and others point to and that materially-oriented composition scholarship points to, an adjustment I argue for and elaborate on in Chapter 2.

Constructing this latent history with these three process scholars is a selection, and thus a deflection. Toward recovering situatedness and physicality in process discourses, I could well have made other choices. I might have exposed the pulsing political contexts reflected and similarly glossed in Ken Macrorie's examination of student voice. I might have highlighted Peter Elbow's focus on the materiality of language in his discussion of conscientious objectors' #150 forms. I might have focused on the political and social justice efforts of the many involved in the publication in 1974 of "Students' Right to their Own Language," those who exposed how writing is ineluctably located in and shaped by individuals' racial, ethnic, cultural, and community contexts. I might have highlighted Barrett J. Mandel, who in 1978 undermined the association among writing and thinking processes and claimed by contrast that writing operates beyond the mind's conscious control. I might have too turned my attention to Susan McLeod or Alice G. Brand's prominent work on affect and process. But I focus on Emig and Perl and Haas, for one and simply, because they are not conventionally positioned in process stories in the ways I uncover here. In the following sections, I close read some of their familiar works and reception in order to bring more of the physical and breathing, local and living dimensions to processes into our teaching imaginaries today.

JANET EMIG: WRITING PROCESSES AS MATERIAL AND PHYSIOLOGICAL

Janet Emig gets a part, and even the lead, in most every composition origin story. Emig so centrally features in broad disciplinary histories that her dissertation-study-turned-monograph, *The Composing Processes of Twelfth Graders,* is often marked as the beginning of modern composition studies. As Steven North is often quoted, Emig's study is "the single most influential piece of Researcher inquiry—and maybe any kind of inquiry—in Composition's short history" (197), making *Composing Processes* a work so well-known it may need no introduction at all. Nevertheless, in brief, Emig initiates her study by observing that writing teachers and students were working only with author accounts and handbooks as resources for writing knowledge, sources that lacked depth, evidence, and relevance. Emig also observes that existing "research on the adolescent writer focus upon the product(s) rather than upon the process(es) of their writing, and, consequently, do not provide an appropriate methodology for a process-centered inquiry" (*Composing* 19). With her landmark study, Emig enacts such a "process-centered" approach, conducting case studies of eight student writers using talk-aloud protocol and interview methods and thereby helping to establish a research and pedagogical trajectory for composition based upon the question, how is writing accomplished?

And while undoubtedly influential, Emig's study in terms of its questions, methods, and implications for teaching also invites critique. In his 1983 evaluation, for example, Ralph F. Voss questions most of Emig's moves, especially her strong condemnation of writing instruction. Voss also questions what he sees as methodological limitations: direct observation and conversation during composing sessions, which "would surely affect students' behavior while they were composing aloud" (280). Yet another concern, echoed in Voss, focuses on the manufactured nature of the writing Emig observed. Rather than studying the emergent processes of "real-life" writing situations, Emig gives short, vague prompts to stimulate writing activity: for instance, participants were asked to write "a short piece in whatever mode and of whatever subject matter he wished"

(*Composing* 30). North and others have, moreover, commented on the interpretive license Emig seems to take in her discussion of student writer Lynn, particularly Lynn's choice to write about a Snoopy cutout instead of her grandmother. Steven Schreiner claims that to the behaviors she observed, Emig applied strong modernist notions of literary authorship (88), assuming rather than actually seeing the difficulty of writing and the "isolation of the writer at work" (87). In Schreiner's reading, Lynn fails to "grapple with her writing the way Emig believes the real writer should or does" (93).

In these ways, *Composing Processes* draws many of the general critiques of Process with a capital P: the pedagogical imperative, disregard for the shaping influences of writing contexts, overemphasizing writer's isolated actions and thinking, seeking generalizability, or manufacturing writing scenarios. *Composing Processes* has in these ways anchored general process narratives and drawn many of its familiar critiques. At the same time, the lines of potential inquiry Emig's study makes available have been interpreted in diverging ways: for one, *Composing Processes* has been said to typify either expressive or cognitive process theories. Schreiner reads Emig as an expressivist who casts schooling as a repressive force, reveres reflexive writing, and links "personal voice . . . with personal authority" (101–2). Martin Nystrand, on the other hand, suggests, "Emig was the first researcher to seriously study writing as a cognitive process" (123). Gerald Nelms echoes, naming Emig's "informing concern with cognitive development" (117) the theme with which she remains most identified. What's more, as Nelms' discussion of the social, personal, and institutional context around *Composing Processes* emphasizes, Emig delivered a range of perspectives on processes before and after the publication of this monograph (112). And this range of work demonstrates nuance, and often contradiction, in Emig's thinking about processes. As Nelms concludes, "[t]he complexity of Emig's thought and work belies any attempt at easy classification of her" (127–8). Surely this complexity is what helps cast Emig as at once as an expressivist and cognitivist, and I will highlight here, how we can see her also seeing and thinking about processes in physical and material terms. While she may in her most reified study equate composing processes to the talk-aloud record itself, Emig also prioritized the inchoate, messy, rhythmic, material, manual, motoric, and physiological aspects of composing, aspects of her process thinking that grand narratives tend to gloss.

Composing Processes, in its overdetermined position in composition history, is perhaps an unlikely place to begin building a lineage for a physical-material, or situated, view of processes. There is no sense in the study, for example, of where Emig observes these writers or how those material locations and other contextual factors may be in play; there is no sense of the sessions' time frames nor the writing tools or other material ephemera that may have been involved. The writing *scene* is decidedly not where Emig imagined the activity of process to take place. Instead, for Emig in the purview of this study, the work of writing unfolds in the compose-aloud record itself. Emig makes this spoken record of the writer's articulated thoughts and concerns essentially synonymous with process. As she claims, "a writer's effort to externalize his process of composing, somehow reflects, if not parallels, his actual inner process" (40). Equating process to the talk-aloud record thoroughly contains process "inside" the writer's mind, a matter of abstracted and procedural thinking. The tight association among process and disembodied thinking holds strong today in everyday conceptions of process, a perspective I am working to disrupt throughout this book. But it is also a perspective Emig *herself* readily undermines.

One important insight gained from Emig's talk-aloud method, and one that recurs prominently in process research and thinking that followed, is the observation that writing is recursive. By listening to Lynn and the other writers speak their writing in fits and starts, Emig concludes,

> composing does not occur as a left-to-right, solid, uninter-
> rupted activity with an even pace. Rather, there are recursive,
> as well as anticipatory, features; and there are interstices,
> pauses involving hesitation phenomena of various lengths and
> sorts that give Lynn's composing aloud a certain—perhaps
> characteristic—tempo. (57)

These blurt and pauses create, of course, a *vocal* tempo in Emig's scheme—the writers generally don't talk, or write, steadily or unceasingly. But, though Emig does not necessarily emphasize this, this tempo also takes on *bodily* and *material* dimensions as it is rendered in the study. This sense is amplified when Emig explores silences in her compose-aloud records.

Emig catalogues "hesitation behaviors," points at which writers' talk was not related directly to the content or focus of their writing. Among these behaviors she includes actions like: "making filler sounds; making critical comments; expressing feelings and attitudes, toward the self as writer, to the reader; engaging in digressions" (42). These hesitations, I note, seem to have to do with the affective dimensions of writing (an area of process inquiry developed by Alice Brand, Susan McLeod, and others, a point I expand upon in Chapter 3) and potentially attention and distraction (an area of much cultural concern, but one that seems to get little consideration in relation to process). Silence, for Emig, is its own brand of hesitation behavior. As she writes, "the silence can be filled with physical writing (sheer scribal activity); with reading; or the silence can be seemingly 'unfilled'—'seemingly' because the writer may at these times be engaged in very important nonexternalized thinking and composing" (42). This is a rare acknowledgment that participants are actually *doing* physical writing or inscription on a page, an obvious but largely unacknowledged reality given Emig's hyper-focus on participants' verbal behavior. She only one other time in the study mentions the physical act of writing when she suggests that the pace of physically writing impacts its "characteristic" tempo. She writes, "Scribal activity seems also to function as an intrusive form of 'noise' in the composing process . . . If oral anticipation thrusts the discourse forward, as Bruner suggests, the physical act of writing may be said, on the other hand to pull it back" (61). In addition, Emig leaves open the possibility that these hesitations may signal that much "very important" thinking activity is happening, but that that activity may fall outside of writers' conscious awareness.

Overall though, Emig sees hesitation behaviors—feelings, digressions, physically writing, thinking activity that is not yet articulable or is perhaps nonverbal—as strictly *outside* the purview of the composing process. She carefully separates "composing behaviors," which are "verbal behaviors that *directly* pertain to the selection and ordering of components for a piece of written discourse," from "those that are not" (41). Process activity does not—not in this study anyway—include wandering, the ineffable, the affective, tools, inscription, nor the movement of the hand on the page. One sees why Emig pledged allegiance to seeing process bound only in these records and only in utterances directly related to the writing; after all, all research must commit to and enact its perceptual frame. But as these small moments suggest, Emig at the same time recognizes that a writers' verbalized sense about what they are doing or thinking isn't the whole story of a writing process. As she qualifies clearly, her efforts provide only a "theoretical sketch of one of the most complex processes man engages in" (44), acknowledging in some measure forces in writing processes that lie beyond the reach of her talk-aloud methods.

I see in just the edges of *Composing Processes* the roles of embodied, material, and nonconscious or wandering action in processes. But in "Uses of the Unconscious," which appeared in *CCC* in 1964, Emig prioritizes the disorderliness and material conditions of writing. Emig here sounds here much like a process critic, arguing that writing processes are depicted in ways much too reductive and oversimplified. Meditating on the "conscious student theme" (46) and its lack of depth, Emig questions especially the way the writing process is constructed in textbooks:

> If one were to believe this inaccuracy, the student-writer
> uncomplexly sits down, contemplates briefly what is left
> carefully unspecified, completely formulates this *what* in his
> head before writing a word, and then—observing a series of

discrete locksteps in the left-to-right progression from planning to writing to revising, with no backsliding—builds a
competent theme like a house of dominoes. (47)

Emig's sentiment here echoes later critiques of process pedagogy, especially what
Anson calls the "process wheel" model, a "digestible scheme" (Anson, "Process"
224) that implies that writers proceed uniformly through stages of prewriting,
writing, revising. This impulse toward procedural order unrealistically reduces
the lived complexities of writing, rendering it instead as a "conscious and anti-
septically efficient act" (Emig, "Uses" 48). While *Composing Processes* focused on
writers' conscious awareness of what they were doing as they did it, in "Uses,"
Emig "suggests that not only are thought and language difficult to separate but
much composing activity goes on subconsciously" (Nelms 118). As I develop
throughout this book, a critical implication of seeing process as physical-material, as Emig emphasizes in this 1964 essay, is that processes are never fully in a
writer's own complete control. This insight will recur in various ways across my
thinking and help to reshape how we imagine the work and purview of process
instruction today.

Emig also emphasizes writing's hyper-local material conditions. Lamenting
the surface-level nature of much student writing, she asks how we could expect
to receive otherwise, considering where students are asked to write. Classroom
environments, with their short timelines and various "blatant assaults on his
concentration" ("Uses" 46), including "scuffling, bookdropping, throatclearing,
ball-point pen rolling" (46) could hardly be expected to yield more than surface
"themes." Emphasizing the susceptibility of processes to environmental factors
contradicts Emig's seeming lack of concern in *Composing Processes* about how
factors like her direct observation might impact or influence those student writers. Further countering the parameters of her landmark study, Emig posits the
importance of control over the material conditions of writing. She emphasizes
both the incantations of ritual and the material practices of habit:

> Habit is that part of the writing self that observes a regular
> schedule; that finds a room, desk, or even writing board of
> its own; that owns a filing cabinet; that sharpens all pencils
> before writing time; that does not eat lunch or take a drink
> before dinner; that cuts telephone wires; that faces a blank
> wall instead of a view of the Bay; even that orders cork
> lining. (50)

Here, Emig makes critical the physicalities of composing work: staging writing
work in a specific space and with specific objects, tools and bodily routines. While

we have no idea with what, or where, or really how the writers in *Composing Processes* produced their text, here in this essay, the stuff of writing matters a great deal to Emig's conceptions of process, as does physicality. Documenting Kipling and Hemingway's preferences for ink and pencil respectively, Emig ponders the importance of the "manuality of the task—the physical necessity to feel a specific pen or pencil pressing against the fingers and palm in a wholly prescribed and compulsive way" (50). In "Uses," writing processes are matters of making space, assembling material tools, and embodied movement. Countering her chief association with the cognitive process paradigm, Emig's early essay shows processes equally to be inarticulable, critically motoric, and materially contingent.

Emig's sense that processes are physical is also realized extensively in a less anthologized work, the 1978 essay "Hand Eye Brain: Some 'Basics' in the Writing Process." As the title makes clear, Emig here advocates for studying the physiology of processes, understanding these embodied realities as more essential to process than articulated thinking or material conditions alone. Considered by Christina Haas and Stephen Witte as one of the only works in composition studies that proposes study of the "embodied nature of writing" (414), Emig's work in "Hand Eye Brain," first published seven years after *Composing Processes,* indeed poses an entirely new set of process questions:

> The process is what is basic in writing, the process and the
> organic structures that interact to produce it. What are these
> structures? And what are their contributions? Although we
> don't yet know, the hand, the eye, and the brain itself surely
> seem logical candidates as requisite structures. (110)

Emig advises that inquiry interested in these questions must account for the plurality of embodiments through the study of writers "with specific and generalized disabilities, such as the blind, the deaf, and the brain-damaged" (111). Emig then meditates on the potential "cruciality" (111) of the physiological to process. She considers the writing hand, which, she suggests, embodies the "literal act of writing, the motoric component" (111). Focusing on the hand emphasizes the aesthetic pleasure of writing, as well as the ineluctable dependency of bodily action and material engagement. Emig underlines this point by casting writing as an act not of abstraction, but of physical creation, likening it to other bodily arts. Emig notes that in the act of writing "our sense of physically creating an artifact is less than in other modes except perhaps composing music; thus, the literal act of writing may provide some sense of carving or sculpting our statement, as in wood or stone" (112). The extended interest in the motoric action of writing by hand harkens back to, but makes much more space for, Emig's tiny acknowledgment of scribal activity in *Composing Processes.*

Emig also sees roles for both the eye and brain in processes. She believes vision might be the sense most closely related to writing; she wonders about the relationship of the brain hemispheres to writing. While this kind of right brain/ left brain scheme doesn't hold up today, Emig anticipates not only the ways that cognitive perspectives will dominate contemporaneous models of process, but also the ways today that distributed and situated cognition perspectives have begun to impact rhetorical and literacy studies (e.g., Mangen and Velay; Rickert; Syverson; Walker). Focusing us on the writing hands, on physical movements and the bodily senses, Emig insists upon process as a fundamentally embodied and emplaced practice.

However, there remains no strong legacy of Emig's emphasis on physicality. Her concluding sentiment in "Hand" is to forecast the need for writing teachers and researchers to learn about the writing body: "All of us, including senior faculty and advisers, must learn far more about biology and physiology than we have previously been asked to learn" (120). It is jarring to realize just how unrealized Emig's forecast is. The long timeline of process thinking in composition, and even Emig's own landmark study, has mostly ignored the specificities of embodiment and environment in processes. Indeed, the master narrative of process—both as its research grows and as critiques emerge—is shaped like a river rock, one that most often sediments into expressivist processes' problematic individualism or cognitivist processes' models and schemes. But what would happen to our stories of process if "Hand Eye Brain" was the essay of Emig's that we primarily associated with the process movement? Or if this essay or "Uses" instead of Emig's case studies were cast as the "single most influential piece" (North) in process histories?

Janet Emig helped remake writing and its teaching. She did so by seeing composing as webs of intricate human activities worthy of close attention. And such study should not just be focused on the activity of famous bards or great writers. Rather, the activity of the everyday student too evidenced rich complexities that defied the banality of handbooks. Emig did not just establish essential insights in the big history of the process paradigm, like recursivity. She emphasized the *physicalities* of writing experience; she believed a range of factors impacted the ways process manifests differently for individual writers' distinct bodies in differing contexts. She emphasized writing's materiality, if overlooking it methodologically. She perceived processes as the movement of the engaged hand, as the rhythms, pace, and interruptions of inscription, and that which could *and could not* be captured in a compose-aloud record. Indeed, silence has more than once lead a process-oriented compositionist to wonder about the roles of the physical body in processes.

SONDRA PERL: WRITING PROCESSES AS EMBODIED INEFFABLE MOVEMENT

In *Felt Sense: Writing with the Body*, Sondra Perl theorizes writing experience through the concept of felt sense, a bodily dynamic both tacit and eruptive in the processes of finding and articulating meaning. Applied by Perl to phenomena she had first observed over twenty-five years earlier and introduced to the field in her 1980 article "Understanding Composing," felt sense is a term originally coined by philosopher and psychoanalyst Eugene Gendlin and described by him simply as a "body-sense of meaning" (Perl, *Felt* 2). Identifying and nurturing felt sense, Perl suggests, can help writers "create a visceral connection between what they were thinking and writing, a connection that was physical" (8) and dynamically linking mind, sense, and motoric action. Aiming to address teachers' persistent questions about what they might "do" with felt sense in the writing classroom, Perl offers a set of practical guidelines in *Felt Sense*, instructions that ask writers to close their eyes, breathe, focus, continue a line of thinking, move away from another, and generally tune in to the rhythms and knowledge of their bodies.

Perl backs off making explicit an argument for writing's embodiment, as she too seems to avoid casting felt sense expressly in writing process terms. And it is telling that she waits until the end of her 2004 book to do so. Supplying the theoretical framework at the book's end performatively enacts her earlier introductory assurance that "One does not have to accept the mind-body connection for the Guidelines to work" (xvi). Given that Perl also declares plainly that, for example, "we are embodied beings; the body is central to knowing and speaking" (54), an assurance that her readers need not accept writing's fundamental embodiment to make use of her guidelines strikes as especially peculiar. Perhaps it anticipates rebuff stemming from ideologies of process as disembodied thinking and social action. Perhaps it speaks more broadly to the influence of Western Cartesian dualism on our scholarly thinking. Indeed, as Jay Dolmage puts it in a manner astute and clear: "we in composition and rhetoric have not acknowledged that we have a body, bodies" (110).

In addition to backing off of the implications of embodiment, it is equally telling that Perl doesn't cast felt sense in writing process terms. For Perl, felt sense is there waiting to become a guide in meaning-making processes; writers can be trained to better listen to and respond to this bodily experience as it manifests. Felt sense drives process through bodily sensation—it manifests as hesitations, sensations, attempts, and familiar phenomenological experiences in writing, like squirming and discomfort (*Felt* 3), unease, waiting, and charging forward. It is, perhaps, a force responsible for that characteristic tempo of composing that Emig observed. Even so, Perl never outright casts it in process theory terms.

This omission perhaps reflects the timing of the book—2004—several years after postprocess discourse has become our deep familiar and process shifted somewhere "deep in the discipline's bones." But it is critical for my purposes to emphasize that Perl discovered felt sense only in the course of her "groundbreaking empirical research" (Blau) on the writing processes of adult writers decades earlier. The ineluctable bodiedness of processes can be said to thus erupt right in the center of traditionally identified, pioneering process history in which Perl is a main character. But, like with Emig, the physicality of processes Perl exposes is not what tends to get retold or stick in our writing process imaginaries. Perl not only uncovered the complex logic and recursivity of the writing processes of "unskilled writers"; she also—and even more so—emphasized composing processes as ineffable embodied movement.

Like the modern field of composition studies itself, Perl's groundbreaking process research was sparked by urgent need. As she describes in a 2014 retrospective, Perl was teaching writing at Hostos Community College of the City University of New York (CUNY) during open admissions. At that time, with an influx of underprepared students and with "no understanding of how our students wrote" (Perl, "Research"), writing instructors became unsure about their conventional teaching methods. And so while Mina Shaughnessy was collecting and analyzing writing samples at City College, Perl took her direction from the emerging belief in controlled research as influenced by Braddock, Lloyd-Jones, and Schoer's 1963 *Research in Written Composition*. What results is her 1979 scientistic dissertation-turned-article, "The Composing Processes of Unskilled Writers." In light of more descriptive methodologies in practice at the time, Perl commences her study expressing need for a more systematic approach, a "replicable method for rendering the composing process as a sequence of observable and scorable behaviors" ("Composing" 318). Perl offers her composing style sheets method, in which she recorded the "movements" (318) of participants' processes as captured through their talk-aloud protocols. By visually mapping their coded behaviors, Perl argues that her style sheets could provide enough detail "for the perception of underlying regularities and patterns" (317) in these writers' processes.

Though, provokingly, Perl calls the writers' process behaviors movements, she identifies patterns in familiar process terms, listing sixteen distinct actions including General Planning, Local Planning, Commenting, Talking Leading to Writing, Repeating, and so on. Across these actions, Perl finds consistency and pattern in her participants' processes, or she puts it, "behavioral subsequences prewriting, writing, and editing appeared in sequential patterns that were recognizable across writing sessions and across students" ("Composing" 328). That these writers enacted comprehensive and logical processes was a significant finding, given that at the time, some educators facing tangled prose wrongly presumed the students who produced it must be cognitively deficient or some-how unteachable. Perl's research demonstrates instead urgent need for an obser-vant teacher who could "intervene in such a way that untangling [a writer's] composing process leads him to create better prose" (328). Perl's study hence established several familiar process claims: the orienting belief that writing can be taught to and learned by anyone, the recursivity rather than linearity of pro-cesses, and as she suggests, the fact that process could be captured in "a replicable and graphic mode of representation as a sequence of codable behaviors" (334). Available too is the conclusion that teacher control, guidance, or intervention in a writer's processes could lead to improved or more acceptable written products. All of these are among the most prominent claims of early process inquiry; all were questioned and critiqued; and some still influence our thinking today.

However, at the same time, "Composing Processes" does not simply resolve in seeing processes as fully observable, codifiable, logical, or intentional actions. In tension with Perl's orderly graphical schemes were the inscrutable "periods of silence" (321) she marked. Since she expected to hear the "movement" of com-posing only through what the participants said they were doing as they wrote, the recording of silence is noteworthy, and provoking. Under her methodolog-ical scheme, silence should indicate a lack of significant composing activity and thus not make it into her style sheets. Recall that Emig too noted silences but she carefully separated them from what she counted as composing activity. But Perl, by contrast, indicated the silences. Perl remained curious about "what my coding scheme could not elucidate" (*Felt* 7): the ways writers would fall into still silence followed by a "burst of composing energy" (7). What was going on in these silent moments interested Perl for more than twenty-five years, leading her to complicate her own suggestion that processes could be comprehensively coded and to investigate how composing is also meaningfully observed in subtle bodily activity and feeling. And it is in this line of thinking that her initial artic-ulation of process as *movement* becomes much more literal.

Perl's 1980 follow-up article, "Understanding Composing," begins to make something of the silences she observed. Perl starts by taking stock of the insights emergent in process movement, among them, that writing is recursive. Recur-sivity, she reflects in the context of her own study, had been "easy to spot" (364), demonstrated by backwards behaviors marked in the talk-aloud protocols, including rereading bits of text and returning to the topic. But Perl remains vested more so in an elusive "backward movement in writing, one that is not so easy to document" (364). To help elucidate this phenomena, she describes the experience of one of her students, writer-teacher Anne, who in her analysis of her own talk-aloud records reflects that process inquiries at once "reveal certain basic patterns" but also demonstrate that "process is more complex than I'm aware of" (363). Perl amplifies this idea of what process inquiries show and cannot show, stating that:

> at any given moment the process is more complex than any-
> thing we are aware of; yet such insights, I believe are import-
> ant. They show us the fallacy of reducing the composing
> process to a simple linear scheme and they leave us with the
> potential for creating more powerful ways of understanding
> composing. (369)

I see much richness in this sentiment—that process activities routinely exceed conscious awareness, that processes are nuanced and unpredictable, that the fleeting and tiny moments in process activity are just as, if not more, important than obvious and repetitive behaviors like recursive rereading, and that "writing is much more of a bodily experience" (Perl, "Watson" 133) than any given process scheme allows us to see. These are not necessarily observations associated with process in traditional or most oft-repeated field narratives.

But they are sentiments repeated by Perl in various ways across the years, both in her characterizations of process and in the modification of her methods for studying them. Reflecting in 1999, Perl laments the unfortunate ways that process became synonymous with cognition and articulates again her enduring interest in what gets left out of these schemes. She observes that, of course, it isn't that a composing process is *not* cognitive,

> but that this is not all it is. It is much richer and far more
> difficult to articulate because there are, in fact, unspoken
> pieces of it—the groping and grasping that we all go through
> . . . [T]he cognition that came out of information processing
> and problem solving, was too narrow to reflect the richness of
> composing. ("Watson" 133)

As her comment reflects, it is the elusive parts of process that compel. It's what is different and changing rather than what is the same that is perhaps most significant: what exceeds any given process model or set of steps, what is ineffable without being unknowable, what is beyond conscious awareness. And, as I argue in this book, emphasizing the contingencies rather than the articulable steps—the differences more than the sameness—of processes is that which can help us transform process teaching.

Felt Sense is yet another place where Perl articulates her process thinking. Again, in that book, Perl calls "attention to what is just on the edge of our thinking but not yet articulated in words" (xiii). Meaning is located in the body, prior to and informing articulation in language and writing. Perl dramatizes felt sense at several points by appealing to our phenomenological experiences of writing, asking us to imagine, for example, that,

> You are drafting a paper. After an initial struggle, trying this, trying that, jotting down a few sentences . . . Everything about the composition starts to feel right. Maybe your body tingles. You lean over your paper or closer to the computer screen. Maybe you jiggle your leg or tap on the table. (3)

Feeling, tingling, leaning, jiggling, tapping, Perl shows us a "bodily connection . . . related to words" (3) and how composing processes, if we pay attention, are always guided by bodily sensations, rhythms, and other forms of subtle movement. Perl closely links language and body, stating for instance "that language and meaning are connected to inchoate, bodily intuitions" (xvii). This link between language and the body aligns Perl's with embodied meaning perspectives (e.g., Fleckenstein, *Embodied*; Johnson; Lakoff and Johnson), which suggest that everyday understanding of language is only made possible by virtue of our bodily experience. But Perl tends to cast felt sense as an extraordinary rather than everyday site, one where language can be imbued with fresh or original expression. For Perl, felt sense provides a way to break free from the postmodern trap of language—from the subtle space of felt sense, "human beings can make new sense" (50) or "new ideas, or fresh ways of speaking" (51). In these ways, felt sense acquires expressivist associations that might see the body as site of individuality, authenticity, or "true" language expression. In short, I see this association turning writing processes inward—a trapping of process thinking I also work across this book to undermine and thus a place where I diverge some from Perl. Nevertheless, Perl's felt sense helps me to situate processes in immediate physical contexts by exposing the shaping roles and rhythms of sensation, bodily action, and unpredictability.

Perl's case for felt sense comes with some hesitation. Again, she does not make express links to writing process discourse, even though much of her description casts it that way. For instance, she provides several illustrations about writers in the process of drafting; her heuristic guidelines are proffered as invention methods, a "'protected space' for writing: to help writers locate topics or research questions that are of interest to them or research questions that have been assigned to them" (xv). Associations with embodiment also makes Perl hesitate. As retold in the introduction to *Felt Sense*, colleagues over the years would approach Perl with interest in, but reservations about, felt sense. Some would tell her, "talking about felt sense makes me uncomfortable. It just seems too touchy-feely" (xiii). Its elusiveness, Perl consents, "can make academics uncomfortable" (xiii) and this is in part, it would seem, why Perl gives readers permission to *not* accept the mind-body connection she constructs, the precise connection upon which the very concept and practice relies.

And Perl's colleagues are not the only ones unsure of seeing writing processes as embodied. Sheridan Blau, in his NWP review of this book, seems to echo the same uncertain response. He begins by summarizing a central claim, that felt sense is "a bodily experience." Blau is skeptical of this, at least initially, but in no-uncertain terms:

> That concept struck me, at first, as not only a counterintuitive idea but one contradicted by my own experience and knowl-edge of the wellsprings for insightful writing and speaking. Aren't our bodies designed more to degrade and misdirect our thinking rather than give us access to the most subtle and elusive thoughts?

Blau here constructs lived bodies as anathema to thinking, perhaps affirming our tacit assumptions about the transcendence of mind and Cartesian split of mind from body. Though Blau does eventually come around in his review to accept "the metabolic rhythm of composition—its movement from aridity to fertility," he does not seem to accept embodiment as itself formative. In summing up Perl's contributions, Blau recasts the physicality of felt sense as something more psy-chological than bodily. For example, Blau constructs one outcome of felt sense in strictly thinking terms, claiming that Perl's work shows the importance of "meta-cognitive processing" in composing processes. He moreover dulls in felt sense its sensational aspects when he emphasizes intuition and knowledge as "most import-ant," identifying "preverbal intuitive knowledge" as the grounds for the "sophis-ticated and subtle verbal knowledge." These terms, while not disallowing physi-cality, certainly do not emphasize it. I note also how Blau's description implies an orderly procedural link between one kind of knowledge and another—intuition to verbal knowledge. Felt sense is a tidy process, Blau seems to imply, as its tension or discomfort reliably shifts into "sophisticated" articulation. But in describing felt sense, Perl by contrast most emphasizes the importance of *not yet* knowing or of not being certain—that sharp feeling in the gut of "no, not this word," for exam-ple. There is, in other words, an important liminality in felt sense. It is inherently or characteristically uncertain; it is a vacillation between knowing just a little bit and not knowing for sure how to proceed. For me the bodily movement of felt sense thus serves as an important disruption in the logical telos that drives peda-gogical constructions of process. The important role of not knowing, of guessing or groping in context, will become especially relevant in my Chapter 5 discussion of improvisation as a figure for teaching writing with situated processes.

In sum, I am certainly not saying that Blau misrepresents Perl's book. Rather, what he focuses on in a book about writing bodies, evident through his turns-of-phrase, is perhaps symptomatic of the field's larger challenge in meaningfully conceptualizing the embodiment of process. His read shows too, perhaps, the endurance of deeply ingrained links between process and cognition.

Ultimately Perl was more interested in the nuance and complexities of writing processes than observable activity like recursivity and rereading. She emphasizes the complexity, rather than the ordered legibility, of processes. She seeks to make the bodily and phenomenological experience of composing more mindfully experienced, rendering aspects that may otherwise go unnoticed or be deemed unimportant or idiosyncratic. She appeals to the data of experience—haven't we all had these sharp feelings erupt in writing? In her focus on what's beyond just the "activities taking place inside the writer's head" (Bizzell 185), Perl raises questions central to the pursuit of situated writing processes: how can we discover and consider dimensions of writing processes that exceed the writer's conscious awareness? What roles do physical bodies play in composing? Bodies, movement, and environmental ambience have indeed been left invisible or relegated to the background. One of Perl's central if overlooked contributions is the always-something-more-ness of composing—the complexities and non-repeatability of processes as embodied movement not amenable to schemas or stabilization.

CHRISTINA HAAS: WRITING PROCESSES AS EMBODIED PRACTICE

In their 2001 study of engineers and utilities staff writing a complicated standards document, Christina Haas and Stephen Witte explore processes of workplace technical writing. They're interested in studying this collaboration for its complexities, for example, in how the writers integrate text and images, standardize their draft versions over time, and "deploy[] multiple production and representation systems" (420). Significantly though, their study is not first motivated by gaps in research on collaborative workplace composing. Rather *embodiment* is their foremost enlivening exigence.

Haas and Witte address this need right at the open of their detailed study. There, they liken the production of music to that of writing, noting that "acts of situated writing clearly entail bodily performances of many kinds: the manipulation of fingers, hands, arms; the orientation or positioning of the body; the use of the visual, aural, tactile senses" (414). While technical writing research had to some extent accounted for context, material conditions, or embodied knowledge (i.e., Sauer), Haas and Witte argue that embodiment takes a formative role not only in the specific practices they observed in their study, but also more expansively as the "essential embodied nature of technical writing" (415) itself.

In a 2007 retrospective interview with Rebecca Burnett, Haas notes that the engineering standards study began while Witte was working with cultural-historical activity theory (CHAT) and she was finishing her 1996 book, *Writing Technology: Studies on the Materiality of Literacy.* "Of course, we were not using the term *embodiment* then" (29), Haas recalls of their separate projects. But what emerged in their data—"the use of space and tools, the interweaving of talk and gesture" (30)—led them to frame their study with embodiment. As Burnett points out though, they might have called upon more established concepts in technical writing research, like expertise or situated cognition. So why *embodiment*? Haas responds that critical theory at the time was taking interest in the body but that "literacy studies had not confronted the embodied nature of writing. And we wanted to do that" (31). Haas establishes this goal in some contrast to the ways she was framing her inquiry in *Writing Technology* "in terms of materiality." She of course focuses on the materiality of word processing and other digital technologies in that book, but I observe that embodiment is too a critical, even baseline, concept there. Though less emphasized in her own research narratives and in reviews of her book, I see Haas' embodied practice as a crux of her argument and critical to my thinking, as in *Writing Technology* she connects local, particular physical situations and movements of writing processes to wider cognitive, social, cultural, technological and historical contexts and constraints. In other words, Haas makes a case for physically situating composing processes as, for her, it is through this local, small-scale vantage that larger social, cognitive and historical dimensions of writing can be enacted, observed, and tracked.

Writing Technology is ambitious and capacious in its focus on technology and literacy, as Haas responds to the assumption "that computers' transformation of communication means a transformation, or a revolutionizing, of culture" (ix). But such seismic cultural change is often only presumed, Haas warns, as "most theoretical accounts of writing treat technology in a cursory way, or ignore it altogether" (xii). Haas thus raises "The Technology Question," or in her words, "[t]he challenge of accounting for the relationship between writing—as both a cognitive process and a cultural practice to the material technologies that support and constrain it" (ix). This question opens up investigations focused on how material tools "change writing, writers, written forms, and writing's functions" as well as "whether, and how, changes in individual's writing experiences with new technologies translate into large-scale, cultural 'revolutions'" (ix). Haas sets out to determine, in other words, how digital revolutions unfold on a range of scales.

Not surprisingly, contemporaneous reviews of *Writing Technology* tend to emphasize focus on computer technology. In his 1996 *Kairos* review, Lee Honeycutt claims that Haas asks us to diminish our blind enthusiasms for computer culture and instead take up "a more balanced view that sees these technologies as material embodiments of our culture." Honeycutt finds Haas' narrative case study about the redesign of a user interface for a campus file-sharing and email system "the most convincing," as it demonstrates that computer systems are not transparent or self-determining but in Haas' words, "an evolving and fluid but nonetheless powerful cultural system" (165). Similarly, in her 1997 *Technical Communication Quarterly* review, Kristine Blair highlights Haas' claims that writing and technology cannot be treated transparently or without considering the specifics of material configuration, valuing the insight especially that "The" computer "does not exist" (225) only computers multiple, with varying configurations that cannot be generalized "from one electronic writing environment to another" (225). Both reviewers also obliquely mention implications for process. Blair suggests that Haas urges scholars to question "the role of technology in the writing process" (225), while Honeycutt wonders if Haas' work might "complicate some of our reigning assumptions about the supposed benefits of computer technology on the writing process." I see in Haas' book, though, more expansive implications than only how discrete material tools differently shape processes (even as that too is an important point). Haas' perspective is bigger—she resolves a rift among cognitive and socio-cultural paradigms in process theories through focus on material writing technologies and her concept of embodied practice. In short, it is only through examining tiny iterations of embodied practice that we may "recognize the symbiotic and systemic relationship between technology, culture, and individuals" (Haas 230).

Haas in part builds the need to examine writing technologies by outlining two established but competing theories of writing in terms of focus and scale: the cultural and the cognitive. She documents both the scholars who established "the cultural forms and social functions of writing and written texts" (x) and those who have focused on "the complexity of the writing process itself" (x), including cognitive researchers like Linda Flower and John Hayes. The reign of these theories, though, presents the vexing problem (one echoed in Patricia Bizzell and Marilyn Cooper's social theories, explored in the next chapter): How can we conceptualize writing as both an individual and social act? Both these social and cognitive paradigms, moreover, tend to treat writing technology transparently (38). For example, Haas notes that in most cognitive models "there seems to be little cognizance that writers live and work in a material space, creating material artifacts, using material technologies. The notion that these material constraints might impinge in any way on the processes of composing, which these theorists seek to examine, is not acknowledged" (39) (certainly this absence is evident in Emig's *Composing Processes*). Examining the materiality of writing, overlooked as it is, Haas asserts, can ease the culture/individual divide in writing (process) theories and research. And this impasse forms the heart of the technology question too—how small-scale shifts in individual technology practice might be understood to precipitate a large-scale cultural (computer) revolution and vice versa.

Though the cultural and the cognitive camps clearly connect Haas' thinking to process, she does not engage expressly in process terms. Nevertheless, she describes writing in ways fitting to the camps we associate with the process paradigm; she asserts that, "writing is at once individual, an act of mind; cultural, an historically based practice; and material, inherently dependent on physical, space-and-time artifacts" (26). By implication, writing processes cannot be just social or cognitive or historical. They are also and simultaneously material. Emphasizing the materiality of composing is not just additive, though—not just another dimension from which to investigate and understand the complex ways writing is accomplished. Rather, it is chiefly through the materialities of writing—the emplaced, socially conditioned, cognitively shaped, and mediated actions of an individual writer—that the full complexities of literacy may be rendered. As I explore in the next chapter, it has been a tacit assumption in composition theory after postprocess that the breadth and complexity of writing may be rendered only through constructing writing's situatedness on massive scales—through ecologies, networks, complexity theories, for example. In short, after postprocess, writing is more so found in its contexts than in relation to individual writers (Trimbur, "Taking"). Haas provides an alternative to this storyline: she sees those massive systems and contexts only through discrete, material, located, and everyday practices.

It's not only that Haas' perspective can be fittingly connected to process history and discourse. Haas should also be viewed as an important connection to recent field interest in the material groundings of literate and rhetorical action. In what has been called a "material turn" (Barnett, "Toward"), of late, writing scholars have worked to complicate more abstracted and fixed social perspectives with insights from new materialism and distributed agency, object-oriented, actor-network, and cultural-historical activity theories. Materially-oriented compositionists question models of autonomous subjectivity and the primacy of human agency in writing and rhetoric while amplifying the roles of things, bodies, affects, environments, and others (e.g., Barnett; Boyle and Barnett; Brooke and Rickert; Gries; Hawk; Lynch and Rivers; Micciche, "Writing"; Rickert). Laura R. Micciche encapsulates this interest as a focus on "the big wide world that both includes and exceeds subjects, altering understandings of agency, identity, subjectivity, and power along the way" (489). Recognizing that "big wide world" in which writing is always already situated has cast net limits on the postmodern dance of discourse and free-floating signifiers in its collisions with flesh, institutions, power dynamics, political forces, objects, and bodies. Materially-oriented theories, in sum, tend to see writing and rhetorical action as practices of more than just agents or communities alone, and rather as acts of "coexistence . . . an activity not solely dependent on one's control but made possible by elements"—like objects, others, tools, environments, and sounds—"that codetermine writing's possibility" (Micciche 498). This interest in materiality certainly amplifies the urgency of situating writing processes I seek in this book and makes a return to Haas' work even more timely.

But with visibility in composition and rhetoric feeling somewhat recent and pronounced, new materialisms can feel a bit like the "Theory du jour." As I think through "new materialisms" with regard to processes and writing instruction, it's important to put checks on its seeming novelty. Indigenous rhetorics (e.g., Haas, A.M.; Grant; Powell) is a decolonialized lineage for relational ontologies and materialisms outside of and before such discourses in Western-European philosophy. Affect theories too hold similar assumptions about the relations among individuals and environments as do many new materialist theories (see, for example, Kathleen Stewart's discussion of environmental "atmospheres"). And Kristie S. Fleckenstein's work on embodied composition delivers similar relational ideas. Building from the work of cultural anthropologist, Gregory Bateson, Fleckenstein describes how place, objects, bodies, and time coalesce to continuously (re)produce the relational and "illusory 'I'" ("Writing Bodies" 288) that writes. This is all to say, and to say all too briefly, what could be quickly glossed as a "new" material turn is better seen as a more longstanding and complex network of relations among myriad influences.

One such extension of or node in this "material turn" that I see as a valuable connection for my interest in situating processes is an emerging "sociomaterial" framework for writing and literacy. In her 2016 qualitative study of individuals with aphasia and their relationships to adaptive technologies, Elisabeth L. Miller advances this orienting term to frame her interests and lists other scholars identifiable with this framework as well (including Dennis Baron's work on the pencil, Paul Prior and Jody Shipka's CHAT study of four academic writers, Suresh Canagarajah's discussion of material access and geopolitical economics for international scholars, and Haas' study of computer technologies, among others). For Miller, sociomaterialism represents "a recent move in writing studies" (35) to unite the material and social dynamics of literate action. Material things of and around writing are actively a part of processes not inert tools transparently deployed by a writer-agent. Writing environments are not passive background staging, but participatory and shaping. Materiality related to writing processes—both immediate and distant like objects, bodies, light, noise, tools, chairs, electricity, pets, and so on—is productively understood as "active, self-creative, productive, unpredictable" (Coole and Frost 9). This is to say: far from a passing interest, materiality has been and continues to be a fertile, if underexplored and ranging, perspective from which to examine writing processes on a range of scales. Haas' work can be said to embody a lineage for current socio- or new materialisms of composition, and, as I'm arguing, for situating processes.

But even with repositioning Haas in the material turn and in process history, what remains even still less emphasized is her concomitant assertion that writing as an embodied practice. This notion earns only a small amount of space in *Writing Technology*; it is mentioned only a few times and in broad strokes. But from any angle, the concept is foundational, more so than material technologies alone, in uncovering the interplay of individual practice and larger social contexts. Here is an extended moment when Haas gives this concept some life:

> [E]mbodied practice is a culturally sanctioned, culturally
> learned activity that is accomplished by individual human
> beings moving through time and space. Certainly writing can
> be understood as an embodied practice. Writers use their bod-
> ies and the materials available to their bodies via the material
> world, to both create and to interact with textual artifacts.
> Writers' bodily movements and interactions are evident in
> the conduct of everyday literate activities: Writers pick up
> and chew on pencils, they rest their hands on keyboards,
> they move closer to their texts in some circumstances, push
> back from them in others; readers hunch over manuscripts
> with pens, stretch out with books under trees, move through
> on-line texts by pushing keys or clicking buttons. (225–6)

Haas emphasizes first writing as repetitive learned habits, the acquired cultural moves that make the making of writing possible. Her opening sentence makes me picture the ways I learned QWERTY keyboarding starting in elementary school, beginning with repetitive punches of the right index finger on the j-j-j-j key then the u-u-u-u key (trying to compose this example only further speaks to Haas' point—only my fingers know now, not at all my conscious mind, which digit is in charge of punching which keys). At the same time, Haas here lingers on the smallest physicalities and movements that make and accompany writing—that which is perhaps idiosyncratic, "everyday," changing, or impro-visational in relation to time and place. Embodied practice is where Haas can "contemplate what she feels are two questions crucial to our understanding" (Honeycutt): "How is it that material tools can shape mental processes? And what is the relationship of material tools to the culture in which they are embedded?" (Haas 224). Embodied practice connects these questions, revealing how micro-focus on something like hands to keyboards can be gateways not to solip-sistic but situated views of writing, enabling access to massive scales of histories, consumer economies, or technological innovations.

Haas no doubt emphasizes word processing and the configurations of material writing technologies. She does say, after all, that writing should be seen as an individual, historical and cultural "act of mind" (26) that is material, or "inherently dependent on physical, space-and-time artifacts" (26). But as she also asserts, "overcoming the culture-cognition impasse in writing scholarship will require refiguring writing, in all its complexity, as of the body and of the mind" (4). In other words, physicality is always already implicated in her argument for the materialities of literacies. Or, as Haas has it, "embodied practice becomes useful in more clearly articulating the connection between the material world of technologies and artifacts and the mental world of thought" (225). It is bodily action that is the critical nexus among minds and objects, and in turn, between individuals and cultures. Haas' contribution for me then is not so much how examining materiality alone resolves the cultural and cognitive impasse but how a physical-material perspective might do so.

It is also the case, however, that Haas doesn't spend time at all, aside from a few gestures to theoretical citations, building embodied practice as a concept. I see my own theory of situated writing processes as informed by the spirit of Haas' embodied practice though; I build upon it in Chapter 3 where I bring together affect, new materialist, ontological, and composition theory perspectives to enliven interaction not only with writing technologies but the ambient, populated environment in which writing takes place. For the ways that Haas focuses on material environments and bodily practice and assuages the seeming choice between social and cognitive process perspectives, I see her work as an integral chapter in writing process stories—and in the not-yet-articulated chapter of situating writing processes that I've begun to sketch here.

Stories of writing processes have not been regularly told from the vantage of bodies, objects, sensations, or inchoateness. The history of process has been one largely focused on cognition or expression and the individual writer. But the physical situatedness of process has certainly been available all along—from Emig's focus on the biologies, material conditions, and physical rituals of writing; to Perl's focus on the body, silence, movement, and meaning; to Haas's less noted emphasis on embodied practice. However, my little story of processes as physically and materially situated is further complicated by other established impulses that have moved us away from the study of writing as individual practice. As Haas shows, we have seemed to enforce or at least allow for an impasse between examining writing on small micro-scales of everyday practice or on larger macro-scales of social and material systems. Indeed, situatedness and scale—a question embodied in postprocess discourses—presents another set of challenges, and exigencies, in pursuit of situating process.

CHAPTER 2

LARGER FORCES OR INDIVIDUAL PROCESSES—SITUATEDNESS AND SCALE ACROSS POST/ PROCESS THEORIES

If the grooves of disciplinary thinking shape process into one thing—like (acontextual) thinking or (apolitical) self-expression—then postprocess is most often fashioned as a *break* from that thing. Many postprocess-oriented thinkers make their break clear—as Thomas Kent puts it, "Breaking with the still-dominant process tradition in composition studies, post-process theory . . . endorses the fundamental idea that no codifiable or *generalizable* writing process exists or could exist" (*Post-Process* 1). Kent's break here is so complete so as to pronounce process always already impossible, even nonexistent. Joseph Petraglia echoes the urge to break up and move on, claiming, "we now have the theoretical and empirical sophistication to consider the mantra 'writing is a process' as the right answer to a really boring question" ("Is There" 53). Petraglia votes to end process in favor of more interesting questions, those focused on the "ecology in which writing takes place [rather] than in the mere fact that writing is the outcome of a variety of steps and stages" (63). In so doing, postprocess acts as a dismissal: "a rejection of the generally formulaic framework for understanding writing that process suggested" (53), a rejection of process as a "regime," of the dogmatism of teachability, and of the illusion that there are any substantive "general writing skills" that can be isolated and taught.

John Trimbur, thought to be the first to advance the term "post-process" in a 1994 book review (Matsuda 65), does not necessarily construct postprocess as a break. He does suggest though that the books he reviews "result from a crisis" and "a growing disillusion" with writing as a process ("Taking"109). Postprocess is for Trimbur more a shift than a break: less focus on writers writing and more interest in "the cultural politics of literacy" (109). Sidney Dobrin has echoed Trimbur's sense of a collective refocusing, defining postprocess in 1999 as "the shift in scholarly attention from the process by which the individual writer produces text to the larger forces that affect that writer and of which that writer is a part" ("Paralogic" 132). Subsequent invocations of postprocess have strengthened its dismantling energy, a force evidenced, for example, by Dobrin's more recent "intent of violence" (*Postcomposition* 2) toward the traditional foci of composition studies—students, subjectivity, teaching, and administration. Postprocess as break is evidenced too, though in a subtler form, in related "postpedagogical" questioning of whether writing can be taught at all (e.g., Lynch).Whether a break strong, weak, or a shift, postprocess in different ways zooms out, leaving behind looking at writers writing to examine instead the macro-scales of writing's expansive contexts and systems.

But often it's not just a shift in focus—incantations of postprocess can also emphasize what we *can't do* anymore. We can't invoke process, Kent and others say, because it doesn't exist. We can't teach general skills because they don't either. This sense of not-any-moreness, of the field being now *after process*, has perhaps had some chilling effect on process discourse. A sense of prohibition, for example, permeates Anson's suggestion that process is now "in the discipline's bones." It likely urges Richard Fulkerson in 2005 to resolutely assert (even if too strongly) that, "we no longer do research into writing processes" (670). It seems to direct Jody Shipka, in *Toward a Composition Made Whole,* to address the "discipline's fading interest in composing process studies" (104) and to make a case for "rethinking the potential and the value of composing process research" (14). It may reflect in the inclusion of "process" in Paul Heilker and Peter Vandenberg's 1996 volume, *Keywords in Composition Studies,* and its subsequent omission in their 2015 follow-up, *Keywords in Writing Studies.* It seems to motivate Pamela Takayoshi, in her 2015 study of social media composing, to argue overtly for "pay[ing] attention to writing as a process . . . through data-based, in situ studies of what writers are actually doing with contemporary writing technologies" ("Short-Form" 2), or again in 2018, to assert plainly that, "we need a return to research on composing processes" ("Writing" 550). That a compositionist would find need to make an overt "pitch" for process as a framework suggests the extent to which a clear if loose "after process" sensibility has taken hold. I note too that express calls for a return to or resurgence of process are concerned largely with process research—making me wonder again: what of our process *teaching* in this long postprocess era?

As we reckon with what postprocess means, it's important to emphasize that the characteristics of process that postprocess aims to break from are not what I and others (e.g., Breuch; Shipka; Takayoshi) are interested in. As Lee-Ann Kastman Breuch has it, the shape of "process" often crafted "by postprocess scholars is the scapegoat in an argument to forward postmodern and antifoundationalist perspectives" (120). Postprocess contributes a range of compelling claims relevant to writing theory, practice, and even to process—those related to the materialities, contingencies, unpredictability, distributedness, relationality, and publicness of writing acts. Indeed, these ideas might take more hold in the field—particularly from my view, in contemporary writing pedagogies—if postprocess was not so regularly conceptualized as *not-process*, if the transformative potential of postprocess claims did not directly appeal to or raise by association "process as the necessary caricature" (Matsuda 74).

Further, mostly unrealized in the long loose influence of postprocess thinking is its potential to see the operation of process (teaching) more clearly and critically. For Dobrin, "posts," like postprocess,

> mark a period in which conversations initiate about not only what we have been doing but what we are still very much currently doing. This conversation occurs in a reflexive, critical way that was not possible during the period prior to the post. This is what is hopeful about the post: the possibility of seeing and knowing the effects of what which is posted becomes greater. (*Postcomposition* 196)

Part of the potential of "post-ing," as Dobrin articulates it here anyway, is that it can help us see the implicit assumptions, ideologies, and associations of that which we've post-ed. That is, postprocess comes loaded with capacity to lay bare the layers of what we have meant by "writing as a process" and what multiple effects those meanings have had. It could help us not only take stock of multiple effects of "the process movement," but also proceed with a renewed commitment to critically interrogate process, to shake this conceptual frame awake, and expand it beyond its tacit associations, particularly in our teaching. (At the same time, I accept that often postprocess thinkers, Dobrin especially, want nothing to do with teaching or traditional field concerns).

My point is that postprocess need not be final abandonment or a full break from process. Postprocess thinking could spur productive disorientation and a constructive rebuilding of teaching with processes that is more nuanced, specific, and dimensional. As Bruce McComiskey writes, a "fruitful meaning for the 'post' in post-process is 'extension,' not 'rejection'" ("Post-Process" 37). But embrace of extension is not to imply sameness or unity across post/process. In wanting to break with the postprocess rhetoric of breaking, I do not mean that all the many differences and conflicts in the scholarship and theory of process and postprocess can or should be smoothed over. Again, variation, or as Kristopher Lotier puts it, "inherent indeterminacy" (362), is a key trait of postprocess. Indeterminacy is also, I underline again, a characteristic of *process* theories and theorists. Accordingly, I am claiming only that any efforts to definitively separate process approaches or ideas from postprocess ones should be interrogated.

Situatedness has been one such dividing line. The situated condition of writing and its practice—broadly, writing's susceptibility to or entanglement with social, material, community, embodied, spatial, cultural, and historical forces—

remains an oft-repeated and expansive creed. Situatedness is a foundational assumption as the core of a range of contemporary writing theories including social constructivism, ecological, activity, networked, complex systems, and postprocess theories. Though it may lack the mantra-style apparentness of "writing as a process not a product," writing's situatedness has been everywhere in our thinking for more than thirty years. For one, situatedness is one of three key tenets of Kent's postprocess theory, as he observes that "writers always write from some position or some place, writers are never no where" (*Post-Process* 3). And while Kent allows that situatedness may be of concern to both process and postprocess-oriented compositionists, he underscores that postprocess tends to "make more out of this claim" (3), meaning that, for one, writing is interactive and deeply relational (e.g., Couture; Kent, *Paralogic*).

At the same time though, a *lack* of concern for situatedness has been the means by which some divide "the process movement" from everything that is more or less "post-process" (Trimbur, "Delivering" 188). For instance, John Trimbur claims that writing process schemes portray writing as intangible and abstract, as "dominant representations of writing typically offered by the process movement all picture writing as an invisible process, an auditory or mental event" (188). Similarly, in his recent work on a longer timeline for postprocess invention, Kristopher Lotier divides process and post- in terms of internalism versus externalism: process-era internalism sees the mind as separate from the world and other minds while by contrast, postprocess externalism sees the impossibility of such "aloneness," as "writing is always already overwritten by other people, and, crucially, other *stuff*" (366). From the vantage of postprocess, process schemes by definition and contrast are acontextual, abstract, isolated, inside-the-head—the transcendent, unsituated solitary mind at work, floating free and of no particular place.

While it will not surprise that I too agree with the clinginess of these associations with process and a need to deconstruct them, it's also true that separating process from post- based on situatedness is not so neat and tidy. The early 1980s, often seen as the "heyday" of process, saw not the reign of unquestioned cognitivism and writing as purely "invisible" mental processes, but sustained dialectical critique undermining assumptions, for instance, about comprehensiveness, protocol methods, and context, (e.g., Cooper and Holzman; Mishler; Odell; Reither) as well as the expansion of process theories into social contexts. And to productively muddy the waters even further: the 1970s, an era associated with expressive, voice-oriented, and many might say, acontextual and apolitical, individualist process approaches, saw at the same time the publication of Students' Right to their Own Language (SRTOL). Lead by Black Power and Civil Rights movements (Gilyard 93) and the NCTE/CCCC Black Caucus starting in the 1960s, this landmark resolution argued implicitly that language and writing processes are inseparable from an individual's intersectional contexts—their communities, ethnicities, dialects, and cultures. In working to make accesss to literacy learning more equitable and just especially for racial and ethnic minorities, SRTOL pivotally situated language processes culturally and socially, doing so much earlier than most disciplinary timelines of process and stories of the "social turn" suggest. STROL, in this way, can be seen as a precursor to the social and community writing process views articulated by Bizzell, Bruffee, Cooper, and others in the 1980s. But some stories about process, like Faigley's in 1986, miss making this connection explicit, instead seeing the "social view" of processes as a "more recent" phenomena (528). Moreover, as demonstrated in Chapter 1, landmark process researchers like Emig and Perl simultaneously presumed acontextuality and situatedness; both staged their studies of processes in laboratory-like conditions and brought attention to writing's immediate material conditions in terms of bodily movement, embodied meaning, and writing tools. Building upon these and other varied moments in our histories associated with situating processes in contexts (among them cultural, embodied, community, and so on), in this chapter, I argue that situatedness is not a stable, distinguishing assumption of postprocess, but one available as a significant part of the varied discourses within "the process paradigm."

In making a unifying gesture though, I preserve an important overarching difference: the scope, or scale, on which writing's situatedness has been viewed and theorized. Again, postprocess perspectives refocus on the "larger forces" (Dobrin, "Paralogic") in which writers find themselves; process perspectives focus on "in situ studies of what writers are actually doing" (Takayoshi, "Short Form" 2). This zoom out in focus beyond the individual writer is suggested in each of the postprocess compositionists I mention above: not just processes but "cultural politics" (Trimbur, "Taking"), no longer individual writers, but larger forces and contexts (Dobrin, "Paralogic"), no longer writers' stages and steps but a complex ecology in which writing finds itself (Petraglia, "Is There"). Such articulations imply a choice between seeing writing in terms of either micro-scaled, individual processes or macro-scaled "larger forces." But I argue that situatedness is a continuum, not a choice. Haas's intervention serves as an example of process theory that doesn't choose but instead ranges across this continuum. She focuses upon discrete writers' interactions with material technologies to in order to situate writing at once within writers' immediate physical conditions and the larger interplay among social, cultural, and cognitive forces.

Writing theories influenced by the assumption of situatedness (and in many cases a generalized spirit of postmodernity and anti-foundationalism), though, have largely operated under a strong impulse to see writing from perpetually zoomed out vantages alone. To exemplify how situatedness has been consistently realized on massive scales, I begin this chapter by close reading the work of Patricia Bizzell and Marilyn Cooper. Perceiving partiality in early cognitive process schemes, these theorists shift focus from contained individual actions to community-situated ones, stretching the scope of writing's activity expansively, even essentially infinitely. I then track this tendency to conceive of writing's (social) situatedness on massive scales in more recent sociomaterial approaches, illustrated by Margaret Syverson and Nedra Reynolds. Their perspectives, which also take keen interest in the material spaces and embodied action of writing practice, directly invite, but largely preclude, the study of writing's radically local physical-material situations. The expansive scales that have dominated the framing of situatedness in composition's theory imagination especially in the 1990s and 2000s—network, complexity, ecological and cultural-historical activity theories—have mostly prevented us from lingering to view writing's physical and environmental situatedness at the level of *in situ* practice. But such situated micro-views of writing creates a critical vantage for the practice of process pedagogies today. Ultimately, I argue and illustrate in this chapter that situatedness and scale is not, and was never, an either/or proposition.

WRITING AS SOCIALLY SITUATED PROCESSES: SOCIAL CONSTRUCTIVIST CRITIQUE ZOOMS OUT

Writing in 1985, James A. Reither aims to modify what he sees as a "truncated view" (622) of writing processes. Reigning models of process started *in media res,* failing to account for the winding backstories of any given writer's knowledge. Reither believes we should chase those infinite backstories, observing,

> If we are going to teach our students to need to write, we
> will have to know much more than we do about the kinds
> of contexts that conduce—sometimes even force, certainly
> enable—the impulse to write. The "micro-theory" of process
> now current in composition studies needs to be expanded
> into a "macro-theory" encompassing activities, processes, and
> kinds of knowing that come into play long before the impulse
> to write is even possible. (623)

In a sense, Reither urges us to adjust the scales on which processes are conceived. The reigning micro-view, he observes, which understands "writing as a self-contained process that evolves out of a relationship between writers and their emerging texts" (622) must be replaced by the macro, a broader and longer view of writing that accounts for previous scenes of learning and activity that inevitably shape how a writer takes up any discrete writing task. In other words, the "substantive social knowing" (626) that initiates writing is, of course, not limited to that moment of penning or typing the first word; rather, it stretches backwards and forwards, across countless social scenes. Reither reflects a view shared by other social-oriented process theorists and that composition still holds centrally today—that which drives and shapes writing is not containable only in small relays between the writer's mind and emerging text. Rather, writing is always *not-just-here*. Reither captures, in the language of micro and macro that I borrow and repurpose, the burgeoning recognition of writing's vast social systematics and in so doing, complicates writing's timelines. Writing becomes an infinite montage, never really lingering upon any single locatable scene.

Reither's interest in the socio-historical situatedness of writing activity is not separate from process topoi; Reither's is a theory about writing processes. What makes it distinct though—and why I think social theories are often collapsed under more contemporary notions of "postprocess"—is its unwieldy scale, a vantage that makes discrete processes essentially unlocatable. Social process theories reveal the vast scope of factors and contexts undergirding writing activity—those *beyond* any individual writer herself. They emphasize how only communities and systems can be understood to host and sustain writing, as I in this section demonstrate through close readings of Patricia Bizzell and Marilyn Cooper's work. Social critique certainly does repudiate certain notions associated with early process research like, for example, that language could meaningfully operate autonomously from sociality. But in dismantling the presumed autonomy of writing as an individual practice, these pioneering social process theorists do not construct a choice between individual or larger community processes, nor do they argue that processes are *only* social. Rather than somehow *after process*, these landmark process critiques advance fluid relationships, a winding complex continuum amongst cognitive and social perspectives, an interest at once in what happens "inside the writer's head" (Bizzell 185) and equally in "an infinitely extended group of people who interact through writing" (Cooper 372). Ultimately I read Bizzell and Cooper calling not for a *break from* process nor a separate paradigm, but rather for a modulation of focus between micro- and macro-scaled perspectives.

Patricia Bizzell's 1992 collection *Academic Discourse and Critical Consciousness* is identified by Trimbur as principally reflective of "post-process" and the "social turn" in composition. As Trimbur puts it, Bizzell reframes the problems compositionists observed in students' writing not as linguistic or cognitive deficiencies, but rather as "cultural unfamiliarity with the registers and practices of a particularly privileged discourse community, the academy" (117). Bizzell makes this case especially in "Cognition, Convention, and Certainty: What we Need to Know about Writing," published originally in 1982. Here Bizzell works to disrupt consensus among compositionists at the time that writing problems are chiefly "thinking problems." In so doing, Bizzell performs what I see, in short, as a *zoom out*—a refocusing of writing theory on macro-scaled, "larger forces" (Dobrin) more than single writers. This zoom is characteristic of social process and subsequent writing theory, like complex systems, ecological, and actor network theories. But, I emphasize, the zoom out need not be a break.

Bizzell begins her process critique by accounting for the common ground amongst inner- and outer-directed theories. Her question becomes not one of *choosing* one camp over the other, but one of emphasis—"what [compositionists] *most* need to know about writing" (77) or where the focus of writing theories ought to linger and as such, where writing pedagogies ought to intervene. The inner-directed camp, as Bizzell identifies it, focuses on language as a matter of "innate mental structures" (77); "language-learning and thinking processes in their earliest state, prior to social influence" (77); seeing writing processes as "universal"; and writers as "problem solvers" (84) with "individual capacities" (77). Outer-directed perspectives, by contrast, are "more interested in the social processes whereby language-learning and thinking capacities are shaped and used in particular communities" (77); the "community context" (89); and the "socially situated knowledge without which no writing project gets under way" (93). Said another way, outer-directed perspectives undermine the tacit assumption that thinking or language could take place outside of "a social context that conditions them" (79). Rather than presuming the immutability, if potential breakdown, of logical, mental writing processes that would carry on identically regardless of differing socio-rhetorical conditions, Bizzell's outer-directed camp puts focus on particular, context-dependent "discourse conventions" (79). In this important distinction, Bizzell shifts assumptions about writing development and instructional intervention. From an inner-directed angle, struggling writers require intervention in their *thinking*. In familiar cognitive schemes, for example, knowledge is something a writer just kind of *has*—the nature of that knowledge taken for granted (93). But, for Bizzell, it is crucially important that that knowledge necessarily comes from *elsewhere*—that it is shaped, received, and accumulated over time and across many social contexts. As such, from the outer-directed vantage, writing problems are *exposure* problems—a lack of experience with the conventions of the varying discourse communities in which writing is always already a part. "[I]f we are going to see students as problem-solvers," Bizzell concludes, "we must also see them as problem-solvers situated in discourse communities that guide problem definition and the range of alternative solutions" (84).

Rather than in the short contained timeline of writing in cognitive schemes, Bizzell suggests it is only a writer's varied background stories, or infinite flash-

backs, that hold keys to helping writers improve, a shift which refocuses pedagogues' interventions on preparation, exposure, and practice. In sum, in order
to know really "what goes on in the writer's head" (183), compositionists must
"research into the social and cultural contexts from which the writer's knowledge
comes" (Bizzell 183). And any sense that thinking processes float free or are universal across writers must be disrupted if interest in cognitive processes remains,
Bizzell insists. Thinking (and language) is really only thinkable if seen as shaped
by local and expansive situated forces and experiences.

I picture Bizzell's critique as though she takes the camera of our disciplinary
interest and suddenly *zooms out* our vantage: where formerly compositionists
were trying to peer "inside the writer's head" (185), now Bizzell pulls the camera
back and up to a tall perch from which we can start to see the myriad social,
cultural, political, academic and community contexts that source and shape any
given writer's knowledge. In zooming out, problem-solvers multiply into communities in which problems are shaped (84); thinking practice spreads out to
become community practice; any given writer is only comprehensible as at the
same time a community of writers. The purview of writing processes gets bigger,
longer. Rather than the writer *right now*, Bizzell focuses on the *elsewhere* and
before: the innumerable social contexts in which any writing and knowing happens, in episodes that even precede and extend beyond any given writer's life-
time, places and times that could not possibly be mapped or known with any
kind of finality. Bizzell's social processes, forged in dialectical relation to cognitive and expressive schemes, emphasizes how writing is never just *here* and *now*.
But Bizzell's zoom out, I should emphasize, does not exclude focus on discrete
writers or defined scenes of writing in time. But it also doesn't encourage us to
linger in any given scene. Bizzell's social process camera is rather in continuous
motion, as it races to keep up with the cascade of potentially infinite situated
forces at work.

Marilyn Cooper similarly traverses and zooms, in her 1986 essay, "The Ecology of Writing." Cooper aims to knock the sheen off process theories' seeming
revolutionary finality by exposing how quickly cognitive process models had
been codified, reduced, and presumed comprehensive. Like Bizzell, Cooper
extends, rather than *breaks* from, this cognitive emphasis by pointing out what
those models still *cannot* see. Cooper writes, "theoretical models even as they
stimulate new insights blind us to some aspects of the phenomena we are studying" (365). Making a generative, additive critique, Cooper diagnoses cognitive
models as probably true but limited:

> The problem with the cognitive process model of writing has
> nothing to do with its specifics: it describes something of

what writers do and goes some way toward explaining how writers, texts, and readers are related. But the belief on which it is based—that writing is thinking and, thus, essentially a cognitive process—obscures many aspects of writing we have come to see as not peripheral. (365)

Like Bizzell, Cooper argues on the grounds of where writing theories must look, as writing-as-thinking models fail to render many of writing's constraints. To illustrate, Cooper constructs her own notion of the inner-directed camp through the figure of the "solitary author" that "works alone, within the privacy of his own mind" (365). In this image, what surrounds the writer alone is unknown or irrelevant. Writing is not simply "individuals discover[ing] and communicat[ing] information" (366); writing is also social action. But also, writing is not social action alone. As Cooper articulates this reciprocal relationship, "Writers do think as well as act; [the social] position differs from cognitive theorists in that we emphasize the dialectical relationship between what writers think and do and their social context—the effects that society has on what writers know and the effects that writers have on society" (*Writing* 108). Cooper here defines the social-cognitive relationship: thinking can only be thinking-in-social-contexts, and contexts quickly enlarge in scope from writers to "society."

Cooper and Bizzell steer composition into the "social turn." Each draws our attention to what reigning models miss in hyper-focusing on writing as something in the mind alone. Cooper's zoom out, though, seems to extend the gaze even further and farther through her choice of conceptual figure. While Bizzell's unit of analysis focuses on discourse communities—a concept that provides at least some sense of being identifiable or locatable—Cooper casts the sociality of writing in terms of *ecologies*. Cooper's ecology compels the gaze of writing theory not to land even in one community discourse but to keep "the camera" *moving* to perceive relations among communities and contexts as massive systems. In Cooper's words:

> an ecology of writing encompasses much more than the individual writer and her immediate context. An ecologist explores how writers interact to form systems: all the characteristics of any individual writer or piece of writing both determine and are determined by the characteristics of all the other writers and writings in the systems. (368)

Cooper's ecological model grants the sense that not much is gained by examining a writer's discrete actions or even by studying a writer situated in her immediate contexts. Individual actions, for Cooper, are not even just community actions, but systemically determined ones; a writer's purpose is only ever a "system of purposes" (370). Cooper's social theory emphasizes complexity and interconnectedness as writing is constructed as a "web, in which anything that affects one strand of the web vibrates throughout the whole" (370). Her ecological figure prioritizes the complex interconnectedness of writing as complex systems, a view that seems to push the zoom out even farther, indeed in a manner "infinitely extended" (Cooper 372).

I want to emphasize a set of points I take away from revisiting of these two compositionists' seminal work, ones critical to the story of situated processes I'm trying to (re)create in this book. If Bizzell and Cooper help instantiate and reflect the "social turn" in composition (a timeline, again, which can stretch further backwards to at least the development of STROL), theirs is not a *break from* established process constructs. It is not that cognitive-expressive process theories had reigned unquestioned and then *suddenly* and fully the field turned to the social (just as too, as many have said, was the field not once fully current-traditional then suddenly and completely process). Cooper makes this clear, for example, as she explains that the sociality of writing was not her observation alone but had long been a part of the work of composition, a "growing awareness that language and texts . . . are essentially social activities" (366). The cognitive model wasn't wrong just too narrow. And left alone to stand in for a comprehensive view guiding process *teaching*, strictly cognitive or expressive models encouraged damaging essentialist assumptions, ones that could see writers who were struggling or seen as "unskilled" as somehow deficient thinkers or writers that simply didn't have "it." Social process methods would instead focus writing teachers and their students on "practice within interpretive communities—exactly how conventions work in the world and how they are transmitted" (Bizzell 101). Cooper and Bizzell contribute to conceptions of how writing comes to be and in so doing, shape expansive social writing process theories that traverse across innumerable contexts of learning, conventions, community discourses, institutions, systems, and history.

One might dissent still that these social theories are not process theories at all but "postprocess." Trimbur from his 1994 book review would likely be in this camp: he sees Bizzell as turning away from processes and walking toward the cultural politics of literacy. Indeed. Kristopher Lotier claims that Cooper initiates "postprocess" inventional models rather than process ones. But, in my view, Bizzell and Cooper do not turn away from processes as much as them make much, much *bigger*. Again, Cooper doesn't indict cognitive models for misrepresenting writing but for "obscur[ing]" (365) its "infinitely extended" (372) social systematicity. Bizzell imagines the relationships amongst cognitive, "personal-style," *and* social camps. Thus, this work is not a shift from "individuals" to "larger" forces, as Dobrin and others subsequently frame it, but a continuum of varying foci, from the micro to the macro. In Bizzell's words:

> Answers to what we need to know about writing will have to come from both the inner-directed and the outer-directed theoretical schools if we wish to have a complete picture of the composing process. We need to explain the cognitive and the social factors in writing development, and even more important, the relationship between them. Therefore, we should think of the current debate between the two schools as the kind of fruitful exchange that enlarges knowledge, not as a process that will lead to its own termination, to a theory that silences the debate. (81–2)

In short, a fruitful exchange is not a making a choice between writers or their contexts. Bizzell and Cooper themselves do not suggest a choice between individuals or larger contexts even as they unify in their call for our cameras to zoom out. And too, efforts to uncover the "relationship" between macro-social and micro-cognitive factors in writing development continue beyond Bizzell and Cooper's early calls (e.g., Flower; Haas; Purcell-Gates et al.).

The sense remains nevertheless—especially in invocations of postprocess—that there *is* a choice to be made, that it *is* individual processes *or* larger contexts. Compositionists interested in situatedness can express aversion to focusing in on discrete writers or writing practice (e.g., Dobrin, *Postcomposition*). Why this sense? There are many possible reasons. First, I do think the language of infinite extension in Bizzell and Cooper (and Reither and others) no doubt contributes. In recognizing writing's situatedness, we have come to agree that writing is never *just* here and *just* now; small-scale investigations of practice feel particularly partial and risk reductionism and oversimplification. Another postprocess factor is an embrace of anti-foundational and postmodern thinking: for example, as Kent writes, "The postprocess mindset takes as foundational the anti-foundationalist claim that writing cannot be produced or understood in isolation from the heteroglossia formed by other signifying elements" ("Preface" xix). Another related reason may be postmodern impulse to unravel the stability of and focus on writers as unified, autonomous subjects (e.g., Dobrin et al. 17; Faigley, *Fragments*). Taxonomic thinking may be another culprit. The stages or eras that tend to anchor historical sketching often present in either/ors—writing as invisible *or* as situated, process movement *or* postprocess. Even nuanced taxonomies can reinforce a sense of having to choose. For example, in 1986, Lester Faigley observed the field's general consensus that approaches associated with "process" were good, but that there was more disagreement than overlap on what was meant by process. He outlines three major views—expressive, cognitive, and the emerging social view of writing processes—but identifies this variance as "[t]he problem" ("Competing" 527) and aims to "contrast the assumptions of each of these three views on composing with the goal of identifying a disciplinary basis for the study of writing" (528). Faigley's approach emphasizes differences, constructs these camps as separate and contrastable more than on a continuum or in relation, and performs explicitly the task of deciding one way to best construct processes. He concludes that, "writing processes are historically dynamic—not psychic states, cognitive routines, or neutral social relationships" (537). Faigley's language emphasizes choice: in order to see processes as historical, they appear to be somehow thus *not* cognitive, expressive, or neutrally social. His move to separate these competing theories suggests their separate reigns, not their overlaps (this is not to say though that there are not significant, even irreconcilable, dissonances among the details informing these three broad process views). But as Bizzell and Cooper demonstrate, camping in process theories may be more profitably understood as a matter of focus—literally of continuously modulating where we look, not making a choice of where to permanently install the camera. Indeed, my view of situated processes in these pages and my emphasis on the embodiments of process is not to say that writing is *only* a local phenomenon. Quite the contrary. As my work with Haas helps illustrate, the living, moving, breathing dimensions of processes is an underconsidered avenue toward helping writers perceive myriad scales on which their writing is situated and shaped.

Bizzell and Cooper's landmark claim that writing is a socially-determined process positions situatedness right in the "heyday" of "the process movement," not *after* process. Situatedness cannot really be a tidy dividing line between process and post-. As McComiskey puts it, the social turn "does not constitute, in practice or theory, a rejection of the process movement, but rather its extension into the social world of discourse" ("Post-Process" 41). This "extension," in my read, is that modulation of focus, the "infinitely extended" zoom out. Bizzell and Cooper's social theories are ultimately additive and extensive, not replacements to previous process thinking. Theories that observe writing on the macro-scale, like Cooper's ecology, do not disclude focus on small-scale practices or all the smaller, tiny, or even incidental dimensions shaping how writing comes to be.

But the macro- may still tend to occlude such zoomed-in focus. Bizzell and Cooper refocus us on writing's infinite systemic contexts; they reveal what initial cognitive models were missing. But their theories alone are not necessarily more comprehensive. In fact, presuming that they *reach* comprehensiveness through expansiveness could, in a sense, return us to the concerns that generated their apt critiques in the first place. Once internal-expressive-thinking processes are expressly "situated," writing's contexts and iterations become essentially infinite.

But imagining situatedness can become so macro-, so infinite and seemingly unmoored, as to *almost* feel acontextual or unlocated again. In other words, trying to see the everywhereness of writing begins in a way to feel like nowhereness again. Indeed, writing activity cannot be staged *only* here just as much as it can never be nowhere. Rather, writing is at once emplaced, local, embodied and locatable and—*at the same time*—cultural, historical, and elsewhere. This is why I see it as imperative to understand social, postprocess, systems, ecological, networked theories too as necessarily partial, and to ask how we might make space in our writing theory imaginaries to also *linger* on the smallest physical dimensions of practice *in situ*.

THE MICRO IN THE MACRO: LINGERING *IN SITU*

Around a decade after Cooper and Bizzell's works are published, Trimbur signals the arrival of the social and a new era of teaching "post-process." As social constructionist orientations settle in, so too do new directions in composition. As Pamela Takayoshi frames it, "[a]fter the social turn, our object of study broadened considerably" and away from individual writers ("Short-Form" 4). Writing theories through to the present continue to build upon foundations of situated social constructions (broadly construed), including actor-network, cultural-historical activity, networked, ecological, and complexity theories. Each differently looks for writing on its macro-scales, stretched across contexts, participants, cultures, discourses, communities, institutions, economies, circulation channels, and so on.

In stretching and sustaining focus on writing's sociality, politics, contexts, and cultures, in recent years and as I discussed at the end of the last chapter, interest in writing's materiality has developed (e.g., Alexander; Aronson; Schell; Selzer and Crowley). This interest—manifest in part in what has been called a "sociomaterial" orientation (Miller; Vieira)—locates, grounds, or moors social discourses, configurations, and worlds in particular material objects, structures, or conditions. That is, study of the local, particular, everyday stuff can reveal "how social values, expectations, and trends are imbricated" (Miller 35) in discrete literate practices. The sociomaterial begins to epitomize, as I've sketched in the previous chapter in relation to Haas' work, a modulation or continuum of focus on micro- and macro-situated forces. Writing processes are not just located out there in social communities or cultures; equally they are not just located inside a writer's head or pinned into a defined span of time from the first word to the last. As Bizzell and Cooper emphasize, we only start to grasp this thing called writing by virtue of many vantages—the more the better.

At the same time, situatedness is *not* a condition exclusively of the macroscale. Situatedness is too significant—relevant and overlooked—in the tiniest micro-scales of discrete writing scenes, too. But to examine processes' micro-scales isn't automatically to turn away or isolate a given scene of writing from the imposition of the macro. This dynamic can be illustrated by writing researcher's interests in writing tools. Miller, for example, shows how the individuals with aphasia in her study partner with and modify various literate tools to create different pathways for access to texts and to writing. Close examination of such individual practice in turn exposes and hopefully works against normative expectations for tools, for literate practice, and for bodily and cognitive behavior. That is, writing tools don't shape local practice alone or in isolation; as things both made and used, tools expose practice as at once idiosyncratic, habituated, learned, communal and cultural. As Haas demonstrates in word processing, writers' thinking processes are shaped by a computer's material configurations that in turn reflect larger shaping forces of culture and history (which in turn change practices, and so on, reciprocally). Tools like computers, pens, software, and keyboards shape processes on the micro-scale in embodied movements, glitches, textures, rhythms, or interruptive updates and simultaneously on macro-scales of design, trends, schooling regimes, economies or political revolutions. Indeed, as Haas shows especially in her short appeal to embodied practice, writing tools are a rich interconnection of selves and stuff, as there is a "coupling between our own physical architecture and the materials and tools we take up for use constrain our activities (and our texts) in nontrivial ways" (Syverson 56). Writing tools contain multitudes (of scale)—the smallest individual moves to sweeping montages of situated social constraints. In this way, focusing on an individual's use of a tool isn't to navel-gaze or ignore the trajectories of that tool or the habituated or hacked use of it. This micro-focus is rather a *place*—a located, situated moment—from which to modulate focus on the range of scaled partnerships and constraints that it takes for writing to emerge.

If it is fair to picture social process theories zooming around to observe the expansive interconnectedness and systematicities of writing, sociomaterial theories like Miller's or Haas' feel like they *catch*. They land upon moments and things, pause and linger on scenes of discrete emplaced practice, *in situ*. The challenge of scale though still manifests, especially in material theories and studies focused on tools, spaces, and physicality. For example, Margaret Syverson's complex systems writing ecologies exposes, as one dimension, how writing acts are populated with a range of things and others at modulating levels of scale, including "pens, paper, computers, books, telephones, fax machines, photocopiers, printing presses, and other natural and human-constructed features, as well as . . . families, global economies, publishing systems, theoretical frames, academic disciplines, and language itself" (Syverson 5). Nedra Reynolds' cultural geography sees writing as the "everyday negotiations of space" (6) and interacting with texts as an act of habitation—"a material act, tactile and physical, made up of movements, motions" (166). These compositionists' ecologies and geographies evidence composing's social and cultural constraints through scenes and spaces populated and emplaced and physical. Each express need for micro-scale focus on the emplacements and physicalities of processes. In other words, they each physically situate writing (processes). But each worry differently about the *scale* and implications of such up-close attention.

In her 1999 book, *The Wealth of Reality: An Ecology of Composition,* Margaret Syverson advances an ecological, complex systems theory of writing. She aims for a "richer, more comprehensive" (2) view, in part, by extending and grounding Cooper's social ecology, as Syverson sees it as "limited to" (24) immaterial abstractions like "social interactions via ideas, purposes, interpersonal actions, cultural norms, and textual forms" (24). Building her framework from distributed cognition and complex systems, Syverson performs detailed case studies of three distinct writing scenes, cases of ambitious scope with analysis of "more factors and influences than any theory that has yet appeared among us" (Killingsworth 309). Syverson's aim is to be exhaustive as she folds together focus of previous composing process theories—social with psychological and cognitive, for example—and draws out the significance of lesser emphasized dimensions, like "the material, physical processes and structures involved in text production" (74). The camera of her writing theory, in other words, is placed at as many vantages as she can imagine, seeing writing acts as "an ecological system of interrelated structures and processes that are at once physically or materially, socially, psychologically, temporally, and spatially emerging in codependent activities" (25).

Syverson's ecology compels in its grasp of scope and scale; it helps her, for instance, uncover the material force of a given classroom (188) and at the same time see how writing done there at once extends well beyond those walls. In examining a poem of Charles Reznikoff, an objectivist poet often considered the epitome of the solitary writer (31), Syverson demonstrates how, on the contrary, the poem is far from a product of an individual writer "whose genius is immutable and largely independent of social, environmental, or physical influences" (35–36). Syverson shows how the many processes leading to this poem are instead meaningfully distributed across multiple authors (including Resnikoff's parents) and across a huge unwieldy timeline of "forty years of reading and rereading, translating, typing, editing, selecting, and publishing material from his parents' autobiographical writings" (43). Far from contained or separable, the scales of Reznikoff's processes for just one single poem are wandering and enormous.

Along the way though, Syverson does linger to view processes on its smallest scales, especially in her focus on embodiment. Embodiment is one of the four attributes (alongside distribution, emergence, and enaction) of writing's systems that she sees as "often overlooked" (7), largely "suppressed" because of tacit assumptions about language, individuals, and thinking (25). Embodiment is a force shaping "conceptual structures and cognitive activities" as well as the "physical activity" (Syverson 12) of literate practices, including "clasping a book, moving the eyes across a line of text" (12). For example, in the instance of "someone writing a book to explain a set of theories" (6), Syverson proposes that we'd do well to consider "the writer's interaction with the environment, including the technologies for writing, the memory aids, the tools and instruments that help shape and support the writing" (6). But the boundaries of this particular scene also (ceaselessly) stretch. The immediate physical situation of writing the book is significant but so too are the broadest channels of circulation and reception, as well as "a larger discourse that is historically situated, and involving historically situated technologies, social relations, cultural influences, and disciplinary practices" (6–7). In her analysis of embodiment in the Reznikoff poem, Syverson finds again these modulating levels of scale: the poem is constructed from descriptions of Reznikoff's (and others') bodily experiences ("physical conditions, actions, perceptions, and interactions" (48)); the poem is impelled by constraints of neighborhood and household "crowding" ("growing up in the crowded Jewish ghetto and an equally crowded household" (52) encouraged walking that would in turn provide Reznikoff "space and freedom" (52) to write poetry); the poem comes to be too by virtue of the "physical and social impact" of Eastern European immigration to New York in the 1880s (48). It is compelling just how capaciously Syverson sees the embodiment of writing—it is on the scene in typing or using a pencil, walking, living in a small space, encountering a text in an archive versus a classroom, or in the movements of large-scale migration. Embodiment is not only the purview of a self or an individual or a contained body. Just as thinking is distributed, for Syverson, so too are writing's embodiments.

At the same time, Syverson's embodiment, as a "physical-material dimension" (18) of complex systems, is provokingly small. A radically local, process-scaled (and, of course, partial) view of writing's physical situatedness, is available—even distinctly emphasized in her discussion. This focus reveals, for instance, that readers and writers are "sensitive to type that is too small, books that are too thick, margins that are too skimpy, screen fonts that are too hard to read, computer monitors that are too small, rooms that are too warm or too dim, and to many other physical features of the text or environment that shape their interactions with the 'content' of the text" (18–19). Syverson underscores how little attention has been paid to the physical-material (with the exception of Haas, she notes). But the force of this observation gets rather lost, almost literally buried, under dimensions stretched across ecologies that are still more familiar to composition theory's imagined scope of relevant situatedness, like sociality, genre, circulation, and reader reception. This makes sense. The physical-material is important but "it is not enough" to get to Syverson's "comprehensive view" (13). After all, Syverson is after the wealth of reality—the seemingly ceaseless situated forces that compel writing at all levels of scale. Her gaze, almost by definition, cannot (and should not) stop with the writer's embodied interactions with local material environments.

Syverson puts unique focus on writing's physicalities. But she also does not set out to linger there. She worries some about the scales of prior process theories—how they tend to be "atomistic" (8)—separating focus "on individual writers, individual texts, isolated acts, processes, or artifacts" (8). She works against "privileging the individual writer composing in isolation" (9) which she sees as occluding the shaping roles of social and environmental structures as disparate as "weather" and "buildings" and "desks" (9). She is no doubt influenced by macro-scaled thinking of the social turn and the emerging postprocess moment in which she was writing. I agree with the richness of Syverson's scales. Writing acts are, of course, never *just here*. But she also makes the case that we have not much considered the physical situatedness of writing acts, that processes are also *always* somewhere (or better, *many* somewheres). Processes can never not be physically located. For me, Syverson makes a compelling call for examining the micro-scales of situated processes (matters of desks, lighting, fonts, rooms, movements, actions, tools, and more) but doesn't aim to linger on them.

Tension in scale and physical situatedness is further exemplified in Nedra Reynolds' 2007 book, *Geographies of Writing: Inhabiting Places and Encountering Difference*. Drawing on discourses of cultural geography, postmodernity, and spatiality, Reynolds proposes that writing be understood as a set of practices "more spatial than temporal" (5). "Geography," Reynolds claims, "gives us the metaphorical and methodological tools to change our ways of imagining writing through both movement and dwelling—to see writing as a set of spatial practices informed by everyday negotiations of space" (6). Reynold's intervention pictures writing as emplaced movement. Such a shift allows Reynolds to explore alienation, access, ideologies, and policing of social difference as constructed by and experienced through spaces material and discursive, and on a range of scales (6). Reynolds grounds writing's sociality, in other words, in its spatial-materiality and in its ineluctable connections to our experiences of space as constructed *place*.

Along the way, Reynolds muses about how we might grapple with writing's *immediate* material geographies—a matter, she points out, that compositionists agree we don't know enough about (176). She wonders what insights those considerations may garner, writing:

> Writing's materiality begins with where the work of writing
> gets done, the tools and conditions and surroundings—not to
> determine a cause and effect relationship between the writ-
> ing's quality or success and the site of its production, but to
> trace the threads or remnants of literacy practices. Along with
> knowing more about where writers write, though, geography
> contributes to a richer understanding of the habits and mem-
> ories and "moves" that characterize our own acts of writing,
> particularly those moves that become habitual but are not
> "taught." (167)

In this rich description, I hear echoes of Haas' embodied practice. I see not only material things, like tools and surroundings, but choreographies of movement, memories, habits, partnerships of things and bodies. Writing, seen through Reynold's micro-scale lens, unfolds *only* among and through things—the tools, conditions, and surroundings in Reynolds terms, as well as technologies, texts, writing chairs, posters, and arrangement of rooms. And attending to these spatial-material dimensions necessarily draws attention to the moving writing body—a look out a window, repetitive punch on the backspace bar, or the tapping of fingers on a plastic keyboard. Here Reynolds depicts writing processes as radically local and shifting geographies with embodied dimensions populated by material objects.

Maybe more than Syverson (who aims for an elusive "comprehensive theory of composing" (2) and thus spends more time in the expanse of writing's systems), Reynolds grapples overtly with the scales her spatial theory entails. She focuses on the "spatial practices of the everyday" explicitly "through different spatial scales: the body, the street, the city" (3). She makes a case for some "staying put" (9) to explore how material structures—built, metaphorical, political, and discursive—shape and are shaped by individuals. She also calls for "new maps of writing," ones that would capture dimensions of writing's materiality, maps that would not only detail "the places where writing occurs, but [also] the sense of place and space that readers and writers bring with them to intellectual work of writing, to navigating, arranging, remembering and composing" (176). Though she expresses interest in traversing a range of spatial scales, zooming-in on emplaced or situated practice remains an interest, but still on the edges, of her overall project. Reynolds herself worries about this omission in a note. She writes, "I haven't done much in these pages to unlock those physical movements that we call writing, uses of a mouse or keyboard, pencil, stylus, screen, or page" (168). She follows this admission, explaining, "more studies are needed that depend upon empirical research to trace writers' moves in composing" (188). I agree with Reynolds call—and for me, there is value especially in writers themselves doing this tracing, as I'll explore more in Chapter 4.

The scales of Reynolds' new geography and Syverson's complex ecologies invite us to situate processes. But, by some necessity too, they push the micro-scales of situated practice to the periphery. Similarly, current composition theories acknowledge that writing is materially situated and distributed at the macro-level of ecologies, hyper-circulatory networks, and social geographies, but as Reynolds indicates, much less so at the micro-level of the practitioner immersed in her immediate embodied environment. Situating process represents a way to bring and sustain this focus. And as these four compositionists—Bizzell, Cooper, Syverson, and Reynolds—make clear, such a zoomed-in or hyper-focus on the physicalities of composing is not to seal off processes from their larger forces. Such micro-looking is not a choice nor a turn away from writing's larger and myriad contexts: it's a moment, to linger.

CONCLUSION: SITUATING PROCESS "TOPOS" OR EXAMINING THE "COMPOSING MOMENT"

In thinking again about John Trimbur's essay "Delivering the Message: Typography and the Materiality of Writing" that I reference at the open of this chapter, I notice how rather ritually separated his concerns about "materiality" are from those of the "process movement." Trimbur draws this dividing line, it seems, because he assents to the notion that composition studies has found itself *after* process. His intervention is postprocess in that he frames and names it that way. I suspect this move in part is owed to a need to emphasize one's separation from the acontextual and oversimplified associations that often stick to process. But, at the same time, Trimbur sees process—"the figure of the composer we inherit from the process movement" (189)—as a valuable conceptual "topos," so long as we emplace, rather than hermetically seal off, that figure in their contexts and conditions. In his case, such a view of situated writing processes asks us to consider writing's materiality from the vantage of typography and labor. The process topos, or view, is valuable and revealing, but as Trimbur underlines, it "requires a thoroughgoing reconceptualization . . . one that locates the composer in the labor process, in relation to the available means of production" (189). In this sense, Trimbur too grapples with scale. He finds it hard to appeal to process at a time when we were supposed to have been done with it, when the macro-scales of social, material, postprocess theories shooed away focus not just on individual practice but also on extremely small but significant material dimensions, like typography.

Seeing processes on their micro-scales is not necessarily to see them as isolated, overgeneralized, or acontextual. In other words, Trimbur too demonstrates the importance of profoundly—and at *modulating* scales—*situating* the individual composer, in his view, in the flows and complexities of expansive material systems of circulation. Similarly, in a recent article in which she makes a full-voiced argument for a "return" to composing process research, Pamela Takayoshi argues that writing acts are always already *reciprocally* shaped in a constant shuttling between broad and immediate forces—social, rhetorical, cultural and other big contexts that both shape and are shaped by any discrete "act of composing" ("Writing" 570). She suggests a fertile and artful concept that might become a guiding focus of situated processes: the "composing moment" (570). In my read, Takayoshi's "moment" recasts and situates writing processes through a productive paradox of anchoring and flux, of intimate and distant contexts. As she writes:

> by capturing the composing moment, we can see that just as literacy is itself in constant motion, so too are the contextual elements that give rise to literacy in any given social interaction. The composing moment allows us to explain and anchor the differences that appear across contexts in terms of how people write, use, and think about composing. ("Writing" 570)

The moment takes as its center literacy as a swirling, changing, giant set of situated forces. Simultaneously, the moment is just that: one *snapshot*, not an enduring or frozen model, of some dimension of a writing act. Exploring, or "anchoring," our look at process in the moment opens gateways to perceiving at least some of how "larger forces" manifest (differently) in living and breathing literate acts. Moments (not models) expose the flux—the enormities, smallest details, differences, and habits—of writing. Processes as moments reveals that situated forces large and small are not eternal nor unchanging but enacted *right now*, in one place or one rich "moment" in time. To me, the composing moment embodies the idea that writing processes are always elsewhere just as much and at the same time as they are always *somewhere*. However its dimensions are construed, stretched, or sliced—processes are located.

There is no doubt that discourse communities, complex ecologies, networks, or expansive cultural geographies remain fitting and illustrative figures for conceptualizing what, where, and how writing is. But we can profitably dispense with monitoring a choice between seeing writing as discrete scenes or as sweeping systems, as the rhetoric of a process/post-process divide can suggest. As Syverson and Reynolds and Takayoshi make clear, there is rich potential in zooming in up-close upon situated processes—for a moment. And like Syverson and Reynolds (and Haas, Emig, and Perl), I see underarticulated value especially in examining composing moments as physical scenes. By lingering and looking closely in this way—or by "trac[ing] writers' moves in composing" (Reynolds 188)—writers and teachers of writing uncover the small, embodied, material actions that give shape differently to all writing acts. With these views, writers can come to see writing processes as located, differentiated, and contingent; they can see the inconsistencies, failures, and material partnerships and disruptions in their everyday writing attempts. But this hyper-zoomed focus is not some kind of navel-gazing or a reflective end in itself. Situating writing processes rather is an *in-road* toward perceiving the larger situated forces at work as processes become seen *at once* as the material and cognitive, cultural and embodied, historical and particularized, the individual *and* larger forces that propel and disrupt "composing moments" as we experience and observe them.

Writing theory has without a doubt situated writing. But especially in our teaching, we still need that "thoroughgoing reconceptualization of the writer at work" (Trimbur, "Delivering" 189). We need to dismantle the lingering tyranny of common Western assumptions: that thinking belongs to individuals and that writing is thinking (Syverson 25); that texts are "bounded object[s]" (36), produced strictly by individuals "largely independent of social, environmental, or physical influences" (Syverson 36); that processes are "invisible" or "mental" (Trimbur, "Delivering" 188); and that "text composing can somehow be isolated from physical and material conditions of production and use" (Syverson 25). We especially need to dismantle how these assumptions control and limit how teachers of writing and writing students imagine and work with the notion that "writing is a process." Process is a most familiar, central, and foundational idea. Student writers know it; it influences how they understand what writing is and perhaps how they sometimes experience it. Thus, targeting *how we picture* and *how we work with processes* is a productive site from which to show writers the many ways that writing is profoundly situated and susceptible. Ways of imagining such adjustments constitute my work in the next chapter.

CHAPTER 3

WRITING MOVES—THEORIZING/ PICTURING SITUATED PROCESSES

How do we picture composing processes? As Linda Brodkey argued in 1987, how we imagine process is shaped in part by what she calls the "picture postcard of writing" (399). The postcard is the image that "many of us find ourselves reading when we think about writing, or, worse, when we are in the very act of writing" (396). This stubborn construction sees the writer as a "solitary scribbler" (398), one who is "merely a clerk" engaged in writing as "transcription" (398), or as Marilyn Cooper describes a similar figure, a "solitary author" (365) "producing propositional and pragmatic structures, Athena-like, full grown and complete, out of his brow" (366). Material conditions on the scene—the "closed shutters of the garret, the drawn drapes of the study, or the walls of books lining the library"—invades this picture as well but operates somewhat counter-intuitively as a means of taking the writer *out* of her contexts or "effectively remov[ing] the writer from time as well as place" (Brodkey 404). In short, Brodkey's postcard embodies Western constructions of authorship as disembodied and transcendent. And this picture is not just pervasive, it is invasive as it compels "those who teach as well as those who take composition courses" to "recreate a garret and all that it portends whether we are writing in a study, a library, a classroom, or at a kitchen table" (397). The postcard encourages us to imagine writing processes as somehow sealed off from contexts immediate and distant; it prevents us from recognizing the social and cultural situatedness as well as the lived experience of writing that Brodkey argued we must reckon with in writing research and teaching.

This image is still afoot—even in spite of how our field has come to account for writing in terms of its sociality and situated cognition (and its politics, its varied communities and locations, its systems or networked relations). I think most can still relate to Patricia Bizzell's description of process in our classrooms as at once revelatory and resisted. She writes,

> Simply to acknowledge that composing processes exist is
> something of a gain for modern composition studies. My
> undergraduate students would like to deny this premise:
> they prefer the fantasy that when they finally become "good
> writers," they will be able to sit down at the desk and produce

>an "A" paper in no more time than it takes to transcribe it.
>Nor are my students alone in this fantasy of instant text pro-
>duction. It is part of a more general notion in our culture, a
>sort of debased Romantic version of creativity wherein verbal
>artifacts are supposed to be produced as easily and inevitably
>as a hen lays eggs. (175)

Processes, in Bizzell's students' minds, are no doubt shaped by the picture post-card—easy, linear, special, continuous, contained in the mind, floating some-how out of time and space.

The picture postcard reflects back to us how routinely we assume that "text composing can somehow be isolated from physical and material conditions of production and use" (Syverson 25). But if we look for processes in the world, we find them inseparable from constraints and pressures of all kinds, within and in excess of the writer's control and awareness—time, others, materials, elec-tricity, tools, deadlines, genre conventions, cultural and financial capital, and so on. Samuel Taylor Coleridge's famous account of the composing process of his poem, "Kubla Khan," illustrates the enduring and routine ways we sepa-rate composing from material life. As he narrates it, this poem simply came to him, fully formed and with no effort, as he slept. He awoke to transcribe it on paper only to be interrupted by a visitor, a knock on his proverbial garret door. With that interruption, the transcendent garret of the poet's mind is disrupted, invaded, and destroyed. Thus, Coleridge concludes, his process was incomplete and the product, the poem, only a fragment.

For this poet, the world is not a part, just an unfortunate meddler. But if we shift our vantage and see Coleridge's processes as instead in and of the world, we see his processes differently. We see how environmental factors—that specific farmhouse setting, the drugs Coleridge took, the work he was reading, his long nap, the loud knock on the door, the hour-long conversation with the "person from Porlock," the cultural ideologies swirling at the time about authorship and creativity—more than a transcendent mind alone shape the famous 54 lines into the version we know still today. And yet it is Coleridge's framing—seeing the environment as a distraction, as the antithesis to his process—that sticks. Our pictures of processes remain in the shadow of Coleridge's story and the picture postcard: writing as rarified and separate. But our lived experiences of them—physical, wandering, located, *implicated*—upend such easy and detached pictures.

In this chapter, I continue to poke at the postcard's control such that we might perceive a knock at the door as much a participant in composing processes as any other present condition or action or individual. To do so, I first locate some residue of the postcard in three recent pedagogical documents that feature process prominently and aim to steer the fundamentals of writing instruction today. Then toward forming a situated and descriptive rather than a picture postcard and prescriptive view, I theorize processes in three intersecting parts: as activity, as physical, and as materially emplaced. By calling this work theorizing, I indicate my interest in exposing and adjusting assumptions around process. As Thomas Kent has it, theories are what operate underneath—"coherent systems of presuppositions" that can "explain and that bring coherence to the practices that derive from our beliefs" ("Principled" 429). I think assumptions can be exposed and questioned especially through contemplating imagery. So I partner "picturing" with theorizing as the main work of this chapter for a set of reasons: for one, to disrupt associations of theorizing with abstractions or rarefied intellectualism; two, to follow Brodkey's lead in her postcard image and its network of assumptions; and three, to continue to build a method of situating processes by looking, locating, describing, or in short, seeing processes as they happen in time and place. Building upon my adjustments to process histories in the first two chapters, I hope this conceptual tour helps us, teachers and writing professionals, continue to work to see an old familiar and its potentials differently.

"SKILLS AND STRATEGIES": PICTURES OF PROCESS IN RECENT PEDAGOGICAL DOCUMENTS

It is likely impossible to know how process is really imagined, talked about, and enacted in contemporary pedagogies, in different kinds of writing classes across the country, at ranging institutions, with differing populations of writers. And given the ways that process has worked itself into our bones (Anson, "Process") or become the very fabric of composition (Foster) or the right answer to a now mundane question (Petraglia, "Is There"), we might find it especially hard now to locate such a defined or unified sense. However, if there were to be such a place, it may be in a set of recent documents interested in the foundations of writing pedagogies today: CWPA, NCTE, and NWP's 2011 document, "Framework for Success in Postsecondary Writing;" CWPA's 2014 "WPA Outcomes Statement for First-Year Composition 3.0;" and NCTE's 2016 position statement, "Professional Knowledge for the Teaching of Writing." Far from backgrounded, processes feature prominently in these documents, a distinct area of knowledge earning discussion alongside other teaching and learning fundamentals including critical thinking ("Framework"), rhetorical knowledge ("WPA") or awareness of writing's range of purposes ("Professional"). In my read, discussion of processes across these documents evidence tension. On one hand, processes are complexly described in relation to rhetorical situations or changing technological scenes. On the other, though, processes are repeatedly defined as a writer's *own* set of strategies. In linking process to strategy, I suspect some influence of the picture postcard at work, where processes are controlled or engineered exclusively by the writer alone.

To be sure, across these documents, the pictures of processes are nuanced and complex, reflecting histories of process critique concerned about overgeneralization and acontextuality, as well as increasing pedagogical focus on rhetorical and genre studies. In NCTE's recently revised 2016 position statement, in which "Writing is a Process" remains as one of its ten epistemological precepts, the document authors underline that processes should not be seen as enduring, singular, or generalized; instead, they will always differ in relation to varying purposes and genres. As such, focusing on process in our teaching should not signal "a formulaic set of steps" that could be learned "once and for all" ("Professional") as the novelty of different writing situations requires different processes. That processes are multiple and responsive reflects elsewhere as well: processes are described as "flexible" in light of differing contexts of writing and "seldom linear" ("WPA"); and "[s]uccessful writers use different processes that vary over time and depend on the particular task" ("Framework" 8). In the "Framework" especially, flexibility is emphasized, echoed as one of the framing habits of mind that urges writers to respond nimbly to differences of purpose, audience, conventions, and disciplinary contexts (1). Writing processes in these documents are multiple; they change in light of rhetorical concerns especially; they are acquired and adjusted by writers across time. "Professional Knowledge" provides perhaps the most capacious articulation of these kinds of differences: processes are said to "develop and refine" across writers' lives and experiences with new genres, "personal and professional contexts," and "writing spaces and technologies;" and they "shift" not just in light of purposes, audiences, and genres, but also "circumstances, such as deadlines and considerations of length, style, and format."

In sum, processes here are plural, multiple, and based on many factors that precipitate adjustments in a writer's procedures. But, even allowing for these differences, I do not see processes as *situated* in the ways I'm after. For example, that processes differ based on "circumstances" is potentially provoking, particularly in the way the document authors exemplify them. Deadlines and format are familiar constraints of school writing; parameters traditionally set and enforced by the writing teacher. Writers enact processes, probably too as guided carefully by the teacher, in order to divide and control time—say, to stave off procrastination or kickstart invention. So, of course, much process activity is in planning and executing in time. But, at the same time, something like a deadline is a constraint that is also profoundly *out of* a writer's control, intentions, or plans. As I think Steven King is famous for saying, writing is never done, it's just due.

So too do other "circumstances" acknowledged in these documents, like technologies or sociality, provoke us to consider what is within and without a writers' control or domain. All the documents in some way recognize profound change in communication technologies. In fact, "Professional Knowledge" cites as impetus for its 2016 revision the ways that "the everyday experience of writing in people's lives has expanded dramatically" with the rise of handheld devices, composing across a range of modal and life domains, and increasing access to and variety of speech and composing technologies. "WPA Outcomes" too emphasizes writing tech across their discussions of rhetorical knowledge, critical thinking, processes, and conventions, suggesting that by the end of first-year writing courses, writers should be able to "Adapt composing processes for a variety of technologies and modalities." This articulation is of course important—we can't talk about writing's production, especially today, without thinking about the tremendous range and learning curve of various composing tools. But, on the other hand, this articulation is also a bit strange when inspected up close. For one, what can "adapt" really mean in this context? It implies writers walk around with their multiple processes—somehow "isolated from physical and material conditions of production and use" (Syverson 25)—and deploy adjustments to them accordingly when employing a pencil versus a laptop versus the interface of Instagram versus an offline Kindle. Processes do certainly change in light of changing technologies (as Haas' and Syverson's studies expose). But those changes are simply not limited to sets of intentional "adaptations" made by the writer alone; they're rather the result of changes in a nexus of relations among environment, tools, objects, memories, intentions, thoughts, time, and so on.

So too with sociality. The documents reflect the social turn; writers should, for instance, "Experience the collaborative and social aspects of writing processes" and "participate effectively in collaborative processes typical of their field" ("WPA"); they should "work with others in various stages of writing" and "use feedback to revise texts to make them appropriate for the academic discipline or context for which the writing is intended" ("Framework" 8). Writing's complex social situatedness is acknowledged here, in peer review, feedback, and discourse conventions (Especially the last quotation above evokes the discourse community perspective initiated by Bizzell). But, again, social contexts are described in a way that suggests any given writer can control them—for instance, how feedback can be "used" to ensure a pleasing, home-run product that fulfills a discourse community's every convention. But within shaping social and cultural contexts, discourse conventions aren't just sitting out there for writers to master in advance or through the rational exercise of "use." An errant zeal for "correctness" or simply the capriciousness of any given reader in those dynamic contexts (of which the writer too is a part) exert their control upon any writer's process.

Any writer alone cannot guarantee something like "appropriateness." In short, writing processes are not ours as much, or more than, they are ours alone.

What I'm eager to expose in these documents is how processes are ultimately controlled in their descriptions by control. Each forge tight links among process and intention; processes may be many and different, but they are writers' *own*. Ownership is exemplified especially in how each document defines processes foremost as *strategies*—the "multiple strategies writers use to approach and undertake writing and research" ("Framework" 8)"; "multiple strategies, or *composing processes*, to conceptualize, develop, and finalize projects" ("WPA"); "a repertory of routines, skills, strategies, and practices for generating, revising, and editing different kinds of texts" ("Professional"). The image of writerly isolation and control is further delivered in recurring appeals to the process wheel: abstractions cast in familiar terms of "prewriting techniques, multiple strategies for developing and organizing a message, a variety of strategies for revising and editing, and methods for preparing products for public audiences and for deadlines" ("Professional"). Strategies indeed denote some context-awareness. And these documents do imagine processes as a capacious, multiple, flexible, adaptable set of strategies fitting to rhetorical situations and constraints. But still, as writer's own alone. Strategies indicate we can plan, control, direct those contexts that are "out there." Strategies imply that "our" processes are *separable* from where, with what, and with whom they are. But processes are never just a writer's plans; they are an amalgamation of ranging, distributed, shaping and participatory forces which include the writer. Such "aloneness" is a fiction, as "writing is always already overwritten by other people, and, crucially, other *stuff*" (Lotier 366). *Situated* forces act in concert and dissonance; the writer is but a force among other forces. Situated forces like technologies, racial or economic privilege, comma conventions, writers, and more—to be now explicitly new materialist or flatly ontological about it—exceed any one actor's or force's control or awareness. Processes in the world are implicated, distributed, situated.

This is not at all to say that the writer has no agency in her processes. And it's not at all to say that talking about and teaching process as strategies is unhelpful. Of course, writers benefit from developing plans and options and techniques for developing complex texts; of course, writers benefit from reflecting on how they and others produce and circulate texts of all kinds; of course, versatile control is emphasized in documents about outcomes and knowledge (chaos, magic, happy accidents, collaboration with a network of writing actors, or improvisation, after all, are not so easy to register in our reigning educational schemes). It's not at all that process strategies are wrong. It's that strategies *alone* is misleading. Processes are never *just* strategies. Writing processes in the world quickly exceed the bounds of strategy as in the world they are mostly unruly, on the fly, constrained, pressed into and merging with the realities and forces of living. Processes are a tangle of intentions, attempts, responses, failures, accidents, others, missed opportunities, things, actions, and movements cobbled together and experienced on-the-spot, not in advance or separately. Processes as strategies, in short, is just incomplete.

Can our notions of process in the classroom account for situated realities, those that exceed the steady, controlled vision of writing epitomized in the process wheel or strategies? Can we still teach with process if processes are more than strategy alone, if processes are *not* ours just as much as they are ours? Seeing processes as situated attunes writers to the susceptibilities, constraints, forces, and differences in writing acts across shifting contexts. Instead of strategies alone, instead of process as writer's pre-fab plans *before* a particular impetus for writing emerges, instead of imagining writers and their processes as somehow *separate from* their swirling surrounds, we can proceed with pictures of processes as implicated in time and place, as situated, distributed, and susceptible *activity* that is *physical* and *emplaced.*

PROCESSES AS *ACTIVITY*

It doesn't feel radical to begin with the claim that situated processes be seen as *activity*. This isn't exactly breaking news. The whole story of the process revolution, as it is known so well, is thought of as a pivotal shift from seeing writing as formalist surface correctness towards observing writing as complex human processes of thinking and acting. Process not product. And yet, in recent years, seeing writing first as human activity has not necessarily been the default. Social constructionist, cultural studies, postmodern, and postprocess are among the influences that have tipped field assumptions more toward writing as heteroglossic textualities or signifying webs and discourses. In such views, the "writing subject" is deemphasized, problematized, or moved entirely out of the frame in favor of what Sidney Dobrin, in his deconstructionist vision, simply calls "a more explicit focus on writing itself" (*Postcomposition* 3).

No longer the default, compositionists recently studying writing as composing activities have found need to make explicit their case for doing so. Jody Shipka, in her study of composing processes as mediated and multimodal, for example, contrasts her intervention to what she sees in the field as a "tendency to 'freeze' writing, to treat it as a noun rather than a verb, and to privilege the analyses of static texts" (104). Similarly, Pamela Takayoshi notes a "deep commitment to and abiding interest in writing—the print linguistic graphic system of marks (letters, words, and other symbols) on a surface or screen" ("Short" 4) among computers and writing scholars, in light of the long social turn. As a result, she laments, we have accounted too little for how writing technologies and digital tools are used, how they shape and alter scenes of contemporary (mobile/digital) composing. That is, for Takayoshi, seeing process as activity is crucial now given how "[w]riting spaces are dramatically different than they were 25 years ago" (4). For Shipka, if we fail to see writing as verb, we leave invisible the multimodal nature of all communicative acts. For me, seeing writing processes as activity stands to help reshape classroom processes from controlled textualities into living and breathing, susceptible and situated ones.

In using the word activity, I don't mean to suggest necessarily specialized or particular connotations (like activity theory, for example), but more simply something like everyday and particularized bodily action. I align with Lee-Ann M. Kastman Breuch's claim that process be understood as "an activity rather than a body of knowledge" (120). For Breuch this postprocess idea understands writing as situational and "indeterminate" (133), and thus beyond the scope of systematicity, closed skill sets, or mastery (127). As open systems, writing processes are specific, contextualized, and distinct across times and places. Seeing processes as activity located in experienced time and place, rather than as writers' *own* pre-fab if adjustable strategies, leads me to three related claims: first, processes leak into life—writing processes are practices of being, inseparable from and encountered across life domains and activities (not just in school); second, processes unfold in the present-tense, not just as abstracted routines that leap out of time to predetermine future action; and third, process activity exceeds the control of textual products.

If we see process as physical activity, then writing stretches out across innumerable scenes, spilling over, into, and through everyday living. Writing processes are living processes, susceptible to many forces and coextensive with other activities. Paul Prior has often emphasized this point with his sociohistoric view of literate activity. I admire this view for how it richly thickens any given composing participant or action with connections to influences and convergences near and far, or "how many voices and moments of activity buoy and flow through the apparently fixed, one-dimensional words of a page" (*Writing* xi). But, Prior notes in contrast to his rich framework, we talk routinely about writing as a condensed, one-dimensional, straightforward, and isolated task. He writes, "Usual representations of writing collapse time, isolate persons, and filter activity (e.g., 'I wrote the paper over the weekend')" (*Writing* xi). But when seen as a "situated" (*Writing* xi) and "actual embodied activity" ("Tracing" 171), clean and orderly reportage about writing processes becomes much more complicated. Far from wholly planful or contained, processes from this view "emerge[] as a confluence of many streams of activity: reading, talking, observing, acting, making, thinking, and feeling . . . transcribing words on paper" (*Writing* xi), as well as "drinking coffee, eating snacks, smoking, listening to music, tapping . . . fingers, pacing around rooms" ("Tracing" 171), and countless other actions. This uncontained view certainly departs from a process as strategies paradigm. More conventional conceptions of process might emphasize procedure with contained identifiable timelines characterized by the "progress" of a text's development. Process as activity, by contrast, exposes the detours, interruptions, failures, abandonments and "fits and starts, with pauses and flurries, discontinuities and conflicts" (Prior, "Tracing" 171) characteristic of writing *experience,* in a phenomenological sense. An activity perspective disrupts the presumption that processes always already yield development or that processes only happen when an identifiable "skill," like reverse outlining or cubing, is deployed. When we look for process as activity, we see writers and writing acts as profoundly vulnerable to material forces and confluences of activity that are situated and unique, not neutral but *implicated* in broader systemic mechanisms of, for example, cultural and economic capital (e.g., Aronson; Brodkey; Canagarajah). Indeed, observing the leakiness of processes into and across life and activity domains attunes writers and their teachers to perceive the rich if elusive contexts that give shape to writing behavior and attitudes.

Processes as expansive activity also invokes ontology: processes as being and living. Prior and Jody Shipka, with their cultural-historical activity theory perspective, illustrate this idea, claiming:

> that literate activity consists not simply of some specialized
> cultural forms of cognition—however distributed, not simply
> of some at-hand toolkit—however heterogeneous. Rather,
> literate activity is about nothing less than ways of being in
> the world, forms of life. . . . It is especially about the ways we
> not only come to inhabit made-worlds, but constantly make
> our worlds—the ways we select from, (re)structure, fiddle
> with, and transform the material and social worlds we inhabit.
> (181–2)

Following this description, processes are imbricated actions, ongoing forms of life and (re)making, not deployable tools. Robert Yagelski reflects this ontological perspective onto writing and its instruction. His phenomenological notion of writing experience is helpful toward seeing processes as activity. He writes, "what if we shift our theoretical gaze . . . from the writer's writing to the *writer writing?* Not writing as thinking, or socially transacting, or 'constructing itself' in a postmodern way, but writing as 'the self *being*?'" (107). This ontological view positions process as a continuous unfolding rather than a telos that might be predetermined in steps. It puts writing activity *in-situ*—in the moment, in the world, as we differently experience it.

This in-the-momentness leads me to a second dimension emphasized in activity: seeing processes as situated in time (and space). As Haas emphasizes, writing (with computers) modifies the "realms of time and space" (226) and thus "how utterly bound to the physical world of bodies is writing" (Haas 46). The right-here-and-now of processes evokes for me too Takayoshi's "composing moment" ("Writing" 570)—those infinite snapshots that momentarily anchor the swirling social factors and other constraints that impinge on writing. But conventional process teaching, as Prior puts it, by contrast collapses time and thus erases the specificities of located processes. Conventional process artifacts like portfolios, drafts, or prewriting condense and limit writing activity into repeated textual steps, "effectively remov[ing] the writer from time as well as place" (Brodkey 404).

Moreover, conventional process teaching would implicitly cast time as orderly and controlled. Process time is regimented, collapsed into steps, the linear deployment of strategies, normative stages, or said another way, "compulsory notions of able-bodied composing processes" (Wood 272). Even recursivity—the supposedly messy back-and-forth movement of composing through time—can often feel boxed into orderly fashion. For example, when recursivity is described as when "a writer may research a topic before drafting, then after receiving feedback conduct additional research as part of revising" ("Framework"), I note how it still marches steadily toward a developed textual outcome. In short, conventional process time is regimented and normative.

"Crip time," a concept from disability studies, helps disrupt normative (process) time and locate processes in experienced time and place. In part an affectionate acknowledgment that disabled persons may need more time or may often be late, crip time embraces the ranging times things take (Samuels; Wood). Any attempt to systematize or regulate time—attempts built overtly and covertly upon certain bodily normativity—will (and should be) exploded by bodily differences, including "a slower gait, a dependency on attendants (who might themselves be running late), malfunctioning equipment (from wheelchairs to hearing aids), a bus driver who refuses to stop for a disabled passenger, or an ableist encounter with a stranger that throws one off schedule" (Kafer 26). Crip time doesn't seek, though, exception or allowance *within* normative time. It seeks instead (characteristic of the disability ethos) to dismantle normative time altogether. As queer, feminist disability scholar, Alison Kafer asserts, "Crip time is flex time not just expanded but exploded" (27); a paradigm not of regiment but "flexibility" (Price 62) keenly aware of and connected to the interplay among space, bodies, moments, and others. Thus, time, from compositionist and disability scholar Margaret Price's vantage, is utterly located and thus *susceptible*—to barriers, avenues, others, architectures, objects, systems, and more.

Time cannot be bootstrapped by individuals or codified as "how long things take." As Price emphasizes, time is an experienced construct always in interrelation with embodied, material, populated, and fluctuating spaces.

Thus, process time cannot be secured or assured in advance. Errant attempts to secure processes for future writing scenes (an attempt a part, it would seem, of defining process as strategies) has been a problem at the core of postprocess critique. The oft-repeated claim that "no codifiable or generalizable writing process exists or could exist" (Kent, *Post-Process* 1) is essentially an argument about carrying processes into the future. Discerning the shape or ad-hoccery of processes might be possible after the fact, says Kent (*Post-Process* 3). But when we enter into a new communicative situation, "we can never be sure that the process or system we used initially will prevail a second time around" (Kent, "Paralogic" 148). We can't assure that any set of strategies can be deployed again. You can't step in the same process river twice, a postprocess perspective would hold. This doesn't mean there isn't anything to learn about processes, it means what matters more is not the strategies alone we carry with us, but our ability to discern on-the-spot where and with whom is our writing. The focus on process in-advance—floating somehow out of, or above, particular moments in which a writer finds themselves—is the issue from a postprocess (and my) view. In very different ways and for different reasons, both Price and Kent emphasize how (process) time cannot and should not be systematized or codified in advance.

The regimented in-advance-ness of conventional images of process, I think, reflects in our students' thinking. In my experience, student writers see processes operating independently of specific times and places. Often my students don't believe they really "had" a writing process at all when I ask them to draw themselves engaging in a recent scene of writing. They limit their experiences of process to just where and when they've deployed certain familiar school strategies like prewriting or outlining or drafting procedures. When I ask them to draw their processes (as I'll discuss further in Chapter 4), most often they show me writing for school—not writing on their phones, on social media, on fan fiction sites, or for their jobs. And they rarely, if ever, show me *where* they are and who they're with. If we put processes in time though, we'd put it in space too; we'd see writing happening wherever and whenever without any preconceptions about what constitutes a "writing process."

Yagelski amplifies this point, as he shows just how much of our instruction equates processes with engineering texts that attain some level of surface acceptability. In our enduring focus on textual features, he observes, we focus basically not at all on the myriad and manifest *experience* of the writing process. He illustrates this in part by describing a scene at an NWP conference—one thousand writers in a big room all quietly and collectively experiencing the act of writing together and then, simply, putting that writing aside. This moment of being and composing, for Yagelski, is itself a profound act, one of inquiry and provocation rarely lingered upon or even acknowledged in our instruction. Through a case discussion of his work with writing student Chelsea, Yagelski exposes how routinely in our instruction, we hyperfocus on writing as making socially acceptable *forms*, a focus which, again, prevents the potential for writing acts themselves to be transformative experiences. He writes,

> Whatever happens to a text after it is written does not affect what is happening to (or in) the writer as she or he is writing that text. Whatever happens to this text that I am composing right now after I have written it will not change what is happening right now as I write it. It is this experience that current theory fails to explain. (105)

Refocusing on the right-now-ness of writing adjusts writing theory and practice: Yagelski's phenomenological, non-Cartesian view exposes how even process instruction, which purportedly focuses on practice over product, thoroughly fails to get at writing as it unfolds in an ongoing present. But focusing on process as activity *in time* might urge us toward radical process descriptivism in our methods. More than future-oriented strategies, processes as activity in time reveal composing as situated and emergent activity—influenced strongly or indirectly (or not at all) by the past (experiences, tools, practices learned and exercised, cultural norms, conventions, etc.) *and* equally why what is *in situ* (new, unthinkingly performed, responsive, never repeated or habitually enacted—in short, improvised).

Teachers of writing may rarely think of processes as living emergent action. Instead, we reconstruct a student's process through collected textual artifacts: drafts arranged in a portfolio, a required prewriting web, freewrites, marginal comments, editing marks, portfolio reflections, tracked revision changes, and so on. Process knowledge is demonstrated in how texts change, not in how a writer has acted. In Yagelski's words: "For all the attention this has received, the process movement seems to have effected little change when it comes to where we cast our collective gaze in our efforts to understand and teach writing: Our eyes remain fixed on the text, like so many test-takers admonished to keep their eyes on their own papers" (144). It should be no surprise that I am taken by Yagelski's image—our process eyes fixate on papers, on drafts, on texts. Meanwhile, the vibrant physicalities of processes (v.) covers its tracks, recedes from view. We maintain a steady, even relentless, focus on texts even if or as we continue to utter our mantra, "process not product." This brings me to my third and final assumption disrupted in casting processes as activity: how we default to search-ing for process as it presents *in texts*.

The link between process and product is as complicated as it is deeply ingrained. The field turned to processes (along with a set of other foci: devel-opmental psychology, the fight for students' rights to their own languages, open access initiatives, civil and students' rights movements, and so on) in part because some writing teachers were faced with written products they increas-ingly did not understand. And as Prior has put it, when we consider why study-ing writing processes is important: "The first and central reason is that writing processes are where texts come from" ("Tracing" 167). Thus, it may be difficult to imagine processes as anything but directly related to products. The familiar process wheel, for example, is trained thoroughly on the path and changes of any particular text from prewriting to publication. It is true too that process theorizing, as evidenced in the last chapter, has increasingly accounted for wide swaths of factors and contexts that influence writing activity as well as the cir-culation and work of texts. This recognition is evident in Prior's claim that "To understand how a text comes into being requires looking broadly at contexts as well as closely at specific situated activity" ("Tracing" 172). While this perspec-tive highlights the complex situatedness of writing activity at both micro- and macro-scales, Prior here nevertheless prioritizes writing as the movement of the text into the world. Tightly connecting products to processes predetermines and limits what counts as relevant process activity.

Perhaps the most restrictive perspectives on product/process relationships are those that have assumed direct correlations between features of texts and specific (acontextual, discrete) writing behaviors. This may feel like an "old" idea about processes. But the NCTE statement I reference above still implies this view. For example, the first point in a list of what writing teachers need to under-stand about processes is "[t]he relationship between features of finished writ-ing and the actions writers perform to create that writing." This suggests that a teacher can "see" process activity in hindsight, as determined through features of "finished" texts. It presumes that distinct behaviors can be isolated and directly associated with specific textual features. It predetermines what might constitute meaningful writing activity. But how can an observer know after-the-fact what specific actions cause changes that move a text toward its final realization? As John Warnock has it, though we cannot really know writing in any other way than through products, texts ultimately confound as a means of "seeing into writing" (7). And plus, even if those behaviors could be isolated and defined, even if writing (n.) and writing (v.) both laid bare its tracks and its relationships, of what use could those behaviors really be in new contexts, for new texts, in novel material and rhetorical situations?

The hope that process and products will offer up clear one-to-one correlations has been perhaps the most errant of process hope. It likely led to well-meaning but ultimately damaging instructional strategies that presumed student writers' processes were systematic texts to be interpreted and debugged by insightful teacher-observers. Perl's study of "unskilled writers" in some ways exemplifies this hope. On the one hand, Perl's methods revealed the complexities, patterns and logics of participant Tony's processes. As Perl writes, "The conclusion here is not that Tony can't write, or that Tony doesn't know how to write, or that Tony needs to learn more rules: Tony is a writer with a highly consistent and deeply embedded recursive process" (328). Perl's assertion is extremely important as it countered anxieties at the time that manifest (much like they can still today) in veiled arguments for academic rigor, "appropriateness," or "back-to-basics" methods and in backlash to calls for language diversity and preservation. Perl demonstrated that Tony, a writer simply presumed to be "unskilled," performs writing processes logically and with sophistication. This was a powerful claim at a time when access to higher education was opening but against a backdrop of insidious social control waged against the fight for increasing civil rights and the recognition of language diversity.

On the other hand, though, Perl suggested that writing processes like Tony's could be modified for the better through instructional intervention. What Tony needed, Perl and others thought at the time, "are teachers who can interpret that process for him, who can see through the tangles in his process just as he sees meaning beneath the tangles in his prose, and who can intervene in such a way that untangling his composing process leads him to create better prose" (328). Embedded in this view is the assumption that processes are amenable to some measure of mechanization and that processes could be stable across contexts. If the processes involved in writing are performed "right," this view implies, "good writing" will result. This interventionist belief also entails the problematic assumption of learner deficiencies: writing problems as problems in thinking rather than—as social process theorists quickly pointed out—relative inexperience with certain social discourses especially those valued and most performed in middle-class, academic contexts. In short, that writing teachers should "intervene in and . . . modify their students' writing habits" (Selzer 276) is predicated on the idea that there are direct correlations to discover between processes and products. But, as Jack Selzer asserts in 1984, the dizzying number of contextual factors potentially at play in processes will always dash these interventionist hopes. Selzer warns, for example, that teachers must understand that student writers who "truncate their writing processes for school writing" or revise "only superficially" may be doing so not out of "ignorance or intransigence" but because they see school writing as unimportant or routine (281).

And, of course, this list of intervening forces which affect the products we receive can expand infinitely—the writer was in a noisy room and under a time limit (Emig); their electricity was turned off; they were caring for an insistent child; they were working a double shift, or in a silent library late at night; their phone or laundry timer or roommate rhythmically interrupted; and so on. Acknowledging processes' always changing environments and situated actions further undermines any sense that process behavior can be tuned or jostled or controlled to reliably generate specific textual features.

For as much as we no longer believe we can untangle or engineer students' processes, products' control of our process imagination remains quite entrenched. In his recent book on process pedagogy, Kyle Jensen takes on this trope of development and control so deeply anchored in process teaching. In Jensen's view, the dominant "how-centered" philosophy of more than forty years of process instruction equates student development with empowerment, a state attained through a carefully orchestrated façade of control. Students produce textual materials that expose their processes for surveillance by instructors. Instructors in exchange "transfer control [back to the student] by providing strategies that facilitate greater levels of proficiency" (2). From Jensen's perspective, this under-interrogated philosophy and the ways it presupposes incremental literate development prevents writing professionals and students alike from fully grasping writing as "a complicated sociohistorical phenomenon" (81). Said another way, because of our preoccupation with the careful engineering of texts, or as Yagelski would put it, because of our driving interest in making texts increasingly acceptable in their surface features, "neither students nor scholars can develop a full intimacy with the complexity of writing processes" (Jensen 13).

Jensen argues that we should shift instead to a "what-centered" conception of process that sees writing in excess of control (6). To make this shift, Jensen positions students as researchers in online writing archives—in "digital interfaces that display every mark of revision" (7)—where they can observe the tiny, seemingly patternless changes in texts as they are marked through time. This view opens up what Jensen sees as an "uncanny space where writing unfolds in surprising ways" (83). Observing myriad textual choices that could be otherwise, Jensen argues, "helps students recognize that material development is not a linear process toward control" (87). Instead, Jensen shows how archival study of process helps writers conceptualize writing as a "multidirectional activity characterized by distributed processes" (87) and unveils the complex, decentered, and "more mysterious dimensions" (117) of writing. This kind of archival looking at a text's tiny and major changes unveils the chaos of emergence.

In his characterization of process teaching as well as his descriptive process methods, Jensen's project aligns very much with my own. He embraces process descriptivism; he disrupts process as orderly, *a priori* development; he values having writers see the tiny detail of processes as they unfold in time. He shifts where we look for process. But where we diverge is in that he makes these adjustments by training student writers' eyes upon process as *text*. Student writers perhaps infer writing as complex human actions as they train their eyes closely on small and major textual changes. While Jensen upsets process commonplaces to good end, he at the same time, from my perspective, doubles down on the stubborn association of processes as products as he casts the "meaning and movement" (Jensen 10) of writing in terms changes marked in the archive. Ultimately, I share Jensen's vision of the pedagogical value of embracing "insecurity" (10) and cultivating curiosity rather than trying to mechanically practice literate control. But I see his "what-centered" view from the perspective instead of bodily activity in space-time—moving physical bodies, affects, spaces, objects, and situated and shaping sociomaterial forces. If writers are to see their writing acts as implicated and susceptible, I think they might do so more readily by observing process as actions with discernable influences than by observing marks in an archive.

Perhaps it is true that we can only distinguish writing activity from the rest of life by virtue of eventual products. But there is value in stretching that process/product connection to its limits. And of course, our instruction will still entail products; we cannot in our teaching, nor should we, erase outlines, portfolios, reflections, drafts, pages, or other text-oriented process artifacts. I'm suggesting rather that there is value in dimensionalizing processes as bodily activities that live and breathe in everyday participatory contexts. This expanded or dimensional view makes writing meaningfully embodied and material, a conception not just suppressed by a process tradition associated most with texts or abstract cognition or controlled literate development. A wider and invasive Western intellectual tradition that prefers mind over matter also interferes.

PROCESSES AS *PHYSICAL* ACTIVITY

Writing is embodied. This is a now familiar assertion in composition and rhetoric. But complicating its familiarity is the range of ways embodiment has come to mean, matter, and do. A. Abby Knoblauch, for example, worries about an "obfuscation of terminology" (51). Such imprecision about what we mean when we say that writing is embodied, Knoblauch suggests, risks further disregard for work invoking embodiment and the marginalized bodies, voices, and lived realities it aims in different ways to account for. I agree with Knoblauch's assessment that what embodiment may signify does vary: to name just a few ways, embodiment is a critical term in feminist composition, methodology, and epistemology (e.g., Flynn; Haraway; Kirsch and Ritchie); in writing pedagogy as signifying bodily performance or performativity (e.g., Butler; Cedillo; Fishman et al.; Kopelson; Lindquist; Stenberg); in theories of language and identity that emphasize racialized, gendered, normative, and class dimensions of composing as well as its systems of difference, privilege, and social and economic capital (e.g., Alexander; Banks; Bloom; Dolmage, *Disability*; Royster; Villanueva, *Bootstraps*; Wilson and Lewiecki-Wilson). But even this set of citations, as any, reduces the ways embodiment may work as a living concept. Indeed, I think it's impossible, and likely undesirable, to reach the conceptual stability Knoblauch seems to seek. Instead, we might reach for, as I hope to here in this section, the clearest articulation possible of what is meant by any given invocation of writing's embodiment. In emphasizing its physicalities, I see processes as located, susceptible, affective, conditioned and improvisatory, differentiated, and particular bodily movement with material things.

The first point to emphasize, again, is that I most often speak in terms of the physical or physicality rather than embodiment. I lean away from embodiment in some measure because I think the term can more often connote textuality or signification. For instance, in her tripartite taxonomy of embodiment in writing scholarship, Knoblauch emphasizes "embodied language" or "terms, metaphors, and analogies" (52) that reference the body (or do not), as well as "embodied rhetoric" which she defines as the "purposeful effort by an author to represent aspects of embodiment within the text he or she is shaping" (58). I have no issue with the importance of terms in Knoblauch's scheme; I just mean to focus not on textualized embodiment but rather on bodiedness which lives, breathes, stops, rests, responds, takes up, moves, does. I choose physicality to direct our (i.e., writers') attention to observable and particular bodily action—the choreographed and improvisatory experience of physical movement and affect that drives any scene of composing. Processes are only accomplished through physical activities, by means of the differing movement of body parts like hands, eyes, mouths and voices, fingers, legs, arms, brains, and muscles engaged with material objects. In part, my work in previous chapters leads me to this assertion: Christina Haas' observation that, "Writers use their bodies and the materials available to their bodies via the material world, to both create and to interact with textual artifacts" (225); Reynolds' call for attention to "those physical movements that we call writing" (168); Emig's emphasis on the "literal act of writing" ("Hand" 112) as physical creation somewhat akin to the acts of sculpting or carving. Located bodies enact writing processes as an ineluctable bodily doing with materials—digital or analog, enduring or ephemeral. Minds alone do not make writing.

At the same time, this physicality is almost too obvious. It risks seeming inconsequential or oversimplifying writing as "mere" inscription. But it is the center of my thinking first because processes in our classrooms are ritually couched in terms of acontextual thinking or textuality, an association which takes writing acts out of time and place as acontextual, floating free, controlled—or in short, picture postcard. In one sense then, seeing processes as physical activity focuses on the bodily action that is available to observation. Aligning with phenomenological traditions, Anne Wysocki similarly suggests that embodiment encourages us to "attend to what we just simply do, day to day, moving about, communicating with others, using objects that we simply use in order to make things happen" (3). Indeed, focusing on physical activity does, to some extent, aim to see "simply" the smallest details of what a writer does, where they do it, and with what. But I am not sure that that bodily doing is best understood "simply." Wysocki addends this kind of attention with a more constructionist perspective. On one hand, embodiment is constructed and socially-situated; it is "knowledge that we are also experienced from outside, observed and shaped as part of a culture and its institutions" (3) and, on the other, it is our "felt experiences of an interior" (11). Wysocki appears to construct this tension familiarly as an inside/outside or self/other dichotomy: embodiment is shaped "through culturally developed identities being placed on us by others while at the same time we come to experience ourselves as sensing interiors" (12–13).

I appreciate the simultaneity that Wysocki reaches for here—embodiment is both individual-interior and socially constructed. But I resist the dividing line, one I think is commonplace in constructions of embodiment: that sensations and "felt sense" or authentic voice are *in* our bodies and social narratives and cultural signification ride outside on bodily surfaces. Embodiment rides instead, it seems to me, always in between and in motion. For one, we know bodies aren't more authentic or originary than culture at the same time that they are always already interpolated (as Judith Butler's well-known work on gender performativity suggests). A body is never outside the interpolation of culture or language broadly construed. At the same time, bodily experience perpetually exceeds or undermines those determinations (see, for example, N. Katherine Hayles' treatment of embodiment versus "the body" as exceeding determination in her reading of Foucault's panopticon). This kind of complex interrelation amongst bodies and signs has been nuanced in this way especially in disability studies. As Tobin Siebers emphasizes, particularized bodies are not blank slates that can be so easily overwritten by language, category, or constructionism. "The body is alive," Siebers emphasizes, "teeming with vital and often unruly forces" (68) that exceed and are "capable of influencing and transforming social languages" (68). I see the physicalities of processes riding in between in this way too—experienced and felt, never outside the imposition of culture, habit, others, and social signification *and* always at the same time "teeming" with transformative potential.

An important implication of this view, one which interconnects sensation and sociality, is that focusing on writing as a physical process isn't at all to narrow its scope or ignore its larger contexts. Quite the converse. Taking cue again from Haas, embodied practice is at once local, sensory, social and historical, learned and idiosyncratic. Writing tools, like a #2 pencil or a MacBook desktop computer in a university library, "have a history built into them" (Haas 229), histories that are shaped by the wider cultural processes preceding (and exceeding) any writing act. Simultaneously, literate tools are the "products both of the uses to which they have been put and of the beliefs that guide those uses" (229). Those histories and uses and beliefs too, I would stress, are not contained just *in* the tool itself either (as Haas emphasizes), but also in relation to bigger *scenes* of use (e.g., the desktop in the university library versus one in a home positioned in a shared family space). Haas nevertheless helps us see the dynamic interconnections of a single writer's moves with writing tools or objects shot through with cultural assumptions, social histories, beliefs (collective and individual), and material affordances. And these relations, it should be underlined, are not of automatic accord or parity. Rather than a baseline of "fit" amongst tool design, beliefs, and specific bodies, the default is better seen as "misfitting" (Garland-Thompson; Miller)—collisions of bodily differences with baked-in assumptions about "the body" (as a universal) as manifest in material tools or writing spaces. As Elisabeth L. Miller exemplifies, for example, "people with aphasia experience a conflict between their bodies, minds, and the normative materials and expectations of literacy—or literate misfitting" (28). Misfitting exposes reciprocal relations amongst tools' actual—that is, fitting, hacked, modified, reinvented, ranging—embodied uses and constraints at a range of scale: material, cognitive, cultural, social, historical. As such, attending to physicality is not to focus processes on interiors or bodies in isolation. Bodies instead are implicated—shaped by and shapers of macro-scaled contexts of community, culture, history. As feminist philosopher Gail Weiss states, building upon Maurice Merleau-Ponty's notion of intercorporeality: "being embodied is never a private affair, but is always already mediated by our continual interactions with other human and nonhuman bodies" (5).

As bodies are never alone nor solely interior, writing's physical activity can be understood as movement *with*. As Laura R. Micciche puts it, "Writing is contaminated, made possible by a mingling of forces and energies in diverse, often distributed environments. Writing is defined, ultimately, by its radical *withness*" ("Writing" 502). Processes are also always thoroughly *with* where they are located. Similar to invocations in feminist, cultural, and affect studies (Haraway; Kirsch and Ritchie; Lu; Massumi; Mauk; Reynolds, "Ethos as Location"), Vandenberg, Hum, and Clary-Lemon offer *location* or *position*—locating bodies in specific contexts (discoursal, physical, cultural, dialect, community, and so on) that are fluid, overlapping, and conflicting—as a means to disrupt universalisms and erasures. Observing the "living human body" (12), Vandenberg and his coauthors assert, "encourages one to recognize gender, skin color, age, and the mild or debilitating physical effects of one's labor. Such observations can become an inroad to the recognition of privilege and difference, or the value-laden 'station' one occupies while engaging others in language" (12). Starting with emplaced bodily experience creates "inroads," as Vandenberg et al. construct it, a place from which to perceive both "a register of life in action, a locus of personal experience as a source of knowledge" and "a reflection of discursive interaction" (12). A living *writing* body similarly spotlights such locatedness: the writer's relations to her interlocutors, her uptake or violations of particular community discourses, her shifting positions of disempowerment or privilege, the changing reception and judgment of her language performance across domains, and so on. The physical movements of processes are then never in a vacuum but implicated in—and a *way in* toward perceiving—the vast contingencies and shaping factors of writing (I say more about this below in my discussion of emplacement).

Next, to see writing processes as physical is also to see affect. Affect in composition studies, somewhat similarly to embodiment, has directed our attention widely, framing considerations related to emotion, psychology, feeling or sensations, "nonrational" action, movement, and relationality. Affect is largely understood as the domain of physical bodies, forces, and sensations, or a "gradient of bodily capacity" (Gregg and Seigworth 2). Affect too unfolds on connective axes of selves/others, evincing how individuals and groups form morphing relations with others, communities, institutions, ideologies, and physical objects and environments. Affect recasts emotions, thought conventionally to be individual and interior, as instead thoroughly social, externalized, and relational forces that hold explanatory power for political and social organizations, allegiances, stances, and fractures, as emotions generate surfaces on bodies and communities that compel and repel (Ahmed).

Compositionists invoke affect and emotion to reconceptualize publics and public rhetoric (e.g., Edbauer-Rice) or reconsider pathos (Jacobs and Micciche); to expose psychological phenomena in composing like anxiety, beliefs and motivation (McLeod) or extra-cognitive (Brand and Graves) or social-performative dimensions of emotions in the teaching and learning of writing (Chandler; Lindquist; Micciche, *Doing*). Alice Brand and Susan McLeod have worked specifically to expand our conceptions of writing processes with concentrated efforts to account for affect, to meaningfully include the shaping roles of emotion in processes and push their constructions beyond control, linearity, acontextual cognition, or detached problem-solving. In spite of these efforts, there remains little focus in contemporary teaching with process on the affective *life* of writing—its physical sensations, rhythms, interruptions, compulsions, and avoidances. Observing the physical and environmental aspects of composing processes will reveal a range of affective relationships writers forge and feel with their writing spaces, the "unconscious, automatic, ineffable, inexplicable" (Brand and Graves 5) ways of knowing and doing. Thus, affect is an important extension and complement to Haas, Perl, and Syverson's focus on embodiment and knowing. Tacit cognitive frameworks can imply sustained goal-directedness and intentionality that affect would perpetually undermine through excess. Observing affect disrupts the sure command, intentions, or predetermined steps conventionally thought to chiefly steer composing. Processes are driven by situated thinking, social conditioning, and affective intensities, among other forces, all of which are likely indistinct or inseparable.

Physical affective dimensions are especially important toward disrupting containment in our pictures of process. Kevin Leander and Gail Boldt's "nonrepresentational approach" (26) to literate activity focuses on any given moving literate body. Through a "strategic sketch" (26) of Lee—a ten-year old boy whom they observe for a day as he reads, plays, socializes and lives through Japanese manga texts—Leander and Boldt portray literacy "as living its life in the ongoing present, forming relations and connections across signs, objects, and bodies in often unexpected ways. Such activity is saturated with affect and emotion; it creates and is fed by an ongoing series of affective intensities that are different from the rational control of meanings and forms" (26). Whereas conventional understandings might delimit "Lee's reading" processes as only those moments when he's moving eyes over a text, Leander and Boldt capture an enormous range of things, movements, and activities that constitute his practice: a comfy armchair, toy headband and dagger, jumping, searching the internet, playing cards, a friend, a porch swing, a play-sword fight (where gender constructs and socialization scripts no doubt give shape to Lee's bodily behavior), just to name a few of Lee's emergent interactions over many hours. This adjusted perspective—Lee-as-body rather than Lee-as-text (29)—undermines highly structured and engineered school literacy tasks, which couldn't register or solicit the indeterminate, unruly, and "unbounded" nature (41) of reading-living-playing practices like Lee's.

Departing from the reigning social semiotic framework of the New London group, which sees "youth literacy practices as purposeful, rational design" (Leander and Boldt 24) within (disembodied or detached) sign systems, Leander and Boldt see processes as movement and mobility, as motivated *and* aimless bodily action rather than as steps or as sedentary and ephemeral mind or sign work. They forefront potential and emergence rather than control; they highlight interactions and composing *with* material objects and tools; they capture movement, desire, feeling, need, and doubt as part of literate action. Their work too echoes my concern about conventional process instruction. Process constituted in terms of texts, drafts, or outlines has focused us too much on "prescriptive shaping" (Leander and Boldt 24)—or engineered literate development (Jensen)—missing how processes are an "emergence of activity, including the relations among texts and bodies in activity and the affective intensities of these relations" (Leander and Boldt 34). Inviting in affective physicality meaningfully into our process pictures focuses us on particularities and differences, specific bodies and things coming together in writing. The particular, physical-material, and affective movements of writing constructively "troubles the writing process" (113) to borrow Dolmage's phrase. Alterity or "broken-ness" (125), understood positively not pejoratively, should be central to our understandings of processes as physical and material. Physicality emphasizes potentiality and disrupts by refusal the conventional "forward march toward a perfectable text/body" (Dolmage 126).

Physicality is thus indeterminate, experienced, culturally shaped, and social. It is also always particular. Focus on embodiment body can by omission become focus on "the body"—a universal standard (which far from applying to everyone, smuggles in dominant normative assumptions), a view from nowhere, the body in general. Writing pedagogies risk the same, promoting under the banner of a supposed "'objective' or disinterested standard" (Vandenberg et al. 16), a generalized subject position that becomes code for able, white, middle-class, hetero, and/or male. Jay Dolmage amplifies this point in relation to processes specifically, noting that the "regime of bodily normalcy is also present, and perhaps even more insistent, in the writing process itself" (112). And though we may acknowledge the ways writing is necessarily governed by the body, Dolmage continues, "few pedagogical approaches allow that the bodies engaged in this process should be viewed as diverse; to ignore the fact that our bodies all write differently is to superimpose a single bodily norm onto the writing process" (112). Following these and other compositionists, I emphasize particularized difference in physical processes: never *the* writing body nor movement in general, never an enduring construct of an "ideal" or "universal" bodily writing experience; and always physicality as particularized, as located, as a view from somewhere, a stand- or sit-point as epistemological social positioning (Dolmage, *Disability* 129). As Elizabeth Grosz writes succinctly, "Alterity is the very possibility and process of embodiment" (qtd. in Wilson and Lewiecki-Wilson 13). Processes as physical activity means to expose and make available rather than elide difference, seeking particularity across the contexts, subjects, and actions that are connected by and constitute writing acts.

My bottom line here, and really in this book, is that I think it's important in process teaching to forefront bodies (and places and things). In their recent anthology, Vandenberg et al. share this call for context-attuned instruction. Embracing process-oriented pedagogies that can break free from inherited constraints and omissions, the authors underline that "while process pedagogies seem amenable to explorations of difference, they routinely homogenize these inclusions under the universalized rubric of 'good writing'" (6). This is to say that, in writing instruction, processes are framed as largely stable and repeatable; that a set of "good" process behaviors will be broadly applicable and result in "good writing" in undetermined future contexts. As such, conventional process approaches occlude the many ways that writing activity *differs* across situations in ways both in and out any given actors' control. The hefty challenge for instruction then—and as the field has recognized for some time and evidenced, for example, in the deconstruction of "general skills instruction" (e.g., Petraglia, *Reconceiving*)—is to help student writers not only build a body of knowledge about writing and practice, but balance that knowledge with what they will need to *learn on-the-spot*. Most instruction, though, ends up stabilizing what is thought to endure about writing in the form of skills or rules—for a simple example, a set of comma *rules* perhaps specific to a given instructor, rather than an exploration of comma conventions or tendencies or what some in power have agreed upon is the case (for now). Contemporary process instruction would more beneficially help writers to *learn how to learn* to write in any situation. By seeing processes first as physical activities iterating differently in every new situation, writers can begin to take on this situated view of writing and focus upon what they need to discover about *where* they are writing.

Syverson too demonstrates how the corporeal can become a dynamic inroad: the micro-scaled study of writing processes as physical and material gives access to the macro-scaled dimensions of writing "observed at every level of scale" (Syverson 23) and that far exceed the spatial and temporal borders of any given writing scene. Syverson puts this idea quite elegantly, as she describes her own train of thought about writing phenomena as it expanded almost wondrously through the course of her studies. She says that most of us, our students and in our field's history, repetitiously knit writing together with thinking, and thinking as "a matter of logical processing neatly managed by a brain in splendid isolation" (xiv). But when viewed from the perspective of an ecology, writing reveals itself to be terrifically expansive: "a complex ensemble of activities and interactions among brains, hands, eyes, ears, other people, and an astonishing variety of structures in the environment, from airplane cockpits to cereal boxes to institutions" (xiv). This view of the breadth of writing, the entailment of writing in place and time and things and life, is made available through a focus on writing bodies moving through spaces and times. I'm taken with Syverson's wonderment at the complexities—the near magic of—seeing writing's processes as *at once* expansive *and* physically located.

PROCESSES AS *EMPLACED* PHYSICAL ACTIVITY

In concluding with *emplacement*, I risk redundancy. I have already emphasized processes as relations among writers' bodies, movement, context, and objects. Process as bodily movement is always movement *with*. Writing is corporeal and material action (Haas). Writing entangles embodiment and enaction: the physical-material-spatial grounding of complex writing systems (Syverson). The affective body is "always in relation to an ever-changing environment" (Leander and Boldt 29), always the "body-*and*" (Leander and Boldt 29), a lively nexus of time, place, material objects, worlds, sensations. Emplacement, in other words, is inextricable from physicality. Writing bodies are never self-contained, not *in* a place but *emplaced*. As N. Katherine Hayles constructs this implicit relation: "embodiment is contextual, enwebbed within the specifics of place, time, physiology and culture" (154–5). Through emplacement, I emphasize susceptibility—writers and processes are an emergent result always of, never isolated from, where they are (on a range of scales). Processes are writer's own as much as they are not.

Kristie S. Fleckenstein helps capture what I'm after in picturing processes' strong emplacement, through her notion of somatic mind. She writes,

> somatic mind is tangible location *plus* being. It is *being-in-a-material-place*. Both organism and place can only be identified by their immanence within each other; an organism in *this* place (body, clothing, cultural scene, geographical point) is not the same organism in *that* place. Who and where (thus, what) are coextensive. ("Writing" 286)

As always already a "view from somewhere" (Fleckenstein 281), emplacement is more than passive background or staging. Rather writing and writers are always already implicated, a part of the place where they are. Change where, with what, or for whom and writing processes change.

In recent years in composition and rhetoric, theorizing emplacement has become a prominent frame, a boon in rhetorical theory sometimes referred to as a "material turn" (e.g., Barnett, "Toward"). Actor-network theory (e.g., Lynch and Rivers), object-oriented ontologies (Barnett and Boyle), activity theories (Prior and Shipka; Russell) and new materialisms (Gries; Rickert) among others, each fit under this material umbrella and share a general impulse: deconstruct the human-as-absolute-agent and proceed instead from the notion that humans and other entities are "thoroughly immersed within materiality's productive contingencies" (Coole and Frost 7). In other words, writers/rhetors, things, and environments are distributed and ontologically flat (not hierarchically arranged) in their relations.

With emplacement, I align my thinking about situated processes with this materially-oriented thinking. Material things of and around writing are actively a part of processes not inert tools transparently deployed by a writer-agent. Writing environments are participatory and shaping, not mere staging. Writers are important but never isolated agents alone acting upon their contexts. Writers are actors in the midst, alongside, or overpowered by materialities immediate and distant—objects, bodies, light, noise, tools, chairs, electricity, pets, and so on—that are too "active, self-creative, productive, unpredictable" (Coole and Frost 9).

To flesh out emplacement a bit more, I turn to the recent new materialist work of Jane Bennett and Thomas Rickert. In Bennett's terms, material things exhibit vitality as "the capacity of things—edibles, commodities, storms, metals—not only to impede or block the will and designs of humans but also to act as quasi agents or forces with trajectories, propensities, or tendencies of their own" (vii). New materialisms like Bennett's understands agency as spread out in a complex, interactive network of actants, rather than contained solely within a human actor. Actants, a term Bennett forwards from Bruno Latour, is a "source of action that can be either human or nonhuman; it is that which has efficacy, can do things, has sufficient coherence to make a difference, produce effects, alter the course of events" (Bennett viii). Disrupting the entrenched human/material, agent/object opposition doesn't slip into a material determinism, nor does it disavow the capacity of human action as a kind of agency. Rather, agency or action is always emerging and reemerging, as actants coalesce and separate differently through time.

Our images of writing process have no means to account for what Bennett names "distributed agency" in a given scene of writing. That agency which we conventionally pour into human actors alone as unfettered textual engineers, under a new materialist frame, would be instead "distributed across an ontologically heterogeneous field, rather than being a capacity localized in a human body or in a collective produced (only) by human efforts" (23). Bennett herself reflects on how we might understand a scene of writing through this distributed framework:

> The sentences of this book also emerged from the confederate agency of many striving macro- and microactants: from "my" memories, intentions, contentions, intestinal bacteria, eyeglasses, and blood sugar, as well as from the plastic computer keyboard, the bird song from the open window, or the air or particulates in the room, to name only a few of the participants. What is at work here on the page is an animal-vegetable-mineral-sonority cluster with a particular degree and duration of power. (23)

Bennett's perspective stretches process. As she underlines, processes unfold as loose and constantly reforming alliances. And those actants themselves entail entwined and divergent histories, prior engagements, and trajectories that simultaneously found and exceed them. This rich picture of implicatedness shifts how we are accustomed to thinking of processes. For one, it makes little sense to "adapt" processes to surrounds or to varying tools as processes are always already implicated.

Thomas Rickert's notion of rhetorical ambience too emphasizes emplacement. His intervention aims to deconstruct over-simplified notions of rhetorical context and instead conceptualize rhetoric as situated and ambient. "To be situated," Rickert writes, "means that one's emplacement is inseparable from the rhetorical interactions taking place, including material dimensions both within and beyond meaning" (34). Like Fleckenstein, Hayles, Leander and Boldt, and others, Rickert binds embodiment with place and things: rhetors/writers are constituted by and in relation to their (material-social-cultural-political-historical) environments. As Rickert describes it, "minds are at once *embodied*, and hence grounded in emotion and sensation, and *dispersed* into the environment itself, and hence no longer autonomous actants but composites of intellect, body, information, and scaffoldings of material artifacts" (43). In other words, Rickert's rhetorical ambience encourages seeing process as material and "embodied and embedded" (34). And, similar to Leander and Boldt's shift away from literacy as rational design, recognizing ambience shifts the focus from rhetorical intention to emergence. The "intent and self-consciousness" of the rhetor "no doubt matter enormously, but they no longer suffice" (36), Rickert writes, because, for one, this intention-driven model cannot account for the oftentimes unruly, accidental, failed, or detoured nature of such action and persuasion in the world. Conceptualizing processes as emplaced similarly emphasizes emergence, affordances, and responsivity to context, which are all important adjustments for contemporary writing pedagogy.

A writer's conscious control will always be infiltrated by situational participants, human and otherwise. The ontological orientation of new materialisms, moreover, exposes how selves continuously interpenetrate material environments and how processes are constituted by living, feeling, moving, emerging. These and other implications of new materialisms have "made inroads into composition studies . . . but the transfer to writing theory and practice remains very much in progress" (Micciche, "Writing" 489). Theories of distributed agency and ambience help generate different questions about the practice and construct of writing processes: What objects and environments are significant (in a given writing place and time) and how does their participatory force operate? How does writing emerge in relation to and as a result of materialities? Methodologically and pedagogically, how can we capture and understand the participatory roles of material objects and spaces in writing processes? How can we teach writers to attune to their locations and practice emergence, response, uncertainty rather than chasing the illusion of control?

CONCLUSION: WRITING MOVES

When I was in graduate school, back when I was just beginning to think about bodies and environments and processes, I recall lingering over a friend's story on social media about the writing blocks she was experiencing. In my memory, she described that in the course of a medical appointment, she suddenly confessed to her doctor her crippling and enduring aversion to sitting in the chair at the desk where she was trying to work on her dissertation. She described spending much time each day trying to get in that chair, moving around it, sitting at it briefly, resolving to order paperbacks, and then quickly fleeing it. A solution offered seemingly in passing, the doctor told her to just associate the chair with something more pleasant—just think about it as something like "her grandmother" or "going to the zoo."

The doctor's casual recommendation sees composing, and this particular writing problem, as a *mental* block. Just *think* about this writing task differently and the problem will be solved. Indeed, the picture postcard of writing seems to shape this likely well-meaning health professional's advice. Writing is a thinking problem. Writing is independent from things and places and objects. But clearly, this writer's ceaseless avoidance of her writing chair very much and meaningfully *is* about the physical, material, and spatial environments in which writing is, or in this case, is not, accomplished. What seems to be going on here is a matter on a different register than thoughts or associations: this object—the chair—the strained dance around it, the attempts to sit down into it, the body's resistance and refusal. Over time the relation of the chair and the body has become laden with physical, not simply symbolic, force. Sensations of the body being strained and pressed, stilted, tensed, fidgety, flighty, pushed and pulled have accumulated on the chair's physical surface. In a sense, the chair shapes the moves that are possible within the writing environment and, in turn, every hesitating, jerky movement the writer enacts adds to the force of the chair. In this way, writing objects and physical habits become laden with a certain affective weight or force—the "writing chair" becomes an un-sittable place as it accrues the physical force of bodily memory. And these sensations exceed the bounds of this room and chair alone—genre, readers, prior histories, memories, conversations, domestic dynamics, and economic anxieties are among the larger forces perhaps felt too through the surface of the chair.

I wonder about what might happen if this writer, instead of *thinking* something different, might have found more relief in *moving* differently—taking up a different chair in a café or library instead of her home, an email window instead of a word-processing document, perhaps. There's no way to know for sure. But my point is this: far from ephemeral, transcendent, or trapped within the two dimensions of the page, writing processes are no doubt impelled by the three dimensions of our lived experience. Our postcard image and process pedagogy changes when we first see processes as emplaced writers moving and making.

In this way, writing processes move. Writing *moves* in terms of physical, emplaced action. They just never hold still enough to be captured as abstracted strategies alone. Writing *moves* too across and within our many life domains and spaces—across our social, civic, personal, familial, work, and political lives. All writing entails processes, and wildly different ones at that. Difference and susceptibility, not sameness and strategy, is the nature of processes as experienced in the world. And, as I explore next, looking at processes in our classrooms as emplaced physical activity can help students perceive writing expansively, differently, and *in situ*, across ranging contexts and as ways of living.

CHAPTER 4

WRITERS AS SITUATED
PROCESS RESEARCHERS

*Figure 3. Alice's photograph of her "very special office
space that I don't use." Photo credit: "Alice."*

I start with an image of process, one that surely feels familiar. In at least a Western
corner of the imagination of many, this is what writing looks like—at least, what
the "official" writing associated with schooling or with highbrow literary culture
looks like. Better, this is what writing *should* look like: writing is precisely this
rarefied, this cloistered, this orderly, this transcendent, this disembodied. In this
image, I see Brodkey's picture postcard, the recreated garret of the "solitary scribbler" (398). I see Cooper's scene of the "solitary author" (365). I see the driving
fantasy of Bizzell's students that "when they finally become 'good writers,' they will
be able to sit down at the desk and produce an 'A' paper in no more time than it
takes to transcribe it" (175). Whatever the particulars, this image strikes us familiarly because, Brodkey tells us, it is the first lesson we learn about writing (397).

This particular image holds personal weight for "Alice," who, at the time she produced it, was a fourth year doctoral student in composition and rhetoric at a large Midwestern university. Alice submitted this photograph as part of my multimodal qualitative study that explored material environments and embodied movement in several graduate student writers' processes (Blewett et al.; Rule). The image shows Alice's wooden desk positioned by a narrow window of her upstairs loft. Bright sunshine cascades through to illuminate the desk's surface, a stapler, an ordered couple of books, stack of papers, and a populated bookshelf nearby and in just enough disarray to suggest deep engagement.

My study design prompted participants to show me in photographs, drawings, and video (methods I use regularly now in my undergraduate teaching with processes) where their processes occurred—the rooms, objects, chairs, background, ephemera, desks, and tools that got involved in whatever they were writing at the time. Because the study focused on whatever composing was happening at the time of the study (rather than what any participant thought of enduringly as their process behavior) this wasn't the only space Alice depicted. In a video recording, she showed me herself writing in an empty college classroom, a materially sterile session in which a wall clock prominently ticked in the background. She drew important comfort items—including a blanket, snacks, water—that she perceived as critical to the embodiment of her processes (items, I note, that do not populate the image above). She gave me a number of selfie-style photographs of her writing in an overstuffed armchair in her living room, laptop on her lap, her two dogs sleeping alongside, and sometimes on top of, her. The other academic writers in the study too showed processes in a range of locations and with and around varied material objects, as Alice did. But what was interesting about this image of this particular writing desk is that Alice gave me several shots of it, even though she told me *she didn't actually write there.*

In our interview, Alice called this desk her "generic office space or my very special office space *that I don't use*" (emphasis added). As I asked participants for the details of where their writing was happening at the time of the study, I wondered why Alice was compelled to photograph this desk at all. And why did she capture it *just in this way*, with the bright cascading light, and without her physical presence?

I think in part Alice thought this is what I expected to see. *This* image is writing—much more so, we assume, than the everyday material conditions and quotidian objects, movements, and rhythms that "actually" produced or got involved in Alice's processes at the time (to name only a very few that she represented elsewhere: water, comfortable chair, pajamas, domesticity, dogs, impromptu workplaces occupied then deserted). This picture, though, remains a strong presence in Alice's mind in relation to her academic writing. As she mused in interview:

> And then I was also thinking about looking at the photos and thinking about what I wrote about the—oh, when I was talking about my generic office space or my very special office space that I don't use and how it's very meticulously cluttered. I feel like it always looks like somebody works there and that's on purpose. I mean it's almost to an obsessive level. I will go up there and arrange the books in a way that I think looks, I don't know, productive. I was thinking that with the photos because I took all of them with my phone but I threw them threw a photo editor before I sent them to you. . . . To just make the light a little better or make the colors pop a little more. I wasn't thinking about it at the time but now that I'm looking at them, I'm like, God, they're so deliberately composed in that way.

Alice doesn't write at this desk, yet she sees making and remaking it an important part of her physical processes and academic writing routines. Alice sees this space as "deliberately composed," "obsessive," "meticulously cluttered," and photo-edited to make the "colors pop." She likely gave me this picture postcard because performing some part of her writing self in this culturally sanctioned space somehow helps her make the messy, wandering, and less idealized daily labor of her high-stakes dissertation writing feel more possible. That's how Alice seemed to think of it, anyway.

But my purpose in starting with this image is not to decide what it did or did not do for Alice at the time it was taken. I raise it rather because it's evocative. I'm interested in how Alice sees this tidy, transcendent image as essential to writing, and in how she unthinkingly enhanced it. I see in Alice's picture the ways my own writing students tend to officialize their conceptions of processes—as steps or uninhabited rational action, always intentional, special and specialized, no labor or life per se—as similarly too "photo edited." Writing students do this, I think, not just because of the ways writing is constructed in our cultural imaginaries, but also because this is how our instruction can cast process. As explored in the last chapter, conventional process teaching might teach the lesson that processes are steps or strategies that are linear, textual and acontextual, matters of disembodied thinking, relevant only to school-based writing—processes as only ever "deliberately composed." And so like Brodkey, Cooper, and Bizzell, I raise this postcard image to undermine it, especially in how it limits the potential and work of process instruction. I raise Alice's image to keep our eyes on *what it misses*, what is not seen in it about the specifying conditions—the tools, objects, movements, technologies, communities, conventions, interruptions, software, and so on—that differentiate processes across myriad everyday rhetorical situations. Student writers benefit from poking holes in this edited image, from disrupting its control over how they work with writing processes in our classrooms and across innumerable writing contexts.

But how to poke those holes? How can we rebuild process images and practices that dismantle myths of disembodiment and placelessness, ease and orderliness, and prefab strategies? We can start by repositioning student writers in relation to processes—no longer (if ever) as replicators of strategies but instead as curious and situated *process researchers*. By this, I mean observers of processes in the world, including those they engage themselves. I mean as generators of insights and actions that are "good for now," both shaped by and suited to real-time and dynamic contexts. Such a vantage shows just how implicated processes are, casting process as a kinetic, improvisatory "making do" with the participating conditions of a writer's surrounds.

But if we encourage students to observe and describe and respond to the details of processes in everyday life, if we teach with processes in excess of prescriptive strategies, if we suggest that processes are not stable steps alone but situationally determined and contingent, then process teaching is surely well out of the control of the writing teacher. Engaging in this kind of on-the-spot process descriptivism necessitates continued reconsideration of the process "knowledge" writing instructors can claim and of the roles that writing teachers and students take. I begin then by exploring (postprocess) pedagogical work which repositions students as (process) knowledge-makers. With that revised perspective, one at stake too in the final chapter, I describe classroom practices.

QUESTIONING PROCESS: TEACHING WRITING STUDENTS AS PROCESS KNOWLEDGE-MAKERS

As do many who take up the postprocess mantle, in his chapter in Thomas Kent's 1999 volume, Sidney Dobrin undermines familiar process assumptions both pedagogical and conceptual ("Paralogic"). Dobrin's main concern is emphasizing power (rather than assuming neutral relations amongst interlocutors), and thus ethics, in paralogic communication theory. His intervention nevertheless entails pedagogy, and not just in his interest in exposing power differentials in liberatory pedagogy. Instead, Dobrin makes meaningful calls to shift the mission and character of contemporary writing pedagogy in general, and of process teaching in particular.

Along the way, Dobrin performs a familiar postprocess refrain: if we can agree that communication is fundamentally neither systematic nor codifiable, then teaching writing is impossible. In Dobrin's terms: "there are no codifiable processes by which we can characterize . . . discourse, and, hence, there is not a way to teach discourse, discourse interpretation, or discourse disruption" ("Paralogic" 133). The assumption here seems to be that only things that are predictable and stable can be taught, and by its complex, situated, and dialogic nature, writing is not that. As such, this refrain resolves into the claim that teaching is "impossible." And as I've established, especially in the Introduction, such a claim of impossibility is often not about teaching at all, but a call to disengage the field from the primacy of teaching altogether. However, in my read of this particular argument of Dobrin's, he doesn't aim to dispense with process theories or pedagogy but points toward how we might practice through its deconstruction.

While postprocess characterizations of the process paradigm can sometimes feel like a strawman or caricature (Breuch; Matsuda), Dobrin in Kent's collection insightfully judges conventional process thinking. For example, building upon Raul Sanchez's claim that "the writing process is often just the teacher's vision of process" (138), Dobrin emphasizes how process behavior is structured for students by the teacher, as it is they who determine "what prewriting is, what editing is, what revising is, what a final document should look like, what is oppressive, what is politically virtuous, how to become critically conscious, and so forth" (138). This view of directive writing instruction is echoed by David Smit, as he notes that most characterizations of process teaching, "conceive of the teacher as facilitator or coach whose job is to help students work through the various stages of composing: getting ideas, planning and organizing, drafting, revising, and editing" (6). And while the field has come to recognize the political and sociocultural contexts of writing and in turn the ways that privilege, positionality, social class, race and gender is entangled with and shapes every language performance, process remains even in "the most politically savvy classrooms" (Dobrin 138) merely matters of "perpetuating inscribed methods of inquiry" (138). As we've seen in previous chapters, processes remain somehow curiously unlocated, even in spite of the ways the field and other aspects of our instruction have recognized writing as situated. The ways today that we talk about and do processes in our classrooms remains still largely *immune from* these situated forces, as "[s]tudents learn to repeat strategies rather than to manipulate discourse from communicative scenario to communicative scenario" (Dobrin 138–9). If we accept situatedness as a baseline though, we can no longer teach process for sameness and strategy and must move toward novelty and difference instead.

That is no straightforward task. Dobrin, while measured in his pedagogical gestures, does provide some direction (at least, again, he did so in 1999). For one, like Kent and others, Dobrin believes that postprocess "demand[s] that we radically reconceptualize not only how and what we teach, but what we think teaching *is*" (134). We cannot simply establish the parameters of processes for our students and then evaluate their performance of our process scripts. We cannot just have students "reinscribe" the knowledge we give them. And this, actually, is not a new concept in writing classrooms at all. We often say now, for example, that we cannot just teach students forms of eternally "correct" or grammatical writing. Instead, we recognize the *situatedness* of language performance and "correctness" as *susceptible* to the shifting and shaping forces of genre, racial and ethnic privilege, occasion, discourse community conventions, and so on. Similarly, we've deconstructed general-skills writing instruction. Even if we have yet to relent talking about them, we at least understand that there are few if any writing "skills" that really can "transcend any particular content and context" (Petraglia, *Reconceiving* xii). As a result, since a general course in writing makes little sense, we've worked to *situate* our instruction in various domains: in and across the disciplines, activity systems, genre ecologies, our *own* discipline through writing-about-writing approaches, and so forth. But process seems to somehow get left behind as a concept that can largely transcend varying contextual specificities. Process remains—as I overheard a first-year writing student say as he observed a set of his class's process drawings hung on the wall—mostly "a bunch of pages."

But if we could help writers *physically locate* writing, then they might be better positioned to see writing and its processes as infinitely varied and sensitive to contexts both immediate and broad, both physical and social. The process "knowledge" that writers need would then not be best understood as stored-up strategies, but as "good for now" insights guiding writing moment-to-moment and discovered *in situ*. Rather than enacting steps from before, students must write where they are, not to practice what they "know" but to practice *figuring out how* to proceed. As Thomas Kent puts it, focused as he is on communicative interaction, "Teachers cannot . . . provide students with a framework that explains the process of collaborative interaction" like process or other strategies, because "the dynamics of collaborative interaction change *on the spot*" (*Paralogic* 165, emphasis added). As Dobrin concludes, "We cannot master discourse" (147) nor processes; we can only become increasingly practiced at perceiving and responding to the nuances of our attempts in living rhetorical situations.

In this way, I am in a sense being "postprocess" as I agree that an all-purpose set of writing "how-to" instructions, even an ever-expanding one, cannot really be taught nor learned. I see value in helping students to be skeptical of how much writing processes—just like any convention or rule we might raise in our classrooms—will hold still, repeat, or be reliable in novel and ranging rhetorical situations. There still are activities or habits useful to learn and enact in future writing contexts but doing so is no guarantee that the resulting product or text will succeed, earn an "A," or be received as we hope with audiences. "[W]e can never be sure that the process or system we used initially will prevail a second time around" (Kent, "Paralogic" 148). I describe process methods in this chapter then that are "postprocess" in as much as I favor teaching processes as, to invoke Thomas Rickert's terms, thoroughly and *ambiently rhetorical*. Writers benefit from looking at processes to discover how they iterate differently in differing contexts, how they are performative, emergent, responsive to others (present, distant, imagined), unruly, ad-hoc, and improvisational.

But teaching—or better, *seeing*—processes in this way requires that, again in Dobrin's terms, we "radically reconceptualize not only how and what we teach, but what we think teaching *is*" (134). I agree. But rather than *start*, the task is more to *continue* to interrogate what it is to "teach" writing. After all, we have been questioning the role of the writing teacher (and the writing student) for composition studies' whole modern life—at least since Elbow's *Writing without Teachers*. And, just as deconstructing teacher authority in our pedagogical imaginaries is familiar if challenging to enact, so too is positioning students in active, constructivist roles. But there is some direction. Activating students' roles, especially in relation to process, is the goal of Nancy C. DeJoy in her 2004 book, *Process This: Undergraduate Writing in Composition Studies*. DeJoy observes how field machinations have greatly minimized the agency and subjectivities of students and teachers. Through conservative appeals to standards and within conventional process pedagogies, writing "students' and many teachers' roles in the writing classroom and in society more generally were restricted in particular ways, ways that favored adaption to and consumption of standards and process 'models' that favored those standards" (4). While DeJoy sees latent potential for agency, liberation, and social progressivism in composition, especially in 1970s-era focus on language rights and student-centered process approaches, she observes how ultimately stronger ideological conservatism continues to win out, propelling policed standards and diminished roles for students as only "consumers" (4) and conformers. In efforts to "right process," DeJoy aims instead to "open spaces in which participation and contribution" become our disciplinary mode, where we approach "undergraduate student writers and their texts" (9) as a contributing part of our field, rather than just our objects of study.

DeJoy outlines several methods to make students contributors. For instance, she describes her own research study in which she partnered with undergraduate students to co-analyze admissions essays, suggesting that "exploring student assumptions about the concepts we propose" (15) is a vital way of making student writers contributing members of the field. Process in particular becomes one such concept to interrogate. In "I Was a Process-Model Baby," DeJoy describes how her own experiences in school led her to see "the real game" in process pedagogies was to conform to and "produce a teacher-identified discourse" ("I Was"163).

She reads into her experience a lack of feminist and critical practices in dominant process models, models which operated on axes of "enthymemic logic, identification, and mastery" (169). As such, in her own instruction, DeJoy dispenses with "pre-scribed and pre-scribable notions of process" ("I Was" 176). Instead, she and her students explore their and others' processes using open-ended questions about invention, arrangement, and revision (176). Emphasizing difference, participation, critical analysis, and co-construction, DeJoy shifts the process pedagogy paradigm from control to analysis. She aims to make process teaching live up to its liberatory potential by unmasking its power differentials and by dismantling its universalizing and standardizing tendencies and its narrowed methods. DeJoy's thinking inspires my own with her crystal-clear shift—seeing writing students as contributors to, rather than just reproducers of, what we know about process practice and by seeing writers as analytical investigators of writing.

This vision of co-constructive accompaniment and analysis aligns my own recent process practices not just with DeJoy's, but also with Kent's call for writing teachers as "co-workers" (*Paralogic* 166) and Kyle Jensen's archival inquiry approach (explored in Chapter 3). Both Jensen and I enact observational methods with students to help them see what lies in *excess* of pictures of prefab processes. While Jensen accompanies students in the textual archive, I ask students to observe living bodily processes in context. For me, through these looking methods, student writers can more readily situate writing and its constraints through focus on bodies writing (v.) in place and time. Process instruction then becomes a kind of *accompaniment*—being alongside writers as they observe and perform situated processes.

ACCOMPANYING CLASSROOM SCENES: TEACHING TO SITUATE PROCESSES

It has become a trope in composition studies books to turn to "application" near the end of a work that might otherwise be historical, archival, or theoretical. This move feels especially warranted in a book like this one in which I've been working to reexamine process for the sake of teaching. I examined the state of process through various materials: compositionists' stock-taking of the process paradigm, composition theory, research studies, pedagogical documents, postprocess critique, and so on. But my look at classroom practice in this section might be among the *shortest* of the sections in this book (and if it is not, it's meant symbolically to be so).

This is because my interrogations of process have not led me to think that some "new" process pedagogy or one kind of "process approach" is desirable or even possible. While process still infuses instruction today, it is far from *the* paramount or controlling conceit. As instruction iterates differently across varying institutional contexts and with the needs of diverse students, how I have positioned my own students to be critical of received process "knowledge" and observe process as emplaced activity will not work the same as it would be in another classroom or at another institution. Just as I am arguing about process, pedagogy too inescapably situates in its varied and dynamic material contexts, which in turn are shaped by institutional, ideological, programmatic, political, and other kairotic constraints. That is, teaching writing, like all rhetorical and composing processes, is always ambient and emergent and thus local and improvisational.

So in lieu of process teaching prescriptions, this teaching section orients around a fundamental guiding question: how can we position student writers to *situate* and *differentiate* writing processes? This big question can be approached through related sub-questions: How can student writers deconstruct and critically engage with their *own* preconceptions of "processes"? How can student writers observe and describe processes (theirs and others) to discover rather than receive ways to proceed?

These questions have helped me to construct, reconstruct, and trouble process with my students in my first-year and intermediate writing classes over the years. Like for many of us that teach college writing, process has been at the center of the courses I teach in different ways. For instance, I've taught the first semester of first-year writing with a reflective, narrative focus on writing processes. My students reflected on themselves as writers by sharing their own writing habits, routines, idiosyncrasies, and so on. Students read and analyzed writers on writing, and we discussed what experiencing writing was like for us. I aimed along the way to expand their textual process strategies for brainstorming and revision. This kind of focus on processes, I think, is pretty familiar. And I think it has some good outcomes. Students tend to develop more of an interest and stake in writing, discover the complexities of their academic writing, and maybe come to see more of themselves as "writers." This approach always spawned good conversation as we shared the dimensional details of what it really means, to evoke Paul Prior, to say that we "wrote the paper over the weekend" (*Writing* xi). And we too revealed some underconsidered embodied and material dimensions of processes, ones I am especially interested in making visible.

However, eventually I began to question this reflective process approach, focused as it was crafting conscious reflection upon habits and enduring practices. This approach, I came to realize, looks very much inwardly; it can keep processes in the garret with the writer alone; it reinforces the idea that processes are writers' own, uniquely "their" enduring process. And it focuses us on what we try to make the *same*—repeated, habitual, and controllable—in our processes and in ourselves. But, so much of writing—even most of it, as Bizzell and

Cooper and others have shown us—is *never just ours alone*. Processes are never dependent on only what we do, never just our will as individual writers but also the will of impromptu local conditions in which writing finds itself.

I've also come to question my own reflective process teaching as a result of some multimodal case study research I've conducted (from which I draw this chapter's opening example) on graduate students' physical processes and composing environments (Blewett et al.; Rule). In that study, I focused on writers' reflective senses of the places they wrote and the importance of objects and physicality in their writing, dimensions the study no doubt revealed. But I also saw just how much of their process activity these writers didn't really control and how much went on in their writing sessions of which they were not aware. These realizations led me to experiment with not just having students *think* about their own processes but having them closely *look at* them, too.

The activities I use now to teach writing with processes as such don't focus exclusively on drafting strategies or habits. That kind of focus is still valuable, but it's not what I think now is most important about having students see processes, theirs and others, inside and outside university. Sameness is actually what I want to counter or complicate to some extent in my students' work with and through processes. It is critical that students experience that producing effective writing is not a matter of hauling along the same process or even multiple processes to every writing situation they'll encounter (nor their same seven comma "rules" or the lasting assumption that academic writing never uses "I"). Instead, writing efficacies are contingent, best built upon first situating writing processes—looking around first to see where the writing is, what constraints can be discerned, and how to proceed. Observational methods can help writers reconstruct writing and its variable processes as ongoing embodied sites of learning, reflection, and responding *in situ*—on-the-spot and amidst the shifting contexts that prompt and differently shape writing activity.

DATA COLLECTION AND BACKGROUND

To illustrate some of how I situate processes with my student writers, I draw on the curricula and collected student texts from two different writing courses. Each data collection was overseen, reviewed, and exempted by each institution's IRB; and in the case where I cite or reproduce students' writing, I have secured their written permissions to anonymously do so. I invoke student work to illustrate practice and generate adaptable pictures of reimagined process work in contemporary classrooms.

The first illustrations come from two Honors sections of a second-term first-year writing course at a state flagship university in the south. This course focuses on rhetorical concepts and analysis, research and information literacies, writing with sources, and multimodal composing. From here, I refer to this course as "FYW," or the "first-year writing" course. I also draw practices from a sopho-more-level intermediate writing course at a large Midwestern university, a course focused on advanced rhetorical and analytical practices, primary and secondary research methods, and practicing writing in context (I refer below to this course as "IW," or the "intermediate writing" course). I'll describe work from one of these IW courses, "Investigating Composing Processes," in which I had students read writing research, observe and experiment with their processes in various contexts, and conduct a qualitative study of the composing processes of a writer or group of writings in a certain context.

Both my IW and FYW courses take on a "writing-about-writing" ethos: I make "writing itself as a topic consider" (Downs and Wardle, "Reimagining" 129) and consider the phenomenology of writing a site to investigate and learn from. I also position students as writing researchers. But I see students as researchers not just in terms of formal research projects on writing, as Downs and Wardle's approach emphasizes ("Teaching" 562). Rather, I more so see writ-ers as researchers first in terms of taking an *inquiry posture* toward every writing experience and process. Said another way, my process teaching emphasizes that *any* writer in *any* context is a researcher to the extent that to be successful, they must investigate and respond as fittingly as they can to the complex contexts in which they and their writing find themselves.

The process practices I describe have been inspired by and repurposed from innovative visual methods in composing process and writing research studies. These methods, which include drawings, photographs, videos, screencast com-pose alouds, and other observational methods, capture the dynamic surround and embodied contexts of processes (e.g., Ehret and Hollett; Gonzales; McNely et al.; Pigg; Prior and Shipka; Shivers-McNair; Takayoshi). Many more practices than I will describe below can be pursued from these researchers' methods. On top of these methods' disciplinary yield, writers themselves benefit from engaging them in our classrooms, and not exclusively as a formal scholarly inquiry, but also toward building an inquiry stance toward writing: an orientation of curiosity and information-seeking as processes emerge differently in different situations.

DRAW PROCESSES

I title recent sections of my FYW course "Rhetorical/Inquiry/Processes" because I emphasize rhetorical analysis of texts of all kinds—methods equally for the analysis, evaluation, and critique of published *and* students' own texts. I focus on inquiry rather than argument as a way to help students expand beyond rote formal features of essay writing they might have internalized (and the manner of one-sided, oversimplified pro/con models of engagement they've learned from living in contemporary cable-news America). And, most significantly for this discussion, processes plural in the title helps us see the rhetoricity and difference of processes as guided by *where* our writing happens. In class, my students and I consider the writing we do in everyday life and across our ranging academic work; we study popular press essays as "mentor texts" to acquire the genre of the "inquiry essay," we examine genres we encounter in the everyday—like podcasts, PSAs, print ads, political cartoons, Facebook posts, and so on—to help students define their own communicative goals and choices in a multimodal recast project. In short, physically situating processes becomes a critical foundation to all of this work as it helps writers *see* that *all* writing is located and shaped by factors that exceed and precede them. In turn, the writing experiences within my class come closer to the rules by which writing plays in the world: one of discovering and adapting to the constraints of *where* writing is.

The wheres of writing processes is something my writing students and I capture regularly with drawings. This practice is largely influenced by Paul Prior and Jody Shipka's 2003 study in which their participants draw and discuss their composing processes and spaces. The drawings help the researchers show, from a cultural-historical activity theory perspective, the "chronotopic lamination" of the writers' ranging process activities—or what the authors define as "the dispersed and fluid chains of places, times, people, and artifacts that come to be tied together in trajectories of literate action" (181). Process drawings depict the immediacies of writing space, time, objects, and activity, but also that which is not contained, like affective dimensions, felt pace of a writing session, memories and inspiration, and more. Drawing thus also stretches conventional conceptions of writing time: while we might think of processes as demarcated by the time a writer is seated and inscribing, drawings from Prior and Shipka's study participants and from my students reveal longer, wandering timelines, as processes blend with everyday activities like laundry, walking, showering, or listening to a class discussion.

Given these affordances, I start the process conversation with drawing on the first day of this course. Supplying paper and various art supplies, I ask students to: "Draw the writing process for something you've written recently. Try not to use any words, don't worry if you're not a good artist, and I don't mean anything specific by 'writing process'—just depict what you recall doing." After some time, students hang their completed images anonymously on the board. Then, placed into groups to meet one another, they work together to closely examine all the drawings, looking for points of interest, patterns, repetitions, trends, and outliers. Groups write up informal notes for me about their collective observations, and each group shares their insights.

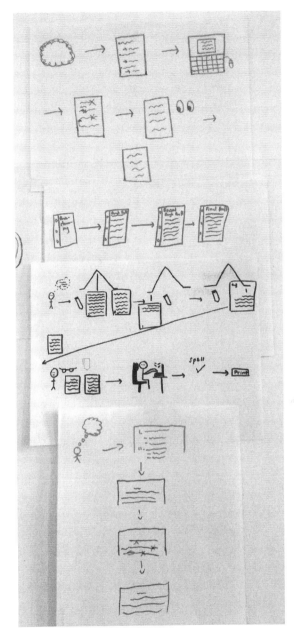

Figure 4. Process as "pages."

To illustrate in more detail, I want to look closer at the drawings and descriptions from just one of my recent FYW classes. As the very first and informal activity in this course, it is no surprise that many of the drawings are general and familiar. Indeed, some drawings appear to be an exact rendition of the process wheel—prewrite, write, revise, edit, publish—an image they might have seen hanging in a prior classroom. Taken as a whole too, students' group observations of the drawings also cast process in familiar terms. The most recurring insights from looking at everyone's drawings had to do with seeing in them generalized "steps" or procedures—in my students' words, "step by step," "multiple steps to each process," "multistep process," or "linear processes." Similarly, students noticed in the drawings the familiar stages of process, given name by writing instruction, like "brainstorming to rough draft," "revisions/additions/edits," "writing & rewriting." Others noted the repetition of representations that indicate "thinking" or an "original idea." Less common insights mention "stuff" like "research," "calendars and clocks," or "distractions." Even less occurring was affective dimensions, like "difficult" and "time consuming." And finally, one group saw simply that "Most, if not all, include a distinct process."

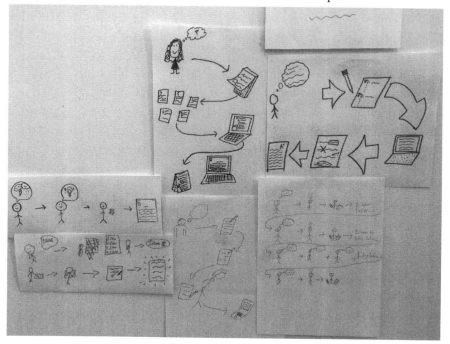

Figure 5. Processes as pages, selves, and stuff.

As I take my turn looking at the drawings, I see about four different kinds of process renditions. The first show writing processes as *pages*—I term it this way as during the activity I overheard one student say as his group was looking, "I guess, I don't know, it's like a bunch of pages" (Fig. 4). That characterization resonated with me. Indeed in at least six of the eighteen drawings, *pages* in various states are really the *only* entity depicted. Similarly, the second kind of drawing I see too prioritizes pages, but also includes selves and stuff, like computers, pencils, or books, or disembodied brains and eyes (Fig. 5). Together, I would say two-thirds of the drawings, all using arrows to indicate linear development, reproduce generalized processes stages. Perhaps I needed not have collated this set of students' drawings to have demonstrated this. We all might have predicted that more than half the class of students would, given the context, reproduce the familiar terrain of processes in school, giving me what they thought I expected to see. Processes, after all, are most often "teacher-identified."

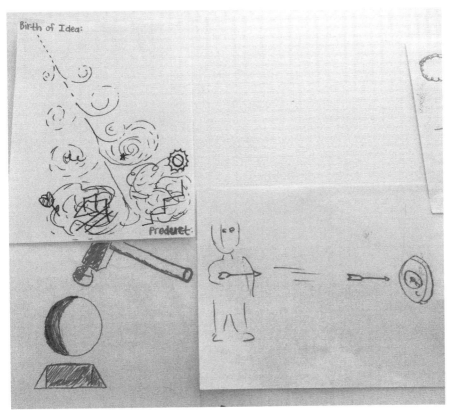

Figure 6. Processes as metaphorical.

But what the remaining drawings show is less similar and familiar. Three of the remaining drawings are rather conceptual or metaphorical—what they might suggest isn't as clear (though I do notice that two of them seem to show something about the "game" of writing: bash one's circle "voice" into the "school writing" square perhaps, or the art of hitting the narrow mark of what's expected) (Fig. 6). The others show scenes or snapshots—writing as experienced while watching TV (or at least sitting in front of it), as a first-person *mise en place* of texts within and outside a screen, and as what appears to be an ephemeral tour of moments of planning and conversation that preceded inscription (Fig. 7).

By here dividing these drawings into "familiar" and "less-so," I do not want to oversimplify any of them. I don't suggest that the "familiar" images are those I eventually want to tap out of writers' consciousness—I don't. What the whole set of drawings do show to me is that writers internalize all the things writing instruction has told them that processes are: development, steps, drafts, the process wheel, thinking, and so on. They show that writers have conceptual stakes in process as an idea that at least sometimes shapes, enables, or inhibits their experiences with writing.

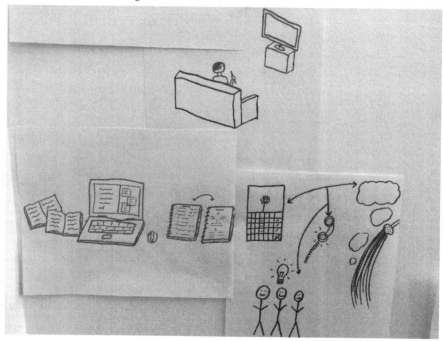

Figure 7. Processes as scenes.

Opening my FYW course with this activity serves critical functions: it displays baseline presumptions about what it means to see "writing as a process." It allows students to start seeing *differences* in processes, to see others' conceptions and experiences alongside their own, and to begin to cultivate a critical and curious orientation toward the particular *wheres*, *whens*, and *hows* of composing. And it serves as the foundation from which I introduce course outcomes related to situating processes, including "engaging in processes of figuring out how writing works differently in different contexts for different purposes" and "practicing writing processes as distinct and varied—shaped by the particulars of environmental and rhetorical situations." To introduce these less familiar process ideas, I can literally point to in the drawings how, for example, all the written texts or products depicted *look so very the same*. None of the drawings differentiate the *kinds* of writing (n.); all are just shown as "a bunch of pages." Writing (n.) in these drawings, in other words, is identical, even though we know—or as we begin to see in this class—that the range of written texts we make each day, and their processes, are quite *different* from one another.

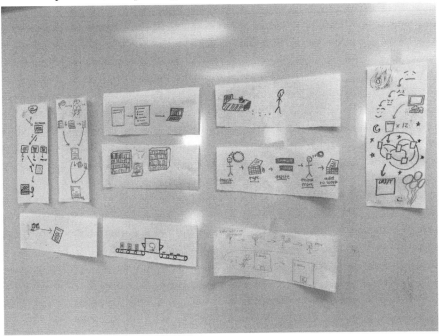

Figure 8. Short draft processes, first class.

Drawing doesn't stop on day one. Students draw again, for instance, as a part of a review activity called "Speed Dating." Working with a short partial draft they have prepared, in rounds of five to seven minutes, students work with a different partner on a focused task. Tasks vary but might include something like the following: "take turns reading each other's first two paragraphs aloud back to the writer; after, discuss what you each notice in hearing the writing." At one of these stations, writers are prompted to draw the *particular* process (or one aspect) of the process they used to produce this specific three pages of draft in their hands. After each partner has finished, they are to again, hang their drawings on the board and discuss what they notice about them all. Embedded as they are in this buzzing, kinetic review structure, I don't get to hear much of the conversation around these drawings. But I notice a few key differences across this particular set I collected recently (Figs. 8 and 9): for one, while I still see familiar process procedure represented, the arrows across the drawings have become less orderly (and much less used). I notice too that the process starts this time with something *else* besides "thinking." For instance, several drawings show engagement with research texts *before* thinking or brainstorming begins. I notice too interesting scenes that seem to be of "not-writing"—getting stopped by a deadline (or a dog or a horse?) (Fig. 7, left top), walking away from writing (Fig. 6), or feeling time ticking by as a writer sits still with legs crossed, at a far distance from the keyboard (Fig. 7, right bottom). This activity, staged in the midst of their working on a text, allows students to render much more specific process experience.

Figure 9. Short draft processes, second class.

Drawing in my courses too does not only just capture what students did when they wrote specific texts. To connect reading and writing processes, for example, we use drawing to collaboratively map the paragraph structure of a sample inquiry essay. Or, as a way to brainstorm a hook of exigence, urgency and timeliness in their own inquiry essays, students draw a dramatic scene they want their readers to *see* when they read their introductions, a scene which can embody the essay's focus and stakes. As my students' drawings accrue and we look to and consider them together, they don't teach processes, they *provoke* critical expansion of this foundational writing classrooms concept. Drawing is a means to access, reconsider, and stretch the foreground of processes to include writer's experiences in place as they grapple with time, affect, disengagement, tools, and environments, and varying situations.

EXPERIMENT WITH AND STUDY PROCESSES

In addition to drawing, my writing students also use a range of observational methods to see processes—video observations, descriptions, interviews, narratives, photographs. The purpose of these methods are manifold: for one, I hope they reveal how situated writing activity well exceeds any process schema offered. Second, observation reveals how writing is embodied and grounded in lived time and space through partnerships with material environments and things. Third, through observation, writing students can broaden what they think counts as "writing" and its processes—writing is pervasive and different, not specialized, not limited only to school-based writing tasks, not one set of rules to master. Perhaps most importantly, these methods show how writing is ineluctably located and shaped—each time a different situation, a different set of constraints, and different processes, depending on where and why writing is.

My IW courses focus expressly on such visual investigations of processes. Students read narratives about authors' processes (e.g., Diaz; Lamott), read writing research about processes (e.g., McCarthy; Wyche), and reflect on their own. Putting extra focus on the emplaced physicalities of writing, we also analyze selections from the *Orion Magazine* blog series, "The Place Where I Write," and based on study and discussion of those narratives, students craft their own detailed essays describing where they write. Students also engage in what I call "Reflections: Experiments in Process." Since the major research project in this course blends secondary and primary research methods, these experiments also give students concentrated low-stakes practice in the challenging arts of observation and interviewing. They allow students too, in an ethnographic sense, to see theirs and others' discrete processes "strangely."

To illustrate, I focus on the first experimental reflection in the course, what I call (in a title that is not so great!) "Zooming in on How Writing Works." The prompt is simple: students choose a time when they are writing something, something for school or not. They can use any means of observation: audio record themselves talking about what they are doing as they do it (compose-aloud), video record themselves, have someone else observe them, and so on.

After listing their observations in detail, they answer reflective questions: What surprised you? What sparked your curiosity in what you observed? What conclusions can you draw about your processes in this particular situation? If you were to do this observation again in similar conditions, what would you watch for more closely?

Looking back on one set of these first observations, I note the great range in kinds of writing students watched themselves doing. Many focused on the making of school-genres: discussion board posts, questions for Marketing homework, a self-introduction for an online class, chemistry notes taken from a PowerPoint, a "specialized lab report for the Anatomy and Dissection of a Rat." Others focused on how they wrote in a professional genre: a study-abroad application letter, a practice response for a GRE essay prompt, a background check form for a new job, a movie review for a student newspaper. Still others observed processes of personal or social writing (several of which, surprisingly, were *letters*): a note to a girlfriend, a "personal letter to my friend," "a letter to my best friend . . . who is now in Prison for the next two years," text messages about evening plans, a post-it note schedule, a to-do list fashioned from a paper plate cut in half, or Facebook chats. Students described writing in study rooms, bedrooms, common rooms, basements, libraries, couches, beds, and other people's living rooms—locations which buzzed with other activity that sustained and paused, halted and enabled processes: music of all kinds, movies and TV watched or as background, texts for reference, phones, family members, pets, drinks, and more. And students described their surprises in watching themselves: for instance, that "the TV and phone didn't play as a big of distraction as I would have thought;" that "It took me 45 seconds to start typing once I put my hands on the Keyboard;" or concern at "the time I actually work verses the time I spend fooling around on the computer with the internet, the TV, and searching for music."

Throughout this book I've suggested seeing writing processes helps writers situate and differentiate writing. But as with the first day process drawings, of course, it's not as though students in this first time observing themselves saw nuanced specifics of how genres might shape their language choices or how what constitutes "revision" will change as they write an application or as they Facebook chat. At first, they all mostly just seemed to see themselves "write" for a while and then, of course, dutifully fix their "errors," no matter what and where their writing was. And too, often their observations were general and glossed: I sat, I drank water, I moved the pillow, I wrote, I stared, I wrote. (And I asked in response, but what did that "writing" really look like?).

So though generalities surely remained, what began to be cultivated in this first "experiment" was at the same time some sharp *curiosity*—the beginnings of conceptualizing how writing across their life domains is *different*. Pondering their first observations, provoking questions emerged, as they asked in their reflections:

- "I would want to know how my writing differs between subjects, i.e., History and English."
- "Did my other actions I was performing simultaneously, such as class and reading, influence my subject matter?
- "What are my behaviors while writing an essay, poem, blog post, text with friend, writing while blocked vs. writing while inspired, different moods, different weather, and so on. I think I need a broader range of observations to come to any real conclusions about my behavior while writing."
- "What are other people's list-making habits?"
- "Another thing I found interesting about this method was the number of things I was able to notice [about what I did when I was writing], which raises the question to me of how many did I miss?"

Here students notice and ask about differences in discipline, genre, situational, environmental and ambient contexts. They want to know about others' writing behaviors. They want to know what they're missing about their and others' processes. Curious investigation of writing continues to be exercised in this IW course through other impromptu studies of processes: interviewing writers about how they write, observing writing in an unusual environment or with unusual tools, closely examining the physical body engaged in writing (inspired by Perl's composing guidelines), and culminating in a formal study of ethnographic-style study of a writer or group of writer's processes.

SEE PROCESSES, SITUATE WRITING

Seeing writing processes is a means to help student writers situate writing in contexts. Describing processes is one illuminating step. Becoming more aware of and responsive to the locatedness of processes is another. This process inquiry posture helps students perceive abstract constraints and factors that shape writing—contextual expectations for language, punctuation, genre moves, structure, and so on. With a final illustration then, I describe how student writers might connect their literal looking at writing activity to processes of "observing" or researching writing (n.) to determine ways to shape their own writing (v.).

As established, my FYW students conduct secondary research directed by an intentionally vague constraint: research must be on a problem or tension related to writing, broadly construed. There is always some palpable initial consternation about this required focus as many students have not thought much about writing at all as more than a transparent tool or set of skills. Certainly, almost none of them have *studied* writing. So as one way of kickstarting their thinking (really as a prewriting exercise unannounced, as students don't know exactly why they're doing this), I send students into their daily lives to observe and record where and how they see writing around them. I make it vague: just observe and record the details of where you see writing all around you during your day.

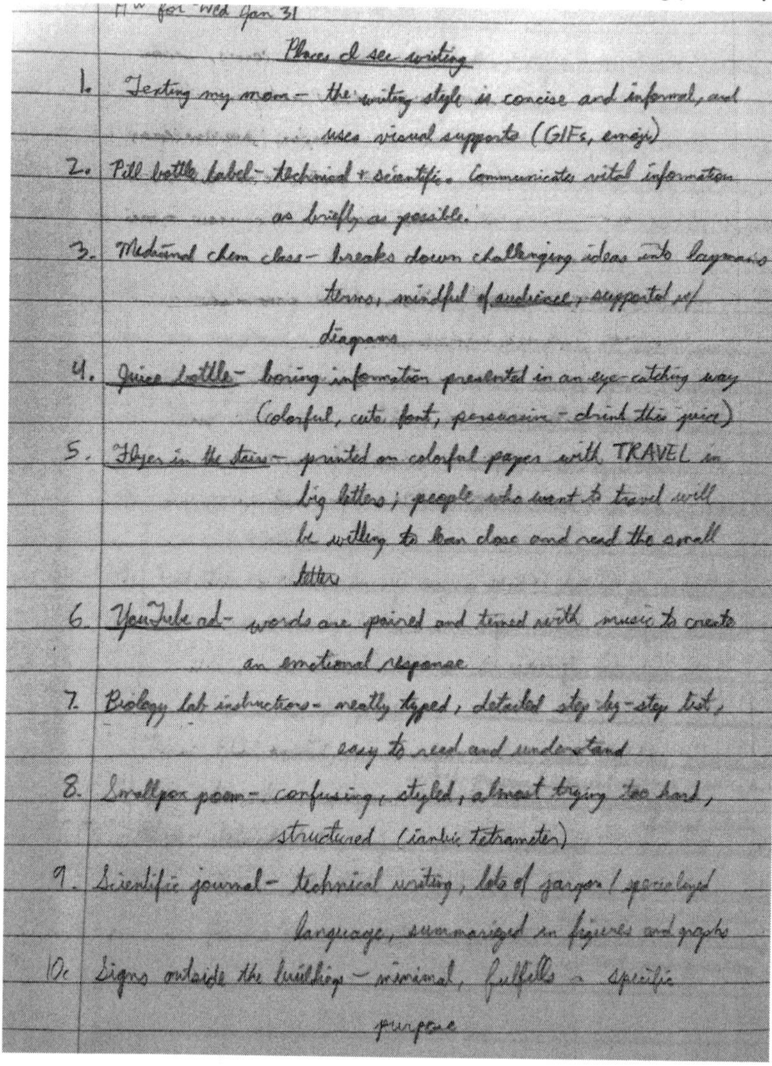

HW for Wed Jan 31

Places I see writing

1. Texting my mom – the writing style is concise and informal, and uses visual supports (GIFs, emoji)
2. Pill bottle label – technical + scientific. Communicates vital information as briefly as possible.
3. Medicinal chem class – breaks down challenging ideas into layman's terms, mindful of audience, supported w/ diagrams
4. Juice bottle – boring information presented in an eye-catching way (colorful, cute font, persuasive – drink this juice)
5. Flyer in the stairs – printed on colorful paper with TRAVEL in big letters; people who want to travel will be willing to lean close and read the small letters
6. YouTube ad – words are paired and timed with music to create an emotional response
7. Biology lab instructions – neatly typed, detailed step-by-step list, easy to read and understand
8. Smallpox poem – confusing, styled, almost trying too hard, structured (iambic tetrameter)
9. Scientific journal – technical writing, lots of jargon / specialized language, summarized in figures and graphs
10. Signs outside the building – minimal, fulfills a specific purpose

Figure 10. Sample "Places I see Writing" Observations.

I randomly collected and photocopied about fifteen of these lists from students' notebooks across two of my FYW sections, from which I form the following analysis. With their observations lists in hand, students get into groups to share the details about where they saw writing. As with the process drawings, seeing, sharing, analyzing the observations of others is a critical extension of this activity. But when beginning to share what they observed, I hear concerns across the room about having "done the prompt wrong." This is because some have described writing (n.) around them—the texts that surround them on campus including, for instance, signs, banners, posters, ads, professor's PowerPoints, notes on a board; or those they see online like Instagram captions, news articles, Snapchats, Facebook posts, and so on (see Fig. 10 for one such example list). Others have described scenes they observed of people "physically writing"—people in their classes writing notes; writing math problems in notebooks with numbers, signs, and words; writing code; professors writing on the board; a person jotting on a sticky note, writing homework in Spanish, a restaurant server writing orders, a friend writing a birthday card, a person doodling. Only a few students' lists described both written texts and writing processes in progress. But this confusion in sharing is productive, as the purpose of the activity is to get students to see writing (n. and v.) everywhere all around them, serving very different purposes and shaped by all manner of constraints. As one student, "Jim" noted in an annotation of his list: "I realize now that I took a fairly close-minded approach to this assignment. I only looked at people in the act of writing instead of pre-existing writing and all the different ways writing exists in the world."

As with the IW students' first observations of their own processes, much on these observation lists was general, rote. But many were able to, through an ethos of curiosity, begin to *see* processes differently, to *see* how situational demands differently shape writing. As "Michelle" wrote as one observation in her list (Fig. 11):

> Sending a text to my grandma today made me think about how often we truly do write and often how quickly we are willing to throw our words out into the digital world. I take time curating a response to my grandma's text, but when my best friend texts me I'll shoot off a response so fast I barely know what I said. I watched my friend spend 5 minutes texting a classmate to ask them to come help them with homework- then shoot off a second text telling their roommate to bring them a book. even w/ small messages, the audience matters.

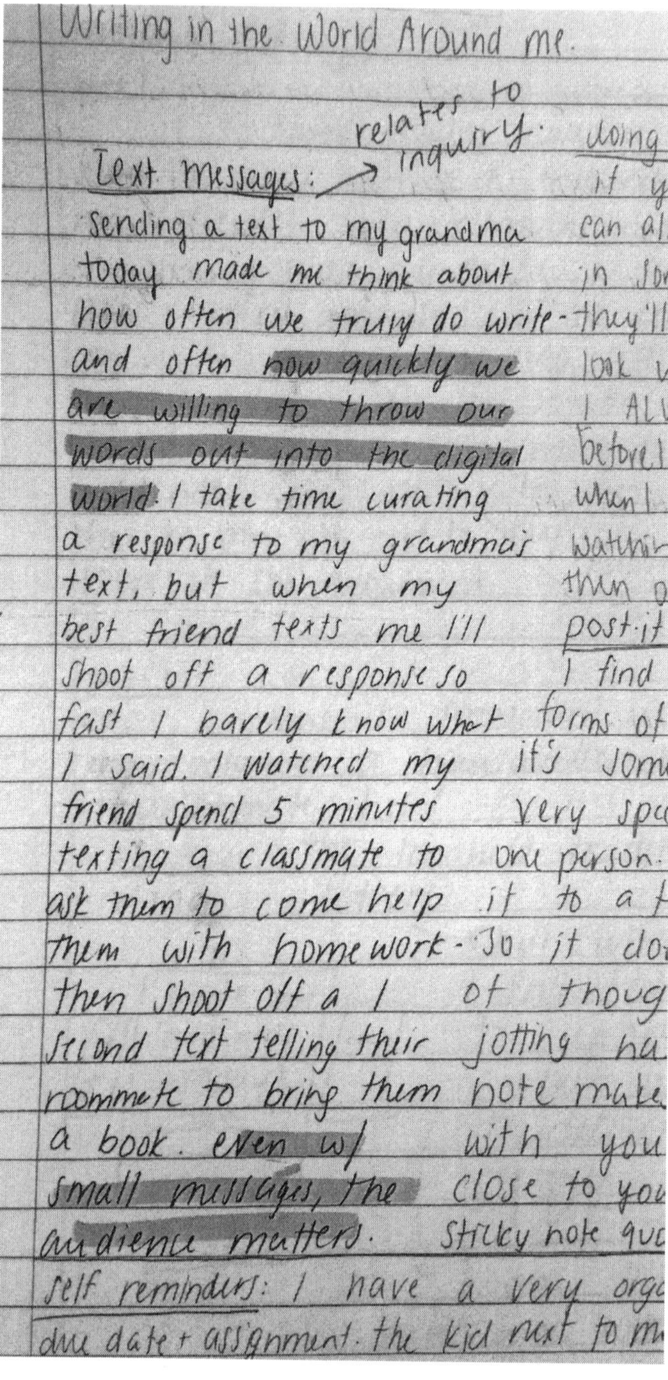

Writing in the World Around me.

Text messages: → relates to inquiry. doing
Sending a text to my grandma
today made me think about
how often we truly do write
and often how quickly we
are willing to throw our
words out into the digital
world. I take time curating
a response to my grandma's
text, but when my
best friend texts me I'll
shoot off a response so
fast I barely know what
I said. I watched my
friend spend 5 minutes
texting a classmate to
ask them to come help
them with homework. So
then shoot off a
second text telling their
roommate to bring them
a book. even w/
small messages, the
audience matters.

self reminders: I have a very
due date + assignment. the kid next to m

Figure 11. One of "Michelle's" observations.

"Michelle's" pause of curiosity about the ways she found herself developing a specific text message that day to her grandmother turned out to be a rich opening for reflection. In her description, she gestures at the reckless speed with which we launch words into the world today. She observes differences in a simple and likely taken-for-granted genre like "texting." To one audience "Michelle" is slow and careful crafting her words; to another, she is fast and unfiltered. Looking closely at her friend texting shows another layer of nuance, based on perhaps, registers of formality versus familiarity. These small quotidian observations lead "Michelle" to perceive broad rhetorical considerations like audience and revision and style in a manner specified and differentiated.

What's more is that "Michelle's" pause over writing this particular text message caused her to become curious about how we keep in contact today more broadly, leading her to pursue an inquiry essay about the art and value of snail mail letter writing today. In seeing this tiny lived process of text messaging, "Michelle" discovered just how nuanced "writing" is; she perceived texting as a situated and differentiated genre. Other students in their observations maybe didn't get as deep or curious as she, but all were able at least to see writing more expansively and as a site of inquiry, eventually each finding a provoking writing-related question to research—topics which included the challenges of science writing for the public, Twitter as a forum for artistic and essayistic writing, emojis in modern communication, factors driving online commenting, the rise and conventions of clickbait, benefits of expressive writing, social media and mental health, and so on. By looking at writing (v.) as it's practiced and writing (n.) as encountered in the world, students through this activity expand and differentiate writing and its processes.

Situated observation continues as a central method of this course. My FYW students don't just observe writing (v. and n.) to locate a writing-related focus for their research or to differentiate theirs and others' processes. We also extend this inquiry habit toward observing sets of particular *kinds* of writing (n.) in the world. That is, these writers also repeatedly "observe" writing (n.) to determine how to write in an entirely new genre to them: an inquiry research essay.

The inquiry essay is not a "real genre," in as much as it would not be identifiable by this name to anyone but my students and I. Rather, as I emphasize, this is a genre I basically have "made up." I do so by collecting a small set of journalistic, essayistic writing from the web and online magazines that serve as our primary inquiry essay "mentors." (In my last FYW sections, we focused mainly on two "inquiry essays" by Robert Rosenberger and Clive Thompson). We also shape this genre's purposes and character through reflective think-pieces on the essay (those, for example, by Philip Lopate and Christy Wampole) as a genre not for air-tight narrow claims with superficial evidence contained in predetermined forms. In other words, the inquiry essay is not the research and argumentative essay students have likely experienced in school. An inquiry essay instead is enacted more in the spirit of Montaigne, a genre through which we doubt, wonder, and discover and reconsider our claims through critical dialogue with ranging source material. Throughout the term we continuously look back to the same set of genre examples to see the similarities *and differences* among them in terms of tone, ethos, kinds of source material (original studies, anecdotes, testimonies, recognizable authorities, etc.), attribution, sentence-style, structure, introduction and exigence-building, and so on. Difference in the inquiry essays we examine is critical, as this method is not about models or imitation, but *mentorship*. And, as we zoom in to examine different characteristics like persona, I bring in additional inquiry excerpts (like Tom Chatfield's on attention, for example) that provide range and confound writers' instincts to do just exactly what one of the examples does.

I am influenced in this practice by "mentor text" methods (e.g., Anderson; Gallagher; Paraskevas) as well as Sarah Andrew-Vaughn and Cathy Fleischer's "Unfamiliar Genre Research Project." In brief, their project starts with having students examine a giant list of genres—scrapbooking, flash fiction, obituaries, sonnets, editorials, and so on—and highlighting ones that seem strange, unfamiliar, or otherwise challenging. Students then select one of these unfamiliar genres to work on. Each assembles and studies a set of genre examples for its conventions, purposes, deviations, and uses; experiments with and enacts the genre based on their research and analysis; and assembles a portfolio including their genre research, criteria that guided their attempts, and a reflection on this process of moving from disorientation to enaction. All of this discovery and experimentation is done, it should be emphasized, *totally without* teacher arbitration, fully without her criteria or control over the genres or students' choices. Rather students themselves mindfully situate themselves in the genre through their research. As such, teaching "unfamiliar genres" is ultimately an observational *research* process—students move from not knowing anything about a genre (like the "inquiry essay") to, through analytical discovery processes, applying newly formed knowledge in the performance of writing that was formerly totally foreign. As I repeatedly underline, the point of closely studying or "observing" this inquiry essay genre is *not* to learn how to write an inquiry essay successfully. The point is the *processes* by which we approximate this, or any, genre. The point is the method itself of *learning how to learn* to write something you've never written before by looking for guidance from genre mentors.

There is much value in these processes of "looking" at writing (n.). The first is in performing ad-hoc and independent processes of figuring out how writing works. This is, after all, how any writer anywhere begins to acquire facility in a new genre. We learn the window of acceptable writing on Facebook, for example (a genre like many which students initially see as a non-genre and as not-writing) by *reading* Facebook and intuiting often subconsciously through violations (public, sappy devotions to a significant other) *and* patterns (Throwback Thursdays) how to shape our writing there. I am not *teaching* genres here, but positioning students to learn how to learn a genre. As such, students discover that to write successfully is always in *situating* that writing (n. and v.) in what can be discerned about the situation, genre, purposes, rules, tone, criteria, available tools, and so on. There is value too in the uncertainty that students experience in shaping their own inquiry essays. Writing, after all, is a game of approximation and attempts, not one of set or defined rules. The measure of a successful inquiry essay is not in what the teacher expects, as the teacher and the student (and all writers) are beholden first and foremost to the machinations of genre and situation and specific Others as audience. As Andrew-Vaughn underlines, both writing students and teachers become "the central inquirers" as to how any particular genre works.

Positioning students as observational process researchers thus takes on several dimensions in my own teaching practice. First, seeing and describing processes variously and repeatedly helps writers see beyond entrenched process commonplaces like ordered textual change, writing procedures, or surveilled school routine (Jensen). Observing processes reveals the infinite material embodied and procedural differences in processes involved in making any everyday text (a diary entry, text message, a tweet or a meme or a Snap, a literary interpretive argument, etc.). Gathering these concrete views of writing activity help writers see processes differently across their and others' experience. In turn, writers *see* and *feel* and better *respond to* broader and more conceptual contextual constraints. And writers enact observational habits too in the close-up study of genre mentors. Broadly, student writers as curious process researchers cast processes as on-the-spot responses to shifting contexts and genres that exert control and shape their writing. Writing and its processes are not one thing, not just what we as writers alone do. Writing processes are rather always a matter of continuously looking to discern and respond to the terrain of *where* writing is.

CONCLUSION: WRITING PROCESSES *ALWAYS* AND *ALL WAYS* EXCEEDING THE PICTURE POSTCARD

Seeing writing processes is revealing for writers, but also for their teachers. I remember one of my IW students describing how he had taken to writing essays for school on his TV screen through his Xbox (still not sure how he configured it, or if I'm recalling correctly his hack that made this possible). He talked about the size of his words on the screen being particularly enabling. Inspired, I recall sneaking into an empty classroom to begin drafting a conference paper I had been avoiding. I wanted to see how seeing my words emerge on the big projection AV screen might make my experience of drafting feel easier. But even more than these rich glimpses into how writing labor is differently staged or enacted, even more than voyeuristic insight or theft of a potentially helpful process hack, I want to end by emphasizing this important point: seeing the *wheres* and *with whats* of our students' processes also reveals exacting social, political, and economic pressures.

These kinds of material and environmental considerations come to light in Anne Aronson's 1999 study of seven adult undergraduate women writers who are also caretakers, parents, partners or spouses, and employees. Through interviews, Aronson shows especially the gendered constraints of "the concrete situations in which [these women] do their writing for college" (284). Situating her inquiry against Woolf's call for a room of one's own (with money to live and a lock on the door) and Ursula LeGuin's narrower material requirements of just a pencil and paper, Aronson reveals some of the conditions in which our students—especially those who are women, adults, and, to varying degrees, socioeconomically disadvantaged—compose for us. Though their writing spaces vary, for all these women, space and time for writing is essentially inseparable from domestic space, with its attendant demands and gendered inequities. The women interviewed "write in cramped spaces that are subject to relentless trespassing" (296) and interruptions. Invoking Tillie Olsen's poetic and bitingly acerbic musing on all that goes unwritten in the world because women and others are saddled with competing impositions on their time and creativity, Aronson has us face how differing conditions—material, economic, political—might lead to different written results for these women and for others.

Aronson's study shows that writing processes in their everyday "concrete" conditions are never *just* about their immediate dynamics. Rather every "right here" of writing is shaped by bigger constraints, and broader inequities. "Private" or domestic material dynamics are public ones as the personal is the material is the political is the economic is the racialized is the gendered. Because she recognizes the strong imposition of these situational dynamics, Aronson is skeptical of LeGuin's belief that all writers require is bare minimum tools, as this

> viewpoint suggests that assuming responsibility and control of one's writing is an act somehow separate from the material conditions of writing. It suggests that internal conviction is independent from external constraints, that our internal selves

can carry on lives of their own apart from the spatial, temporal, and other resources of the external environment. (298)

Aronson's point rings to me with devastating accuracy. Writers simply cannot bootstrap themselves beyond or outside of the material-social-economic
conditions that shape lives and writing. Writing processes are always and all
ways of their places, and of the world—never independent of it nor willed to
transcendence.

Aronson's work leaves me feeling how important but overlooked writing is
as a material practice. She leaves me concerned about space-making and the
inhospitable designs of universities and colleges (Mauk). She leaves me thinking
about silences precipitated by students' night shifts, single parenthood, depres-
sion, hunger, fear of violence, housing insecurity, intellectual difference, or other
sociopolitical and systemic vulnerabilities, ones which we can see and those we
may never. She reminds us of what we know, but that which nevertheless feels
so far beyond our intervention: that literacy is largely determined by economics,
access and privilege (and that it is less the bridge to mobility we might believe it
could be). Aronson reminds us, as literacy teachers and as citizens, that we must
continue to dismantle systemic disadvantage and inequities of all kinds.

She makes me think at the same time, though, that we should fight another
familiar message, one that seems on its face less concerning, but one that is
still insidious. We ought to kick around too that picture postcard myth that
"real" writing is always cloistered, private, sustained. Writing processes are not
just matters of cloistered focus, not just a set of somethings that "real writers"
always do and have, not just or ever well-preened, disembodied, "photo-edited"
writing desks. Privacy is also ideological, not an abstract good-in-itself but a
small tyranny reproduced especially, as Kristie S. Fleckenstein has discussed, in
the (re)production of academic spaces and the status imbued in the academic's
closed private office door. But, Fleckenstein emphasizes, "The need to control
the degree of disruption in a physical writing scene evolves with the belief that
an academic must shut out life, must separate the life of the work from the life
lived, the body from the mind" ("Writing" 300). This ideological network of
seemingly commonsense assumptions in turn would devalue "the discourse (and
knowledge) that evolves when scholars write standing in their kitchens or sitting
by the kitty litter (Sommers; Bloom)" (300). While spatial norms are conse-
quential, they are also not static nor categorically determinant. As Fleckenstein's
concept of somatic mind suggests, we are "always placed; yet we are always on the
verge of new placements that disrupt and reconfigure materiality and discourse"
(303). That is, as women, who might be more "culturally predisposed to carry
with them their peopled space" (Fleckenstein 303), continue to attain higher

and more conventionally cloistered academic offices or as increasingly unsteady markets of academic labor continue to undermine both spatio-economic privilege and security, the meanings and experiences of academic space too shifts. Ideologies around material conditions and knowledge always might be otherwise (and of course, not necessarily for the better or the more liberating).

Undoubtedly the experiences of the women writers in Aronson's study are constricted by the weight of gendered norms and the specifics of their material environments. We ought to fight still for Woolf's door lock for them and for all, for equities and access, for ever more equitable planes of discoursal authority. At the same time, we can undermine the mythic ideology of the picture postcard of writing. Who says effective, impactful, beautiful writing can't be forged in the middle of, rather than separated or cloistered from, complex domestic lives and multiple social roles? In spite of the impossibilities and partialities, we should look for *all ways* writing unfolds *always* in excess of official spaces and sanctioned means. Multiplying images of processes shows writing as inseparably of the world. And by accruing images of processes' differences, the materialities of access and writing might be (re)cast differently.

CHAPTER 5
PROCESS AS IMPROV

. . . we may know all there is to know about how texts work and how readers read, and we still may create documents that fail to communicate effectively.

— Thomas Kent ("Paralogic" 149)

Joke-writing is my thing, it's like a passion. What it is, is basically: you have an idea, you write it as hard as you can, but at the end of the day, it's like you gotta get it on stage. And it's not a joke until a crowd laughs at it.

— Dave Attell ("Friday," Bumping Mics with Jeff Ross and Dave Attell)

If you've ever been in the room when a seasoned stand-up is trying out new jokes, you have viscerally felt the composing processes by which stand up is forged. I once saw comedian Rob Delaney perform at Cincinnati's Taft Theatre. I thought he was supposed to be in the main theatre—the regal, expansive, theatrical stage—but he wasn't. Instead, he performed in the theatre's basement. I was never clear on why the change was made—perhaps it had to do with the number of seats sold, perhaps Delaney himself chose the closer quarters of the basement with its lowered ceilings and rows of ragged chairs to get the feel of an intimate dingy comedy club. Regardless, the ad-hoc nature of this performance space seemed to encourage him to do what he did at the end of his well-crafted, essentially scripted show. He tried new jokes. And they didn't really work— basically, they bombed. He told us after that the new bits didn't work, not yet. He had kernels, but next time (probably for many next times) he'd need to try a different pace, fill out that part of the story and shorten this part, move more quickly to the punch line. Read the room, the city, the region, the particular bodies in the audiences at particular times. Repeat.

Comedians are of course funny in themselves. Comedians practice and refine their bodily control and performance chops, creating worlds that the audience can inhabit through description, gesture, timing, delivery. They too have particular ways of seeing their world and delivering those visions; they have penchants for the structure and the art of the joke, word-play, and the call-back. Said another way, as Dave Attell's words above attest, comedians are at the core professional writers. But arts like stand-up comedy or theatrical improv—or writing more broadly—are far from solo performances. This is easy to see in improv as it most often commences with a suggestion from the audience from which the players build a scene. But effective stand-up too is just as relational an art as is improv, even though there is just one person on stage. Stand-up is built over time and by attuning to, reading, and adjusting to changing audiences—discerning between the sighs, gasps, chuckles, guffaws, and polite laughter in infinitely different rooms night after night. This influence is often imperceptible to any single audience member though. Nevertheless, it is the Other, the laugh, that serves as the final engineers of the joke. As Viola Spolin, foremother of the American improv tradition, states simply in her theory of improv, "Without an audience there is no theatre" (13).

We can say too without much of a stretch: without an audience there is also no writing. In other words, what comedians, improv performers, and postprocess rhetorician, Thomas Kent, equally recognize is that writing is not merely *staged* in social and material contexts—it is *susceptible* to those contexts and to others. And it is not *just* audiences that shape writing or stand-up: composing processes are equally subject to their places, moves, scenes, positions, objects, tools, privilege, props, presuppositions, resources, genres, language, capital, timing, and more. What I'm driving toward here is another way of saying what my claim has been all along: Situating a process (or a slice or sliver of one) in place and time exposes composing as a matter of physicalities, positioning, and positionalities. Situating processes helps writers become more responsive to the fluctuating contexts in which they find themselves; it helps writers respond on-the-spot to the presenting constraints immediate and distant. In short, situated processes are supremely contingent on where, with what, and for whom they unfold. Or, even shorter, process is improv.

Recognizing the on-the-spot contingencies of writing processes, though, is to embrace some measure of uncertainty. It is to accept that bombing on writing's stage is possible at any time, no matter how much or how long we've worked on our craft (or our draft). Emphasizing situated susceptibility exposes what can't be secured or learned in advance, the "ghostly" quality of processes that reveals that "writers are unable to control [or "consciously locate"] what influences them" (Jensen 15). And while that may be right and we might accept it, such a revelation also makes a problem for writing instruction. Teaching writing wants more secure outcomes than "you'll have to see when you get there." Teaching writing relies in some measure on the sustaining mirage that it basically serves as an "inoculation" (Kent, "Righting" xvii) guaranteeing total immunity from all "bad writing" in all future contexts. Teaching writing, especially as instantiated in first-year courses, pledges at least some allegiance to "general writing skills instruction (GWSI)," some complicity with the tantalizing myth that "writing is a set of rhetorical skills that can be mastered through formal instruction" (Petraglia, *Reconceiving* xi) and that those "skills [can] transcend any particular content and context" (*Reconceiving* xii).

Today, I do think that many pedagogues would agree that "there is no autonomous, generalizable skill or set of skills called 'writing' that can be learned and then applied to all genres or activities" (Russell 59). But how we, or if we, make that clear in our teaching practice is another story. And how we help others, like our writing students or faculty across the university, accept this situated and contingent view of writing remains a tremendous challenge, too. Compositionists have worked variously to do so: David Russell and others, for example, situate writing acts in complex and overlapping activity systems. David Smit, like many others thinking with a WAC/WID framework, disperses college writing instruction into specific disciplinary contexts, making writing studies professionals into in-context "facilitators" (12). Conversely, with their writing-about-writing approach, Elizabeth Wardle and Doug Downs put writing instruction firmly in our own disciplinary context, calling for us to "teach the knowledge of our field" ("Reflecting" 6) rather than aim for skills or "how" to write. Still others dare to call the whole thing off: some advance a postprocess "postpedagogy" (e.g., Ceraso et al., Dobrin, *Postcomposition*; Dobrin et al., Rickert, "Hands"), which holds that writing is "too complex, too particular, too situated to be rendered in any repeatable and therefore portable way" (Lynch xiv), and as such "nothing exists to teach as a body-of-knowledge" (Kent, "Paralogic" 149). And moving in quite the opposite direction, still other compositionists have focused us on teaching for transfer (e.g., Anson and Moore; Nowacek), recognizing the uncertainties of context by helping writers secure means to make their know-how emerge anew in times, places, and contexts unforeseen.

I'm interested in this final chapter in the two latter responses to the deconstruction of general skills, and the ways that situating processes might help rectify them. Postpedagogy and transfer seem like polar opposites. Transfer aims to craft writing knowledge that can travel and reemerge in new ways across time and situation; postpedagogy undermines our ability to predict and control future (and present) writing situations. Either our instruction can time-travel or it is impossible in the first place, these two views would hold. At the least, these discourses do not interact—their assumptions (and citations or conference panels) do not overlap. In oversimplified terms, one (transfer) lives in circles of compositionists expressly focused on teaching writing; the other (postpedagogy) lives in circles of compositionists mostly focused on writing theory. But I argue for the benefit of their mingling, particularly in focusing writers on the immediacies and instabilities of where they are writing now—in the moment, on-the-spot.

Such embrace of context-contingencies, though, raises that big and familiar problem in writing pedagogy today: how can writing instruction teach writers to navigate situations that aren't stable and that we can't predict? How can we teach something so wiggly as context-contingency? I turn to theatrical improvisation—its practice and pedagogy as imagined by Viola Spolin, pioneer of the American improv tradition—as a final visual figure to imagine teaching with situated processes and to address this challenging question. Process as improv embraces writing as a situationally contingent art of figuring out how best to respond to unique rhetorical situations, conditions, and discoverable and unknown constraints. If we aim today to keep pushing the teaching of writing beyond demands for acontextual writing skills and aim instead to hone rhetorical and genre sensitivities, emphasize shaping contexts, disrupt privileged "standard" language performances, and so on, then teaching with processes must emphasize located, nimble, and on-the-spot responsivity. Imagining situated processes as improv is one such way to help us do so.

TRANSFERRING UNCERTAINTY: INVITING THE COLLISION OF TRANSFER AND POSTPEDAGOGY

The drive to expand writing instruction—to make its relevance or scope bigger—is one way to read the arc of composition and its teaching. This story might go like this: in the old days of current-traditionalism, instruction was trapped in dimensions of the page—the weekly theme built of careful penmanship, decorum, formality, and correctness. Then came process and instruction got bigger, more dimensional. It looked beyond the page, accounting more for spheres of human activity like development; cognition and thinking processes; language varieties and difference; voice, personal expression, or political expression. Then, recognizing that writing can never be just the action of one individual, instruction expanded again to encompass the social—communities, discourse, disciplines. Then too, seeing that social entities are never not implicated in the political, ideological, and cultural, came a critical orientation that situated everything: in communities of practice, political landscapes, writing in the disciplines, community literacies, workplace writing, activity systems, ecologies. And, with implicatedness came even more sweeping expansions to the *where* and *what* writing is: global Englishes, new media, the extracurriculum, writing across the lifespan. This story is, of course, a sketch—and a stretch. I've implied that the swellings of instruction's scope have come just in this order (they didn't); I've implied that this story is comprehensive (it isn't). Nevertheless, the arc of this story creates some context for one recent and prominent crescendo of the drive to make our instruction bigger and to deal with the contextual susceptibility of writing: transfer.

Transfer—an interest in how (writing) knowledge, aptitudes, and learning might be applied or repurposed in contexts beyond the classroom—has been an express focus in composition studies for at least around ten years. But, as Chris Anson and Jessie Moore emphasize, the implicit *assumption* of transfer has always been embedded in the ubiquitous first-year writing course in the very fact of its being required (3) and understood as a foundation for writing in the university. It's only more recently that this premise has been questioned and expressly investigated by composition scholars through critical questioning, reframing, and extensive and complicated research endeavors. That is, while transfer may now be a focus, it remains a struggle, as transfer scholarship is the pursuit of supremely "complicated" phenomena (Wardle). Even the term itself engenders debate, as "transfer" can imply ease or straightforwardness, an implied mechanization (Yancey et al. 7) or an oversimplified "carry and unload" association that is largely rejected but nevertheless clings to the term (Wardle). As transfer scholars make clear, to conceptualize, study, or teach for transfer involves getting a handle on a dizzying array of actors and factors, each which constantly change and differently relate to one another: individuals, histories, memories, tasks, institutions, contexts, classrooms, dispositions, habits, and so on. That is, transfer processes are not uncomplicated cause and effects; and those working on transfer as an emerging paradigm for college writing instruction are doing so with the recognition that transfer isn't easy, and neither is it one thing, predictable, or wholly controllable. But in the face of its challenges, even what we might identify as impossibilities, transfer scholars make us believe it is nevertheless worthy of the efforts.

Transfer pedagogues certainly take this nuanced position—that it is worth exploring the best or most likely ways to encourage transfer processes even while acknowledging that instruction may never be able to finally pin them down or surely secure them. Transfer pedagogies are future-oriented and their aims far-reaching, as the measure of transfer is the usefulness of instruction in *future* situations. To secure such trajectories, transfer emphasizes the writer herself as an active knowledge-maker with some measure of agentive control exercised in instruction through various means: question posing about "writing situations and developing strategies for examining unfamiliar writing contexts" (Anson and Moore 341), rhetorical knowledge and concept building (e.g., Beaufort), and reflexive practices including meta-awareness, "reflective processes," meta-cognition (Moore and Anson 8), and "mindfulness" (Anson, "The Pop" 532). Transfer pedagogues ask in short, "how can we help students develop writing knowledge and practices that they can draw upon, use, and repurpose for new writing tasks in new settings?" (Yancey et al. 2) and assumes that writers—armed with strategies, concepts, reflection, mindfulness—can be empowered as agents of transfer (Nowacek).

In their 2015 pedagogical project outlining a "teaching for transfer (TFT)" curriculum and its qualitative study and evaluation, Kathleen Blake Yancey, Liane Robertson, and Kara Taczak pose the question above, viewing writers as potential transfer agents. Their TFT curriculum builds upon a bedrock claim: given that research has demonstrated that transfer often doesn't happen because students don't expect it to and also that transfer may be complicated but it has been shown to be possible, first-year writing curricula ought to expressly teach *for* it (12). And teaching for it, according to these pedagogues, means helping writing students build a conceptual "passport" (33) that can help make writing "travel" or "boundary crossing" into new writing situations better, more satisfying, and instructive (33). This passport vision of writing instruction—a framework which forefronts students' acquisition of, reflection upon, experience with, and subsequent stretching of "key concepts" (76)—is a flexible repository for students' learning about and mindfully practicing writing. The passport helps "ensure[s] students can theorize about and practice writing using key terms and concepts learned in the course" (58) but also supports writers "moving forward to new contexts, where through 'retrieval and application' of prior knowledge they can write anew" (137). In addition to focus on concepts, the TFT curriculum engages students in reflective processes which help them develop a working theory of writing, a method that helps students develop "as reflective writing practitioners who are able to abstract their theories and employ them in new contexts" (58). Through comparative qualitative study of the TFT curriculum with an Expressivist course focused on voice and agency (5) and a cultural studies, media-focused course (5), the pedagogues find not unsurprisingly that the TFT approach "is shown to provide more conceptual grounding to students" (35) and therefore, better realizes transfer.

Yancey et al. offer a compelling vision of first-year instruction, one that speaks not just to the goal of transfer but also to several priorities driving writing instruction today: genre awareness and writing in multiple genres (56), reflective practice (4), teaching key disciplinary concepts or building a "language for writing" (34), and situating and specifying discourses instead of teaching overgeneralized "academic discourse skills" (1). TFT makes good sense—it makes sense that students are more prepared to see how their learning might apply in future writing situations if they are expressly and repeatedly asked to do so. If students imagine how new writing knowledge (whatever that is) squares with or complicates what they previously knew or if they are asked to modify their practices in new writing situations, then they are more likely to take this adaptive posture outside of our classrooms. The TFT curriculum thus focuses on stacking the odds for successful transfer by designing a climate for writers to practice it. In this way, we might say Yancey et al. maintain in their curricular vision a "glass as half full" perspective on transfer, to put it in David Brent's terms: these pedagogues acknowledge the complexities of transfer but maintain "that it can happen under certain pedagogical conditions" (Brent 404).

In their glass-half-full vision, Yancey et al. focus their attentions most on equipping the writer. The notion of building the writer's passport creates a stable locus for instruction, a focus on what the instructor might arm the writer with that might help prevent future disorientation. And there is always more a transfer researcher or pedagogue might consider about the learner herself, including "less explored writerly factors such as language preferences, the degree to which certain habits and practices have become sedimented, and aspects of writers' identities, cultures and prior experiences in particular communities" (Anson, "The Pop" 539). One writer famously and exhaustively considered in the transfer literature is Dave, the subject of Lucille McCarthy's 1987 case study of how this writer wrote, and struggled, across the curriculum.

Dave is famous in our literature for being lost. McCarthy documents how he struggled unevenly as he wrote in his composition, biology, and literature courses with the pervading feeling that writing in each of those courses was profoundly different. He was a "stranger in strange lands," it seems, because Dave believed "that he had no prior experience to draw from" to help him (qtd. in Yancey et al. 29). But Dave's feeling of disorientation was unfounded, as from McCarthy's perspective, "we know he had had related prior experience" (29). In other words, Dave may have just failed to see the *opportunity* for productive transfer of knowledge. Yancey et al. see this missed opportunity too. They read Dave's difficulties as an "inability to call upon prior knowledge and, more generally, to frame the new in any way relating to the old" (29). And though they don't say so explicitly, one assumes that Yancey et al. would believe that Dave *could have* been instructed out of his feelings of struggle and disorientation in different writing situations. A TFT approach might have stepped in to orient, guide, and equip Dave with a beefy conceptual framework that might have eased his sense that writing in these classes was so different.

I don't quarrel with this assumption; Dave surely would have benefited if his composition course helped him develop flexible concepts for writing situations (rather than focusing more so on overgeneralized "academic discourse" skills or essay forms). But I wonder also if Dave wasn't on to something in his feelings of being lost.

Dave's disorientation reminds me of another writer profiled in a 2016 study of transfer: Chris Anson's "Martin." Martin is an accomplished academic and a prolific writer, by all accounts an expert. But this mastery is shaken when Martin undertakes the job of writing game summaries of his son's Pop Warner football games for a local paper. Martin does a lot of things, even *everything*, right in trying to acquire this new genre, all things we would want our own writing students to do. He revises a first draft based on feedback he solicited from his kids (who laugh at the draft's ornateness and academic-feel); he carefully studies the final edits made to his first revised and submitted summary in order to try to discern the conventions; he studies the genre "almost obsessively" (Anson,

"The Pop" 530). Martin's summaries demonstrate his many competencies—"sophisticated vocabulary, expert control of syntax, a penchant for smart phrasing, organizational skills, rhetorical savvy, impeccable grammar" (531). But, in this particular context, Anson emphasizes, "such ability was beside the point" (531). Writing aptitudes are not, it seems, measured as qualities "in Martin" nor "in" his writing. The measure is much more "in the context"—in the moment, in this new rhetorical situation, in the response and changes by those controlling Martin's writing, in the constraints controlling the genre at that moment, in that newspaper, with those particular editors. Even though Martin tried valiantly to read the nuances of writing in this context and made powerful even extreme efforts to adapt his writing knowledge to perform fittingly in this new context, he ultimately evaluates his performance on these summaries at best as a "self-determined level of C+" (531).

The question is *why*? Why is "Martin," a veritable writing expert with a well-equipped "passport" doing all the right things to study and adapt to this new context, unable to feel success or acclimation in this writing situation? In a "spoiler-alert" twist, Anson reveals at the study's end that *he* is actually Martin. Anson's detailed self-study injects healthy skepticism into transfer, pouring out considerable volume to come much more to a "glass half empty" view (Brent 401) and leading him to several insightful implications. For one, Anson's nagging disorientation demonstrates the need for what he calls a "principle of uniqueness" (Anson 541) applied to our constructs of ours or other writers' selves, knowledges, and contexts. Rather than assume stabilities, "we must see every writer, and every context into which the writer moves, as a unique amalgam of situation and human agency" (Anson, "The Pop" 540). And just as the writer is never an orderly locus of rationally filed and deployable knowledge, neither are contexts, genres, or discourse communities stable and codifiable. Discourse communities, for instance, are not unified and clearly demarcated entities; they are better seen as at best "a fragmented social collective" (Anson, "The Pop" 537) that may or may not offer up finally legible conventions.

But this fluctuating uniqueness is in my read not the most significant takeaway. Anson doesn't much feature in his study those individuals who ultimately arbitrate, control, and change his summaries. Indeed, Anson pieces together *on his own* the specific changes made to his first summary in order to try to discern patterns and generate situation-specific knowledge about the expectations. Anson's dogged pursuit of the genre's logic is admirable—again, a process we'd hope our own students would do. But Anson's self-determined inability to ultimately master the summaries, his inability to successfully transfer even in spite of his highly credentialed "passport," makes me wonder: what if there was never a logic, not even a complicated and convoluted one, buried in the situation to be found at all? I wonder too about those ghostly editors—what would they say about their evaluation and edits to Anson's summaries? Could they explain why they made the edits they did? Were they prompted to, would the logic they articulated in hindsight be the same that provoked them in the first place to cross out that phrase and replace it with this one? That is, what if there wasn't really any consistency in these writing situations that could yield conventions for Anson to discover and enact?

Certainly, the challenges experienced by Anson, and Dave, support the notion that writing in new contexts "require[s] continued situated practice and gradual enculturation" (Anson, "The Pop" 541), even more gradually than we may expect. But it is also true, I am underlining, that their experiences show that "full" enculturation may *never happen* and even may be impossible. Given all Anson tried in order to please the editors and avoid the red pen, we can conclude that he may never be able to overcome the slight discourse differences or idiosyncrasies held not just by different *people* editing his summaries, but different people holding those idiosyncrasies differently at different times with different drafts read in different environments and states of mind. Full acquisition of this new discourse— or, his sought-after "A+" performance on those summaries—might only ever occur if Anson *himself* occupied the empowered position of editor. To the point: given a fundamental changeability in every situation, a measure of disorientation or failure in writing *may never be finally nor fully overcome*. Disorientation may just be a *part* of what it is to experience writing. The most credentialed of "passports" and express efforts to transfer still cannot fully safeguard against feeling lost or failing to write successfully in one situation or another.

I am now deep into transfer skepticism; more than even half-empty now, I may have tipped over the transfer glass entirely. More skeptical views on the transfer question hold that instruction can never fully prepare students for specific workplace communicative contexts. Though instruction may be able to approximate some of those demands, this perspective holds, a gulf necessarily remains between the instructional and any "actual" context (Brent 401) in which writers might find themselves. But it's not just that Anson or any other writer must acquire conventions and processes in the same context in which they are attempted. Instead, Anson's case raises the implication that—no matter their preparation or detailed study of a context, no matter how reflective they are or the extent of their training and mentorship (both prior and in context)—writers still may fail. That is, "no matter how much we know about writing conventions or the writing process or the elements of style, we nonetheless may miscommunicate" (Kent, "Righting" xviii).

As is likely clear, in pushing to forefront this uncertainty, I am taking on a "postprocess mindset" (Kent, "Righting" xvii). Kent emphasizes the "interpretive complexity" (xv) of any communicative situation, one constituted by triangular interactions among two or more language users and "a world of objects and events" (xiii). While language users, like Anson and Dave and the rest of us, do gain useful guidance from prior experience, interpretations, knowledge of conventions, and the like, the sticking point for Kent is that these guides never *ensure* that communication in any scene will be successful or effective. This instability is there essentially because all contexts are fundamentally "particular and unrepeatable" (Kent xiv) in their relations to varying writers, interlocutors, and material conditions, all which change moment to moment. And this changeability ensures that the Other's interpretation and the communicator's intent will never completely align. As such, all we can ever do is "*guess*, generally in a highly effective manner, about the meaning of one another's discourse" (emphasis added, Kent xiii). And while guesses can be educated, they will never stabilize sufficiently into a reliable process, procedure, or *a priori* strategy. Instead, guesses are only ever "fleeting," (Kent xiv) because every *situation* is only ever fleeting—different, contingent, susceptible, changing slightly moment to moment, and built upon interpretation, rather than stable conventions that hold still "out there" to be discovered.

This last point is how the "postprocess mindset" bleeds into a postpedagogical one. Postpedagogy aims the baseline of postprocess—again, "that nothing exists out there to ensure successful communication" (Kent, "Righting" xvii)—at the very premise of teaching. Postpedagogy questions if there is really a set of "somethings" out there to be learned, and that once those things are learned, then "satisfactory communication is more or less assured" (Kent xvii). Kent describes this common view of teaching as an "inoculation conception" (xvii) of writing, a belief held by many (especially those outside of writing studies) that instruction provides a vaccinating concoction precipitating total immunity from all "bad writing" in all future contexts. Kent's image of inoculation reminds me of Yancey et al.'s passport metaphor. I do think the passport is more skeptical or tentative than the inoculation myth—a passport only gets you across borders and isn't the *only* necessary condition for "successful travel." But in spite of these differences in figure, I think Kent would be similarly skeptical of the transfer passport as it assumes that writing is amenable to systemic logic that is accessible, demystified, containable, portable in a passport, and remixable in new situations. Postpedagogy undermines this perceived travel security.

So why mingle these pedagogical discourses? Why attempt to put them into conversation? In short, I invite postpedagogy in here to more deeply situate transfer (even if some postpedagogy would resist such use out of hand). The disassembling energy of postpedagogy, though, can (de)constructively reimagine teaching and transfer. For instance, Kent's work has had much to say (as I detail more below) about how postprocess shadows our pedagogical scenes differently, scenes that will roll on anyway in spite of their contingencies (recognized or not), and our lack of control over them and over writing (again, recognized or not). As discussed previously, in his discussion of paralogics and ethics, Sidney Dobrin dismantles conceits of mastery, systemization, and the narrowed boundaries of pre-set and reinscribed knowledge in our instruction, especially in process teaching. Thomas Rickert's vision of post-pedagogy "declines to participate in the dialectics of control" ("Hands Up" 314) and "commodification" (315). As the uncertain and paralogic nature of both writing and teaching explodes pedagogy's drive to control and codify, in Paul Lynch's words, "we might encounter teachable moments, but no pedagogy can reliably occasion them. The best we can do is create the conditions in which they might occur" (xiv-xv).

Postpedagogical relinquishment of mastery and its focus on "conditions" sometimes end in calls to stop talking in terms of pedagogy at all. But at the same time, I notice, these claims do not seem too far off the insights of some transfer and other contemporary pedagogues, who also emphasize the need to face up to the many unknowns in writing experience and instruction. For instance, Doug Downs and Elizabeth Wardle's "writing-about-writing" pedagogy, which focuses on our own disciplinary knowledge, is based largely on accepting all that we actually *don't know* about writing, even in nearby academic contexts:

> Our field does not know what genres and tasks will help
> students in the myriad writing situations they will later
> find themselves. We do not know how writing in the major
> develops. We do not know if writing essays on biology in an
> English course helps students write lab reports in biology
> courses. We do not know which genres or rhetorical situations
> are universal in the academy, nor how to help FYC students
> recognize such universality. ("Teaching" 556–7)

Also stressing what writing teachers cannot know, Matthew Kilian McCurrie questions career and college "readiness" as a guiding standard for education today. What can "readiness" possibly mean, McCurrie asks, given that rapid change seems to be the only constant in work and communication domains today? (Min-Zhan Lu and Bruce Horner pose a similar question about skills and in light of ongoing "environmental, geopolitical, social, cultural, and economic" instabilities (126)). Novel and uncertain is the future students need to be "ready" for, as labor statistics project they may have more than ten different jobs before they're 40 and that "almost 70% of those jobs that don't exist today" (McCurrie). Given all that we don't know, the writing teacher surely cannot be the knower of or gateway to all modes and scenes of communication; she cannot "simply continue to tell students what we know and expect them to master it" (McCurrie).

Postpedagogy and transfer, in this way, are not so different. But postpedagogy willingly, even eagerly, risks the baby and the bathwater of writing pedagogy's entire enterprise. Postpedagogy exposes how certain constructs of teaching and learning interfere—those that, for instance, presume there are reliable conventions "out there" to learn and to take along for successful future writing "travel." Putting postpedagogy on the transfer skepticism scale releases steady surety so thoroughly baked into to instruction's, including process instruction's, traffic in outcomes, strategies, and system. Postpedagogy can, in other words, help us imagine teaching (situated) writing (processes) with a baseline of uncertainty and contingency.

Teaching for transfer *with* situated uncertainty would change how we understand writing and learning writing. For one, it adjusts the view of Anson's and Dave's feelings of disorientation. Dave thought that writing in each of those classes was entirely different. As McCarthy and Yancey et al. read it, Dave instead could have seen those contexts similarly, or at least as more navigable, if he had been able to repurpose or remix what he already knew about writing. That's certainly still true. But, at the same time, Dave's perception of those differences is apt and valuable. Dave was right when he discovered that writing in college was not one accessible thing or even multiple, but basically still rationally navigable, things. Dave's sense of difference might have led him to reconceptualize writing as a deeply challenging and always different enterprise requiring continuous realignment and unsure attempts in situations with varying interlocutors that never hold still. That is, Dave's disorientation might have led him *both* to seek ways to transfer his writing knowledge *and* to complexly reckon with the notion that *difference* is a—maybe *the*—primary characteristic of writing, much more so than sameness or codified strategies that can traverse contexts. Dave might have discovered just how much one needs to discover about the contexts in which their writing is situated. Dave might have learned, too, that challenge and feeling lost in unfamiliar compositional terrain is, well, *normal*.

Anson's self-study already leads him to skeptical awareness of context-specificity and difference. Being unable to become excellent at that summary genre leaves him cautious on transfer, warning against approaches that suggest writing's messiness might be fully atomized by instruction. Anson rightly warns of the "dangers of simplifying and mechanizing the kinds of knowledge that facilitate transfer" (541). Knowledge may indeed help writers more ably navigate the "vast topography of discourse," but, Anson stresses, "it does not create new, situationally determined knowledge" (542). Anson's study shows that what writers bring along with them to a new context isn't necessarily the key; teaching for transfer might also help writers experience *on-the-spot* what they don't know and need to know more about where they are writing. Situating writing processes in our instruction, in some of the ways I imagine in the previous chapter especially, is one such method to begin doing so.

Injected with postpedagogy, Anson's experience resolves into productive and deep skepticism: situational knowledge, or better, those situational *guesses*, will not offer themselves up systematically or clearly or possibly at all. Failure is always an option in writing no matter how much instruction or experience or reflection tries to guard against it. Yancey et al. are interested too in failing and transfer, naming "failure" at their study's end among six issues they see as needing more attention. They think it is important to investigate how "challenge and failure facilitate transfer" (145), as they believe that those who can see writing failures as opportunities to learn, or those that will "make use" (145) of failing would be more apt to identify as writers. Significantly, the researchers reframe failure in writing as "critical incidents" (135); not as a lack or an impasse or disorientation, but as a challenge that prompts "learning in ways that perhaps no other mechanism can" (135). Failures here are opportunities. Challenges, if approached "critically," become more learning that in turn decreases the odds and occurrence of future failures. And ultimately, this logic suggests, with enough learning, all future failures could be avoided. Failures here, in other words, become moments to seize further control of writing.

It is a common and valuable trope to help learners shift their views on writing and failure, to recast miscommunications as not a worthless or "meritless performance" (Yancey et al. 135) but "failure-as-opportunity" instead (135). Resilience and reflection are desirable qualities in learners, and in writers. But arbitrating failure is still never going to be in any single writer's full control. Writers do learn from less-than-successful attempts—potentially from all attempts. But still, writing will never not be an asymptote: we approach the axis of mastery, but for infinity we'll never touch it. Writing is radically interpretive and relational, contextually bound, and *different*. Failures—small ones, grand ones, C+ performances—are a *feature*, not a bug in writing's enterprise. (And this strikes me as a terrifically important revelation and message especially for students who seem to fail often in writing as it's measured and monitored and policed in schools. For one it doesn't kowtow to the myth that writing is a bootstraps endeavor. One cannot *alone* engineer successful communication. Writing is always ours and it is always not ours.)

Teaching writing (processes) *from* uncertainty does not mean that teaching is impossible; it does not mean that there is nothing one can learn about the art of writing; it does not mean that writers can't learn anything about writing from their purported failures. It does not negate in any way the efficacies of teaching for transfer. It makes them stronger.

But teaching writing *with* uncertainty is recognizing that all writing acts are not controllable, that writing is a collaborative contextualized act in which meaning is only ever approximated in exchange with others, never transmitted. Writing, like teaching, is *experience*: action, response, reflection, as Paul Lynch puts it, processes that yield knowledge but "guarantee[] nothing" (Lynch xxii). But, luckily, "uncertainty does not undermine wisdom. In the realm of praxis, wisdom without uncertainty is not wisdom at all" (Lynch xxii). To teach for transfer as context-contingent guessing is to see writing and its processes as improvisation.

PROCESS AS IMPROV

I've had occasion for several years around the holidays to see a Second City show at the Cincinnati Playhouse in the Park. It's a combination of scripted play and improv comedy, a show that exposes a fundamental truism of rhetoric *and* improv: play to your audience. With jokes about Jerry Springer; the woes of all the local sports teams, their owners, and stadiums; and more recently, the downtown streetcar, Second City's performers earn laughs by knowing what the audience will identify with. Laughs fill the theatre by virtue of adaptation and apperception. Indeed, this traveling Second City show carries the spirit of its origins as an American improv group that has always been local.

The story of American improv starts with community work—a vision of theatre performance that connects audience and actors as players, and the stage with shared lived experience. Its origin story most often begins with the work of Viola Spolin, who through her Works Program Administration work in Chicago around 1939, began working with children on theatre games focused on "problems of the neighborhood in which the people who attended Settlement House lived" (Feldman 128) and which developed spontaneity, physicalization, focus, collaboration, self-realization, and creativity. Building upon Spolin's social work, years later, Spolin's son, Paul Sills, met David Shepard in Chicago and circumstances manifested such that they collaborated on a new kind of theatre, which would, in Shepard's initial vision, be "close to where people lived so they could come without dressing up . . . where the circumstances would be informal; and where they could see plays that had to do with the life they led, and not with another class or another culture or another country" (qtd. in Feldman 129). Eventually, this work and involvement with other collaborators evolved by 1959 into Second City, the longest running American improv theatre group. Second City has yielded many stars in comedy and continues to provide workshops and education in its communities, keeping with Spolin's vision of improv as foremost a way of being, a collaborative human art and experience that puts in close collaboration players and audiences.

Improv and its teaching—especially as a both a "worldview" and an "anti-authoritarian" art (Tung 59) by the preeminent improv "teacher-director" Viola Spolin—is an apt figure for situating writing processes and, more broadly, for writing pedagogy after the deconstruction of general writing skills instruction. I mean by "figure" a concretized image, one like the "picture postcard" but enabling rather than inhibiting. Improv emphasizes how practicing writing is local acts of on-the-spot learning and best attempts. Improv as a final figure for situating processes emphasizes vulnerability: that all acts of writing involve risk in which bombing is always a possibility, and that processes are profoundly vulnerable to forces on ranging scales in excess of the writer alone.

I've long been interested in comedy, joke writing, and stand-up as a written and performed art built on deep audience awareness and attunement, as well as robust and ongoing revision. And as I hope is utterly clear now, I am arguing for writing processes as performative, embodied, emplaced and improvisatory *action*. But this connection to improv solidified for me ultimately with a passing reference in Kent's discussion of postprocess. He writes:

> [w]hen we write, we elaborate/passing theories during our acts of writing that represent our best guesses about how other people will understand what we are trying to convey, and this best guess, in turn, will be met by our readers' passing theories that may or may not coincide with ours; this give and take, this hermeneutic dance that moves to the music of our situatedness, cannot be fully choreographed in any meaningful way, for in this dance, our ability to improvise, to react on the spot to our partners matters most. (*Post-Process* 5)

I see in Kent's comments how writing and improv are physical and located, relational, emergent, and beyond the control of any single actor. Both require being *in* the moment and *in* the situation; they demand reading, listening, living, and responding to situational elements. Improvisation and writing are, simply and artfully stated, "openness of contact with the environment and each other" (Spolin qtd. in Tung 59). The most important choices and conditions in writing and in improv are those *right here*: what we can discern as constraints in the moment, in the space, with others. And both arts are conducted routinely with contingency built-in: we cannot know what reactions might be coming or how our partner players and audiences may act or respond. In raising improv, I don't exactly mean to invoke it as a metaphor for effective teaching (e.g., Sawyer, *Structure*; Talhelm) though in the course of this discussion, I will consider the writing teacher as expert versus collaborator. I also don't mean improv as a call for theatre exercises in the writing classroom (e.g., Barker; Esposito; Paden) even though these approaches are too valuable. Instead, like compositionists have with many other kinds of bodily arts, I look to improv to help me further imagine situating processes: as embodied, dialogic, and contingent activity.

Seeing writing practice as akin to other bodily arts is a now familiar move in composition. Some, for example, have linked writing to meditative, yogic, or otherwise inward-looking feeling and focusing practices (e.g., Campbell; Gallehr; Perl; Wenger). Others have made connections to music and jazz performance (e.g., Clark; Dixon and Bloome; Elbow, "The Music"; Haas and Witte); or to athletics and physical training (e.g., Hawhee; Chevillle; Rifenburg); or to live performance of various kinds (e.g., Bell; Fishman et al.; hooks; Love). Recently, Jennifer Lin LeMesurier invoked dance and its pedagogies to reconsider writing instruction, especially genre pedagogies (293). LeMesurier emphasizes context and the "performative immediacy" (293) of feedback in dance training, connecting the bodily uptake of learning dance as a way to expose the situated and embodied knowledges activated and inseparable from genre performances (293). I value the ways LeMesurier exposes in writing and in dancing relations between the writer/dancer and her contexts, and how feedback is collaborative and *in situ*. The adaptive, emergent nature of dance and its instruction is similarly why I turn to improv. And, like LeMesurier, I see improv as illuminating on two planes: first, the bodied work of dance and improv uncovers the phenomenology of writing processes as living performance; and, second, the pedagogical philosophies informing these arts are instructive for our own pedagogical thinking. At the same time, I see characteristics in improv that distinguish it from other bodily arts. One is the improviser's relationship to performance audiences *and* to their stage collaborators, without whom there can be no writing and no improv. Other embodied arts like athletic or musical performance do not seem to entail interlocutors or social susceptibility in the overwhelmingly collaborative ways that improv or writing does (in fact, some of these arts, like Perl's focus on the felt sense and the body, can feel focused entirely inwardly). Another distinct characteristic of improv is its endless possibility. The improviser/writer works in a wildly open system with all possibilities in language and scenario. What worked yesterday will never work in the same way today because too many contingent factors differently constrain a given performance. Improv, writing, and the teaching of both arts, in sum, must find ways to teach for difference. The improv pedagogy of Viola Spolin, I argue, is instructive for our writing pedagogies in our present disciplinary moment: one *after* postprocess, postpedagogy, and the deconstruction of general skills.

As with my view of situated processes, at the center of Spolin's improv teaching and practice is *experience*. She opens her discussion of the theory founding her improv instructional practice asserting that,

> Everyone can improvise. Anyone who wishes to can play
> in the theatre and learn to become "stageworthy." We learn

through experience and experiencing, and no one teaches anyone anything. This is as true for the infant moving from kicking to crawling to walking as it is for the scientist with equations. (3)

I hear Peter Elbow in these comments: everyone can write (and improv) without teachers. Experience is the guide. Spolin's "experience," moreover, strikes in two ways: first, more conventionally as repeated practice but also, more importantly, experience as *living* and observing and reflecting, or experience in the phenomenological sense. Or perhaps, in Dobrin's terms, in the sense of direct "participation" in communicative interactions ("Paralogic" 147). Or the experience of writing processes as lived, bodily action in place and time, a perspective I've framed in previous chapters with phenomenological and ontological perspectives (e.g., Ehret and Hollett; Leander and Boldt; Yagelski).

In practice, experience in Spolin's improv is about presence and focus, observation and description. For example, her first introductory exercise called "Exposure" puts half the students on stage and half in the audience and presents a simple prompt for action, "You look at us. We look at you" (Spolin 53). After palpable discomfort sets in, stage players are given an easy task by the teacher-director, like to count the seats in the theatre. This task becomes the felt introduction to the "focus" that is so central to each of Spolin's games. After the exercise concludes, players describe every moment as it unfolded in their bodily experience, as prompted by nonevaluative questioning: how did you feel at first standing on stage and looking at the players in the audience? How did your stomach feel? How did you feel when you were counting the seats? (Spolin 54–55). Through structured bodily experiences and nonevaluative descriptions, in this exercise, players begin to *feel* how focus, as the core of improv practice, is forged by *doing* something within the space where they are (and not in thinking about what comes next or the next line to say). In turn, focus on *doing* begins to mitigate fear, overthinking, uncertainty, and discomfort. In oversimplified terms, students slowly acquire improv by doing it and by describing it. I see similarities in my own practices of having students observe slices of their writing processes and describe them.

In Spolin's view as well, experience is embodied and emergent as it is also implicitly *emplaced*: "Experiencing is penetration into the environment, total organic involvement with it" (Spolin 3). Improv is inconceivable if it is not situated in place; improv is inconceivable if not unfolding and emergent, a series of tightly connected choices plucked from infinite possibilities. So too writing processes. In his study of everyday conversation as collaborative and improvisational, R. Keith Sawyer demonstrates through a simple eight-line improv scene how each short line "provides its own unlimited possibilities" (*Creating* 13) from which "a combinatorial explosion quickly results in hundreds of other performances that could have been" (13). But exposing this kind of situational possibility and contingency in writing processes feels almost impossible. As Nedra Reynolds puts this problem: "we can follow a pedestrian through a street to see the moves she makes, the turns she takes, but we can't follow a writer into a text—or it's proven very difficult to 'study' how writers write" (166). Writing (n.) covers its tracks, severed from the emergent time and place of its production.

Chris Kreiser, in his discussion of improvisation and writing, helps further address this situated unfolding, or the improvisational quality, of writing. Kreiser discovers his connection between improv and writing instruction differently than I as he explores Quintilian's understudied comments in the *Institutio Oratoria* about extemporaneous speeches, what constitutes improvisation, and the relations among preparation, skill, and performance. Kreiser takes from Quintilian what he identifies as an emergent model of improvisation (88), a working concept that helps him to overhaul his peer review workshop. Dispensing with the familiar review model in which students exchange drafts to tinker with a draft's surface features or defer to the sense that the text is probably fine the way it is, Kreiser instead opens space for emergent possibilities through whole-class collaborative "interviews with the author." Like the ethos of Jensen's archival process journeys, as students proceed slowly through an author's draft, they locate specific choices and ask the author why she made them. Students, author, and teacher all work together to imagine many possible alternatives, or multiple ways the choice might have been otherwise. In so doing, "the whole class improvise[s], collectively harnessing a developed repertoire of communicative moves, making choices within and for a particular rhetorical situation" (98). This is a powerful intersection of writing and improv as this practice embodies an essential rhetorical maxim: not just the faculty of writing acceptably in a situation, but of observing the *possibly* persuasive in each case. And Kreiser's methods expose how effectiveness doesn't just measure how a text *on its whole* is or is not suitable to its situation, but how *within* a given text, choices are impinged on by location, timing, and the possibility to be otherwise. In other words, he shows how process is perpetually susceptible to environmental forces at the level of tiny textual choices considered in collaboration with others.

And though he doesn't emphasize it, in Kreiser's methods too is an important leveling of participation imperative in practicing processes and/as improv. Kreiser, the writing teacher, serves in these author-interviews mostly as a participant, playing possibilities right alongside students rather than directing them. In improv instruction, as in writing, the role of the teacher is much considered. Most often, the teacher is a problem to be solved, just as they are and have been in process, writing-about-writing, postprocess/pedagogy, critical and liberatory, expressivist, and other writing pedagogy discourses. As Charles Deemer says in 1967, the writing teacher is a "flagrant misnomer" (122). The contingent arts of writing and improv complicate common images of teaching and learning. As highlighted throughout my discussion, the (process) writing teacher can no longer if ever be master, authority, knowledge or standards bearer. Because contexts and factors and Others change, teachers cannot give a reliable "framework that explains the process of collaborative interaction" (Kent, *Paralogic* 165). So if we accept (and I think we do) the situatedness and susceptibility of writing, then the "nature of how we envision teaching is obsolete" (Dobrin, "Paralogic" 134). But of course observing need for a different role for the writing teacher has been one (repetitive) thing in the long history of composition; enacting it remains another. In a way, Viola Spolin too argues that improv teaching is postprocess and postpedagogy. In fact, she says explicitly, "Do not teach. Expose students to theatrical environments through playing, and they will find their own way" (42).

But what does that mean? What does it really mean to ask writing and improv teachers to "not teach," to call them to "relinquish[] their roles as high priests" (Kent, *Paralogic* 166) and become instead "facilitators" (Smit 12), or "collaborators" (Kent, "Paralogic" 151), or "mentors" engaged in one-on-one dialogue (Breuch 143–144), or "co-workers" or "students themselves" (Kent, *Paralogic* 166)? And too, how can we afford to deconstruct writing teacher mastery in these ways given Downs and Wardle's seemingly opposing but important call for writing teachers to be nothing less than credentialed disciplinary experts?

In her recent (postprocess) iteration of this call, Lee-Ann M. Kastman Breuch laments that descriptions of postprocess dialogic co-instruction remain too "broad and abstract" (144) to see how it might work. Others, including David Smit and Thomas Kent, focus on immense institutional change as the only change capable of repositioning the writing teacher as collaborator or mentor. For them, writing instruction should no longer be centralized but permeate across the curriculum with writing "professionals" situated as "facilitators" (Smit 12). For Downs and Wardle, the institutional problem is of a different sort: as they worry about the ongoing minimized positioning of first-year writing a service course, they imagine a more conventional view of a disciplinary expert teaching and a disciplinary novice learning. So as we wait for concrete co-instructional practices, or for the "glacial" pace of institutional change (Kent, *Paralogic* 170), or for our "full disciplinarity" (Downs and Wardle "Teaching" 578), and as we all continue trying to defeat the myth of universal writing skills, Spolin's vision of the improv teacher-director can guide us at least a little, helping to resolve some of this seeming tension among expertise, impossibility, and getting out of the way in the teaching of writing.

In improv, there are no teachers and no students at all, only players. As Spolin emphasizes,

> The need for players to see themselves and others not as students or teachers but as fellow players, playing on terms of peerage, no matter what their individual ability. Eliminating the roles of teacher and student helps players get beyond the need for approval or disapproval, which distracts them from experiencing themselves and solving the problem. There is no right or wrong way to solve a problem: there is only one way—the seeking—in which one learns by going through the process itself. (iii)

Especially important here is the work to arrest the drive of what Spolin calls "approval and disapproval." This drive, "years in building" (9), is reflected in the "authoritarianism" (Spolin 8) permeating myriad social domains and roles: parent, teacher, employer, and so on (8). Approval/disapproval in the scene of learning has us asking and needing to know, is this good or is this bad? Am I good or bad? So ingrained is the desire to get approval, Spolin warns, that attitudes and language around approval/disapproval "must be constantly scourged" through "constant surveillance" (8) on the teacher-director's part to ensure that she does not tread back into these familiar grooves of judgment. And this monitoring, it should be underlined, is not just to avoid language of criticism, but equally to avoid praise and approval. Praise, in many ways, is worse as it inevitably signals progress in the teacher's terms and not the students' own (Spolin 8).

To break the approval/disapproval paradigm, evaluation or assessment processes become especially important to Spolin's improv. Evaluation occurs routinely after players have finished each performed scene or theatre game. Evaluation focuses on "direct communication made possible through non-judgmental attitudes" and questioning through "objective vocabulary" with "group assistance" and "clarification of the focus of an exercise" (Spolin 24). That is, nonevaluative and descriptive questions are posed to the players, including the teacher. All participants in this discursive process use the focus and aims of the given problem as the guide. As demonstrated above with the "Exposure" exercise, the teacher-director poses objective, descriptive questions about what the audience observed on stage (e.g., Was concentration complete or incomplete? Did they communicate or interpret? and so on). Evaluation is thus non-evaluative, contextual, and collaborative as the "teacher-director does not make the evaluation but, rather, asks the questions which all answer—including the teacher" (27). The student audience and the teacher-director are only able to engage the evaluation if they are so focused as to be also "in" the scene or work on stage and involved themselves in the choices of the players in that performative moment. Thus, for evaluation processes to be effective "the teacher-director must become the audience together with the student-actors in the deepest sense of the word" (28).

Continuing emphasis on proximity and involvement, Spolin describes how "teaching" also happens through what she calls "side-coaching" (28), or interjections from the teacher-director contributed "in the same space, with the same focus, as the players" (28). These are nudges that call players' bodily attention to where they are and what they are doing as a scene unfolds. Side-coaching is still non-evaluative and non-directive in that it does not tell what a player should do next, but instead gives voice to the "realities" unfolding in the scene ("See the buttons on John's coat!" or "Write with a pencil, not your finger!") or calls players to attune to the performance space ("Share your voice with the audience!" (29)). Because side-coaching is dictated by the very same situation and rules the players are inhabiting and constrained by, the teacher-director cannot rely on tropes or maxims or "disappear behind a veil or aphorisms regarding the . . . process" (Kent, "Paralogic" 151). Side-coaching is only ever spontaneous, on-the-spot, in the moment—a command fitting only to the moment it is uttered. For Spolin, as for Charles Deemer's pedagogy of the happening, the improv and writing class must be "a class of students actively aware and participant, a class that does not swallow the 'teacher's' remarks but *considers* them" (Deemer 123).

But with descriptive nonevaluative language and collaborative discussion and diagnostics of scenes, what guides improvement? If the teacher-director ruthlessly avoids evaluation, "good/bad" language, both praise for achievement and concern for mistakes or failures, how could growth possibly be achieved and measured? As Spolin poses this question in a manner more abstract, "How can we have a 'planned' way of action while trying to find a 'free' way?" (9). For Kent and other postprocess thinkers, this kind of decentered unpredictability means teaching is "impossible." Writing is just too situational for there to be anything to teach, this view concludes, so the writing teacher must transform into a "collaborator" with relinquished authority dispersed across the curriculum. For Downs and Wardle, calling for instructors to be disciplinary experts and students to be novices would appear to conflict with postprocess deconstruction, even as they are too working toward the same (postprocess) goal of dismantling general-skills instruction.

However, these views are not necessarily contradictory. The writing instructor should, even must, have a range of knowledge and expertise—about language, grammar, language attitudes, composition research methods and findings, pedagogical histories and methods; threshold concepts like genre, kairos, exigence; process practices and habits, to name just a very few areas. At the same time still though, that disciplinary expert, for all she knows, cannot claim expertise over the behaviors of language, writing situations, or situated processes in the world. Writing teachers, as anyone, cannot anticipate entirely what writers will encounter (Downs and Wardle, "Teaching" 556–7). The writing teacher or disciplinary expert, no matter their training, will never be a master of processes nor be able to define them in advance for our students or for themselves (just ask Chris Anson). The situational contingencies of writing in the world will always exceed even the most thorough and extended regimes of instruction. Said another way, being a disciplinary expert is not the same as being a misstep-free master of all writing acts themselves. As Dobrin says, "We cannot master discourse" (147). None of us. We are *all* only players. We and our students can become varying degrees of expert in the knowledge of writing studies, but that doesn't ensure that we will practice writing in context without any failure or miscommunication, disorientation or uncertainty.

This characteristic uncertainty of writing and of improv means that the direction that *all* players must follow, including teacher-directors (as disciplinary experts or co-collaborators or something else), "is the demands of the art form itself" (Spolin 18). It is the very situation—the situatedness of writing and its processes—that is the "master." Said another way in Spolin's words, the master is the "needs of the theatre" (9) itself, "for the teacher too must accept the rules of the game" (Spolin 9). In Kent's terms, similarly, this means that "*good writing* and *good reading*" cannot be objectively judged from some distanced position. The only measure is the "good sense" of some particular utterance in "some particular situation" (Kent, *Paralogic* 170). The demands of the *situation* in which writing finds itself, not the teacher's or writer's alone, must be met. Through improv, we see that writing can never be arbitrated between just teacher and student, no matter how dialogic that relation may be. Writing and its instruction is simply more collaborative than that: players (students *and* teacher-directors) inhabit, describe, and dialogue together with the given situation in which play unfolds, working to discern the dynamics of scene, genre, audiences, tools, discourses, purposes and so on. Writing *in its situation* is the guide.

In casting situated processes as improv, I linger on the stage—but not Donald Murray's formal public stage for the performance of professional writers. Instead, I picture writing processes as a living stage of players, objects, responses, influences, constraints, Others. Situated processes as improv are never just our intentions, habits, or strategies alone. They are attempts, our best guesses as to what might work in the moment in which we find ourselves and the materials and spaces at hand. I hope my discussion of Spolin helps my reader picture differently the potentials of process instruction—our assessment, our relationship with genre, conventions, the rhetorical situation, and our images of the writing teacher as *at once* a disciplinary expert *and* a player equally alongside our students. It is our responsibility as writing teachers to play our teacher-game too according to the demands of the situation. There may be some baseline writing facilities that might more easily cross boundaries—perhaps broad skills of fluency and language convention, or guiding schemas about genre, audience, adaptation (which each, at some point too, become *profoundly susceptible* to writing's *wheres*). Ultimately though we must recognize that "what we call writing ability may be very context-specific, a matter of knowing what we need to know or be able to do in whatever situations we find ourselves" (Smit 166). In other words, what we may call writing is improv.

CONCLUSION
SITUATING WRITING PROCESSES

Writing about ongoing research back in 1984, Jack Selzer observed the range of detail and insight emerging about the nature of composing processes. Though he found this work illuminating, Selzer warned against impulses that would turn that wealth of observation into "overly prescriptive interventions and modifications" (276) to the way student writers were expected to write. As process research fueled process textbooks, Selzer hoped to see emphasized not just generalized similarities like recursivity, but more importantly, variation in processes. "The books sometimes acknowledge that differences in habits of composing exist among writers," Selzer notes, "but never within a single writer who is confronted with different writing tasks" (279). In the midst of the burgeoning "process movement," Selzer emphasized the *situated differences* of processes, especially those shaped by differing purposes. Not only are processes not uniform *across* writers, they also are not uniformly held by any *single* writer. A writer's process will necessarily differ as shaped by "different writing tasks." Indeed, as Donald Murray declared—and as he viscerally experienced in Berkenkotter's one-hour protocol in that library room—writing processes are always "a matter of the conditions" (Berkenkotter and Murray 169). As I have explored in this book, conditions range—not just as differences in broad contexts or rhetorical situations or an unfamiliar library versus a home study, but also in the tiniest, most immediate of conditions (like bodily movement, hesitations, interruptions, or interactions with tools, glasses of water, dogs, books, and others) and in the most distant and abstract macro-constraints (including genre, audience, historical moment, community discourse, and so on).

Throughout, I've forwarded the (postprocess) claim that when we let these ranging "conditions" into the frame—especially as I've seen them here as embodied and emplaced experience—living composing processes explode the bounds of modeling or repeatable strategies alone. But this insight on its own isn't exactly novel: while we still to some extent prescribe process routinely as part of our curriculums or equate processes with drafts, we also highlight in our process teaching the multiplicity Selzer valued. We recognize that writers are different, that each have their own complex histories, experiences, positionalities, and psychologies around writing, especially in school. We accept that processes are complex, plural, and never fully prescribable (even if, again, we also have writers do one set of prewriting activities or we specify expectations for revision).

We engage student writers in dialogue and reflection about multiple procedures to get writing underway or to revise at the sentence-level. We ask student writers to read professional writers talking about the life of writing and have them perform similar reflections and narratives.

My efforts in this book have been, in part, to ground those constructions of writers' processes in the specifics of bodies and things and writing places. I have urged less focus on processes as steps or "thinking" and more focus on the physical and material life of process—the range of tools we take up and those we have access to, the infinite sites outside of school which engage us in processes of all kinds and configurations, the affective pace and rhythms of writing as a contingent and susceptible life activity which collides and overlaps with countless others. And too, seeing this physical grounding has potential to encourage important environmental mindfulness—the idea that writers should become conscious of and reflective about how they partner with writing places, space, time, and things. Susan Wyche's study comes to mind on this point. Wyche's own prolonged experience of painful writer's block caused her to examine the shaping, and it turns out, inhibiting role of the environmental conditions in which she was attempting to write. Unblocking for Wyche was not a matter of getting control of her planning processes nor of closer study of the genre conventions of a masters' thesis in her discipline. Instead, Wyche gets relief and progress in her writing by virtue of considering her emplacement, by modifying her writing space and rituals. Guided by the effects of her own environmental overhaul, Wyche then describes how she has her own student writers similarly take stock of their spaces and habits in order to adjust them, to ensure that their environments and object-oriented rituals were properly engineered to better secure good, or at least *completed*, writing projects. Practicing awareness of our writing environments and their participatory shaping roles is certainly important to writing work of any kind today. We all could use more discipline in knowing when to turn off the WIFI if we notice ourselves fleeing too regularly to Facebook or Twitter for a distraction (though I note at the same time too, much writing happens *in* these hectic digital contexts). Reflective awareness and mindfulness about writing spaces remains a very important outcome of situating processes in our teaching.

I've noticed too over the years in presenting my research on writer's spaces and objects just how much *looking* at the material surround of writing engages us. The photographs and drawings I show tend to spark animated conversation around the labor of writing that would otherwise go unvoiced or remain invisible. People just *like* talking about—and even more, peering into—writing spaces. As Brian McNely has put it, in short, we seem to just like looking at "what others' desks look like" ("Taking" 49). This fascination reflects more broadly in culture, too: in our interest in authors' homes; in images of Einstein's or other genius' offices; and in how regularly we share research studies about what a messy desk says about us, our intellect, creativity, or writing talent. I know I share this fascination in looking. Writing in cafés has become a bit of a liability for me if I find myself next to someone who appears to be writing. I'll inevitably watch them. I try to see what kind of writing they might be doing, how fast they seem to be able to go, what's in the document they keep clicking over to, or how many times they've looked out the window or cracked their fingers.

Just as often when I talk about the environmental and physical dimensions of writing processes, people spontaneously confess things to me. They tell me about their own unusual habit or their specific environmental requirements—like absolute silence or taking up writing on their smart phone in the car. They seem to want to know from me: Is this weird or is it normal? They especially want to know: is it good? Implicitly, I feel like with these questions, writers want me to interpret or diagnose their behavior or writing spaces and prescribe some enabling adjustments. What's the *secret* underlying where we write?, many seem to want to know. Where and with what should we be telling our students to do their writing? What have I found about the best environmental configurations that might produce the "best" writing?

As I have worked on this book, these kinds of questions have left me off-kilter, unsure, bothered (in a good way). My first instinct has always been in the moment to think something like, "well, optimization or interpretation isn't the point exactly. . . ." There is, of course, no single optimal environment for writing, or even multiple "best practices" in writing space design. And I don't know how I would know if your habit of needing to write by a window or only with a cup of black tea is "good" or helpful or not. It just *is* a habit—along with countless others, some of which you know as reliable, much of which unrolls without your awareness, and even more which change all the time depending on right where you are when you take to the page or screen or begin that internal monologue.

But if engineering or taking control of the physical situatedness of our processes is far from the point, then what is? If it is not optimization nor interpretation nor relating well-organized environments to well-organized written products, then what *is* the point of observing and rendering situated processes? My inability to give good answers to these questions had me feeling like I was missing something about my own interest in seeing processes this way.

After some time and much thinking, I think now that it is this that I was missing: in the ways writers and writing instruction conceive of them, processes have come to be something each writer *has* and holds on to. We have come to see processes thoroughly as a *"writer's own."* "My" process is unique—that which

I've tried out, repeated, ritualized, habituated, reflected upon and refined. Process, this entrenched assumption holds, is what *I alone do* when I write. Process is *my* preparation, *my* plan, *my* idiosyncrasies. Processes are snowflakes; no two writers' are alike. Processes, we have assumed—whether we see them as problems to tackle with cognition, conventions to discover in social communities, activities in dynamic physical environments, or all these dimensions simultaneously—are ultimately *ours* alone to fashion. I realize now that this was what gave me pause in those questions about optimization or interpretation: our tacit, implicit allegiance to this sole control mythos.

I came to see this small tyranny of process ownership through these types of responses to my work over the years. I came to this view especially after looking and relooking at those pedagogical documents (Ch. 3) which each reproduce the virtues of process engineering. I came to this view thinking closely about what it means really to dismantle our allegiance to teaching general writing skills. I came to this view puzzling over what to make of postprocess theory. I came to this view after years with my writing students and our joyful conversations about our strange habits and needs around our complex (be)labor(ing) of writing. Ultimately, I came to complicate process ownership by *looking*, by inviting my writing students to look, by reimagining processes through those big metaphorical glass observation boxes.

When we look at processes where they unfold, we see just how much they are not just *"our own"* predetermined habits or familiar spaces. Processes are just as much the unstable, incidental, accidental, tiny, random, susceptible, and varied actions and objects and constraints that operate outside the reach of writerly control or reflective awareness. What "really" happens in writing processes always exceeds whatever we tell ourselves that what we do when and where we write. And most often—or at least much more often than we focus on, I think—writing processes are not fashioned choices but ad-hoc responses, improvisations. Processes are much more accurately on-the-spot reactions to whatever's going on: to circumstances, a new coffee shop or chair, unfamiliar genres, varying audiences, discourse demands or rules, and other infinite and shaping "conditions." Processes are *never just* ours alone. Seeing processes in their physical and material instantiations reveals this clearly.

This disruption in the mythos of process ownership is no small thing. We in composition have told the stories of process for so long and so loudly that process is not just a critical and shaping concept for writing teachers, but also just as much perhaps for writing students. Many or most who write have at least some purchase in this concept—again, as research on transfer has shown: "For several decades, we have been teaching process, and according to our students, they transfer process" (Yancey et al. 28). But the stories of process we seem to keep telling can reinforce the false idea that writing is a *solo act*—one we can engineer, one we should ably guide with our own strategies, one that happens somehow independently of where we are and what's on hand. And yet, basically all the other stories we try to tell about writing shows a different picture altogether—especially those more recent stories about context and situatedness but also all those oldest ones we keep telling about rhetoric. Our many other stories of writing—of audience awareness and adaptation, of discourse communities and communities of practice, of rhetoric as identification, of language conventions and the policing of "correctness," of writing-in-the-disciplines, of inventing the university or of Burke's parlor, of genre as social action, of jargon and discourse expectations, of the myth of voice or the unified writing subject, of the social turn, of the rhetorical situation, and many more—resoundingly tell us that writing is *never* a matter of the writer alone. Writing is *not ours* ever much more than it is ours alone.

So why would we keep telling it otherwise in our stories of process? And what could happen in our instruction if our main storyline of process *aligned with*, instead of contradicted, these many other stories of writing as a relational, contextual, and contingent team sport?

Complicating process control, or situating writing processes, does not mean that we shouldn't still help writers be mindful, reflective, and environmentally aware. It does not mean that the only thing left to do is emotionally reckon with writing's distributed chaos (Jensen 15). We should still, as I still do with my students, reflect on who we are in our processes and what seems to work for us. But, at the same time, *really looking* at writing as it unfolds casts processes a much more "co-dependent" (Micciche, *Acknowledging* 8) activity than our process teaching has yet to acknowledge. Writing is not ours *and* it is ours. So too are writing processes always already a team sport—with players both human and not, both local and distant, both here and not.

In embracing this realization, I'm reminded of an intermediate writing student who brought a memorable "attitude" to a narrative essay in which I asked students to artfully describe where they write—where they staged their writing processes and what kinds of things participated alongside them. Others described beautifully a "new drafting table" or being "underneath the awning hanging from the café" or in a "small attic room . . . of my rented, century-old house" (I notice, this last student was, or at least she made it seem like she was, writing in a literal garret). But this student, "Jay," seemed to sniff out a lie or impossibility in my very prompt. He wrote,

> I don't really know where I write. . . . I could say the place
> where I write is the rut I wear into the floor from pacing

around, stumped. I could say that the place where I write is any random website I call upon to distract me when I cannot focus. I could say that the place where I write is the twilight period between good time management and the night before something is due—the list goes on. Yet, there is not one specific place. They are all places where I write.

I was both irritated and delighted. Irritated because I didn't really see the lie when I wrote the prompt, and he did. Delighted because he was right. We do not wholly own or control writing or its processes. We cannot claim full domain over or fully strategize process. Of course, we can always learn to better guide, move, reflect, attempt, and improvise. But, ultimately, processes reveals themselves to be more responsive and ad-hoc than pro-active and planned. And seeing how differently processes are emplaced across ranging situations shows how situated writing processes are never about the writer all alone. As Emig, Murray, Reynolds, Brodkey, Cooper and others in different ways, and most importantly, as "Jay" has it in his own words—any situated writing process "all really depends on the circumstances."

WORKS CITED

Ahmed, Sara. "Affective Economies." *Social Text* 79, vol. 22, no. 2, Summer 2004, pp. 117–39, http://cr.middlebury.edu/amlit_civ/allen/2012%20backup/scholarship/affect%20theory/22.2ahmed.pdf.

Alexander, Jonathan. "Transgender Rhetoric(s): (Re)Composing Narratives of the Gendered Body." *College Composition and Communication (CCC)*, vol. 57, no. 1, Sept. 2005, pp. 45–82.

Anderson, Jeff. "Zooming in and Zooming out: Putting Grammar in Context into Context." *English Journal*, vol. 95, no. 5, May 2006, pp. 28–34.

Andrew-Vaughn, Sarah, and Cathy Fleischer. "Researching Writing: The Unfamiliar-Genre Research Project." *English Journal*, vol. 95, no. 4, Mar. 2006, pp. 36–42, https://doi.org/10.2307/30047086.

Anson, Chris M. "The Pop Warner Chronicles: A Case Study in Contextual Adaptation and the Transfer of Writing Ability." *CCC*, vol. 67, no. 4, June 2016, pp. 518–49.

———. "Process Pedagogy and its Legacy." *A Guide to Composition Pedagogies*. 2nd Edition, edited by Gary Tate et al., Oxford UP, 2014, pp. 212–30.

Anson, Chris M., and Jessie L. Moore. *Critical Transitions: Writing and the Question of Transfer*. The WAC Clearinghouse and University Press of Colorado, 2016, https://wac.colostate.edu/books/perspectives/ansonmoore/.

Aronson, Anne. "Composing in a Material World: Women Writing in Space and Time." *Rhetoric Review*, vol. 17, no. 2, Spring 1999, pp. 282–99.

Banks, William P. "Written through the Body: Disruptions and Personal Writing." *College English*, vol. 66, no.1, 2003, pp. 21–40, https://doi.org/10.2307/3594232.

Barker, Lisa M. "Invoking Viola Spolin: Improvisational Theatre, Side-Coaching, and Leading Discussion." *English Journal*, vol. 105, no. 5, 2016, pp. 23–25.

Barnett, Scot. "Chiasms: Pathos, Phenomenology, and Object-Oriented Rhetorics." *Enculturation: A Journal of Rhetoric, Writing, and Culture*, vol. 20, 2015, http://enculturation.net/chiasms-pathos-phenomenology.

———. "Toward an Object-Oriented Rhetoric: A Review of Tool-Being: Heidegger and the Metaphysics of Objects and Guerrilla Metaphysics: Phenomenology and the Carpentry of Things by Graham Harman." *Enculturation: A Journal of Writing, Rhetoric, and Culture*, vol. 7, 2010, http://enculturation.net/toward-an-object-oriented-rhetoric.

Barnett, Scot, and Casey Boyle. *Rhetoric, Through Everyday Things*. University of Alabama Press, 2016.

Baron, Dennis. *A Better Pencil: Readers, Writers, and the Digital Revolution*. Oxford UP, 2009.

Bell, David. "Rise, Sally, Rise: Communicating through Dance." *TESOL Journal*, vol. 8, no.1, 1999, pp. 27–32.

Bennett, Jane. *Vibrant Matter: A Political Ecology of Things*. Duke UP, 2010.

Berkenkotter, Carol, and Donald M. Murray. "Decisions and Revisions: The Planning Strategies of a Publishing Writer and Response of a Lab Rat: Or, Being Protocoled." *CCC*, vol. 34, no. 2, May 1983, pp. 156–72, https://doi.org/10.2307/357403.

Beaufort, Anne. *College Writing and Beyond: A New Framework for University Writing Instruction*. Utah State UP, 2007.

Bizzell, Patricia. *Academic Discourse and Critical Consciousness*. University of Pittsburgh Press, 1992.

Blair, Kristine. "Review: *Writing Technology*." *Technical Communication Quarterly*, vol. 6, no. 2, Spring 1997, pp. 225–27.

Blau, Sheridan. "Book Review: Felt Sense: Writing with the Body, by Sondra Perl." *The Quarterly*, vol. 26, no. 3, 2004, http://www.nwp.org/cs/public/print/resource/1988.

Bleich, David. *The Materiality of Language: Gender, Politics, and the University*. Indiana UP, 2013.

Blewett, Kelly, et al. "Composing Environments: The Materiality of Reading and Writing." *CEA Critic*, vol. 78, no. 1, Mar. 2016, pp. 24–44.

Bloom, Lynn Z. "Freshman Composition as a Middle-Class Enterprise." *College English*, vol. 58, no. 6, Oct. 1996, pp. 654–75, https://doi.org/10.2307/378392.

Braddock, Richard, et al. *Research in Written Composition*. NCTE, 1963.

Brand, Alice G. "The Why of Cognition: Emotion and the Writing Process." *CCC*, vol. 38, no. 4, Dec 1987, pp. 436–43, https://doi.org/10.2307/357637.

Brand, Alice G., and Richard L. Graves. *Presence of Mind: Writing and the Domain Beyond the Cognitive*. Boynton/Cook, 1994.

Brent, Doug. "Transfer, Transformation and Rhetorical Knowledge: Insights from Transfer Theory." *Journal of Business and Technical Communication*, vol. 25, no. 4, 2011, pp. 396–420, https://doi.org/10.1177/1050651911410951.

Breuch, Lee-Ann M. Kastman. "Post-Process 'Pedagogy': A Philosophical Exercise." *JAC*, vol. 22, no. 1, 2002, pp. 119–50, https://www.jaconlinejournal.com/archives/vol22.1/breuch-postprocess.pdf.

Brodkey, Linda. "Modernism and the Scene(s) of Writing." *College English*, vol. 49, no. 4, Apr. 1987, pp. 396–418, https://doi.org/10.2307/377850.

Brooke, Collin, and Thomas Rickert. "Being Delicious: Materialities of Research in a Web 2.0 Application." *Beyond Postprocess,* edited by Sidney I. Dobrin et al., Utah State UP, 2011, pp. 163–82.

Bruffee, Kenneth A. "Collaborative Learning and the 'Conversation of Mankind.'" *College English*, vol. 46, no. 7, Nov. 1984, pp. 635–52.

Burnett, Rebecca E., and Christina Haas. "Explicating 'Writing as Embodied Practice:' A Conversation with Rebecca Burnett and Christina Haas." *Journal of Business and Technical Communication*, vol. 21, Feb. 2007, pp. 23–36.

Butler, Janine. "Bodies in Composition: Teaching Writing through Kinesthetic Performance." *Composition Studies*, vol. 45, no. 2, 2017, pp. 73–90.

Campbell, JoAnn. "Writing to Heal: Using Meditation in the Writing Process." *CCC*, vol. 45, no. 2, 1994, pp. 246–51, https://doi.org/10.2307/359010.

Canagarajah, A. Suresh. *A Geopolitics of Academic Writing*. U of Pittsburgh P, 2002.

————. "'Nondiscursive' Requirements in Academic Publishing, Material Resources of Periphery Scholars, and the Politics of Knowledge Production." *Written Communication*, vol. 13, no. 4, Oct. 1996, pp. 435–72.

Cedillo, Christina V. "What does it Mean to Move?: Race, Disability, and Critical Embodiment Pedagogy." *Composition Forum*, vol. 39, Summer 2018, http://compositionforum.com/issue/39/to-move.php.

Ceraso, Steph, et al. "Learning as Coordination: Postpedagogy and Design." *Enculturation: A Journal of Rhetoric, Writing, and Culture*, May 2019, https://designpedagogy.giyhub.io/introduction/.

Chandler, Sally. "Fear, Teaching Composition, and Students' Discursive Choices: Re-Thinking Connections between Emotions and College Student Writing." *Composition Studies*, vol. 35, no. 2, Fall 2007, pp. 53–70.

Cheville, Julie. *Minding the Body: What Student Athletes Know about Learning.* Boynton/Cook Heinemann, 2001.

Clark, Gregory. "Virtuosos and Ensembles: Rhetorical Lessons from Jazz." *The Private, the Public, and the Published: Reconciling Private Lives and Public Rhetoric*, edited by Barbara Couture and Thomas Kent, Utah State UP, 2004, pp. 31–46.

Coleridge, Samuel Taylor. "Kubla Khan; Or, A Vision in a Dream." http://www.victorianweb.org/previctorian/stc/kktext.html.

Coole, Diana, and Samantha Frost, eds. *New Materialisms: Ontology, Agency, and Politics.* Duke UP, 2010.

Cooper, Marilyn M. "The Ecology of Writing." *College English,* vol. 48, no. 4, Apr. 1986, pp. 364–75, https://doi.org/10.2307/377264.

Cooper, Marilyn M., and Michael Holzman. *Writing as Social Action.* Boynton/Cook, 1989.

Couture, Barbara. "Modeling and Emulating: Rethinking Agency in the Writing Process." *Post-Process Theory: Beyond the Writing Process Paradigm*, edited by Thomas Kent, Southern Illinois UP, pp. 30–48.

Deemer, Charles. "English Composition as a Happening." *College English*, vol. 29, no. 2, Nov. 1967, pp. 121–26.

DeJoy, Nancy C. "I Was a Process-Model Baby." *Post-Process Theory: Beyond the Writing Process Paradigm*, edited by Thomas Kent, Southern Illinois UP, 1999, pp. 163–78.

————. *Process This: Undergraduate Writing in Composition Studies.* Utah State UP, 2004.

Delpit, Lisa D. "The Silenced Dialogue: Power and Pedagogy in Educating Other People's Children." *Harvard Educational Review*, vol. 53, no. 3, Aug. 1988, pp. 280–98, https://doi.org/10.17763/haer.58.3.c43481778r528qw4.

————. "Skills and Other Dilemmas of a Progressive Black Educator." *Harvard Educational Review*, vol. 56, no.4, Nov. 1986, pp. 379–85, https://doi.org/10.17763/haer.56.4.674v5h1m125h3014.

Diaz, Junot. "Becoming a Writer." *O, the Oprah Magazine*, Nov. 2009, https://www.oprah.com/spirit/junot-diaz-talks-about-what-made-him-become-a-writer/all.

Dixson, Adrienne, and David Bloome. "Jazz, Critical Race Theories, and the Discourse Analysis of Literacy Events in Classrooms." *Literacy Research for Political Action and Social Change,* edited by Mollie V. Blackburn and Caroline T. Clark, Peter Lang, 2007, pp. 29–52.

Dobrin, Sidney I. "Paralogic Hermeneutic Theories, Power, and the Possibility for Liberating Pedagogies." *Post-Process Theory: Beyond the Writing Process Paradigm*, edited by Thomas Kent, Southern Illinois UP, 1999, pp. 132–48.

———. *Postcomposition*. Southern Illinois UP, 2011.

Dobrin, Sidney I., et al., editors. *Beyond Postprocess*. Utah State UP, 2011.

Dolmage, Jay Timothy. *Disability Rhetoric*. Syracuse UP, 2014.

———. "Writing Against Normal: Navigating a Corporeal Turn." *Composing (Media) = Composing (Embodiment): Bodies, Technologies, Writing, the Teaching of Writing*, edited by Kristin L. Arola and Anne Wysocki, Utah State UP, 2012, pp. 110–26.

Downs, Doug, and Elizabeth Wardle. "Reflecting Back and Looking Forward: Revisiting 'Teaching About Writing, Righting Misconceptions' Five Years On." *Composition Forum* 27, Spring 2013, http://compositionforum.com/issue/27/reflecting-back.php.

———. "Reimagining the Nature of FYC Trends in Writing-about-Writing Pedagogies." *Exploring Composition Studies*, edited by Kelly Ritter and Paul K. Matsuda, Utah State UP, 2012, pp. 123–44.

———. "Teaching About Writing, Righting Misconceptions: (Re)Envisioning 'First-Year Composition' as 'Introduction to Writing Studies.'" *CCC*, vol. 58, no. 4, June 2007, pp. 552–84.

Edbauer-Rice, Jenny. "The New 'New': Making a Case for Critical Affect Studies." *Quarterly Journal of Speech*, vol. 94, no. 2, May 2008, pp. 200–12.

Ehret, Christian, and Ty Hollett. "Embodied Composition in Real Virtualities: Adolescents' Literacy Practices and Felt Experiences Moving with Digital, Mobile Devices in School." *Research in the Teaching of English*, vol. 48, no. 4, May 2014, pp. 428–52.

Elbow, Peter. "A Method for Teaching Writing." *College English*, vol. 30, no. 2, Nov. 1968, pp. 115–25, https://doi.org/10.2307/374011.

———. "The Music of Form: Rethinking Organization in Writing." *CCC*, vol. 57, no. 4, 2006, pp. 620–66.

———. *Writing without Teachers*. Oxford UP, 1973.

Emig, Janet. *The Composing Processes of Twelfth Graders*. NCTE, 1971.

———. "Hand Eye Brain." *The Web of Meaning: Essays on Writing, Teaching, Learning, and Thinking*. Heinemann, 1983.

———. "Uses of the Unconscious." *The Web of Meaning: Essays on Writing, Teaching, Learning, and Thinking*. Heinemann, 1983.

Esposito, Lauren. "Saying 'Yes, and' to Collaborative Prewriting: How Improvisational Theatre Ignites Creativity and Discovery in Student Writing." *English Journal*, vol. 105, no. 5, 2016, pp. 42–47.

Faigley, Lester. "Competing Theories of Process: A Critique and a Proposal." *College English*, vol. 48, no. 6, 1986, pp. 527–42.

———. *Fragments of Rationality: Postmodernity and the Subject of Composition*. U of Pittsburgh P, 1992.

Feldman, Lee Gallup. "A Brief History of Improvisational Theatre in the United States." *Theatre*, vol. 5, no. 4, 1974, pp. 128–51.

Fishman, Jenn, et al. "Performing Writing, Performing Literacy." *CCC*, vol. 57, no. 2, Dec. 2005, pp. 224–52.

Fleckenstein, Kristie S. "Writing Bodies: Somatic Mind in Composition Studies." *College English*, vol. 61, no. 3, 1999, pp. 281–306, https://doi.org/10.2307/379070.

———. *Embodied Literacies: Imageword and a Poetics of Teaching*. Southern Illinois UP, 2003.

Flower, Linda. *The Construction of Negotiated Meaning: A Social Cognitive Theory of Writing*. Southern Illinois UP, 1994.

Flower, Linda, and John R. Hayes. "A Cognitive Process Theory of Writing." *CCC*, vol. 32, no. 4, Dec. 1981, pp. 365–87, https://doi.org/10.2307/356600.

Foster, Helen. *Networked Process: Dissolving Boundaries of Process and Post-Process*. Parlor Press, 2007.

Fraiberg, Steven. "Composition 2.0: Toward a Multilingual and Multimodal Framework." *CCC*, vol. 61, no. 1, Sept. 2010, pp. 100–26.

"Framework for Success in Postsecondary Writing." Council of Writing Program Administrators (CWPA), the National Council of Teachers of English (NCTE), and the National Writing Project (NWP), 2011, http://files.eric.ed.gov/fulltext/ED516360.pdf.

"Friday." *Bumping Mics with Jeff Ross and Dave Attell*, season 1, episode 1, 2018. *Netflix*, https://www.netflix.com/title/80216094.

Fulkerson, Richard. "Composition at the Turn of the Twenty-First Century." *CCC*, vol. 56, no.4, June 2005, pp. 654–87.

Flynn, Elizabeth A. "Composing as a Woman." *CCC*, vol. 39, no. 4, Dec. 1988, pp. 423–35, https://doi.org/10.2307/357697.

Gallagher, Kelly. *Write Like This: Teaching Real-World Writing Through Modeling and Mentor Texts*. Stenhouse, 2011.

Gallehr, Donald R. "Wait, and the Writing Will Come: Meditation and the Composing Process." *Presence of Mind: Writing and the Domain Beyond the Cognitive in Brand*, edited by Alice Glarden Brand and Richard L. Graves, Boynton/Cook, 1994, pp. 21–30.

Garland-Thomson, Rosemarie. "Misfits: A Feminist Materialist Disability Concept." *Hypatia*, vol. 26, no. 3, 2011, pp. 591–609.

Gilyard, Keith. *True to the Language Game: African American Discourse, Cultural Politics, and Pedagogy*. Routledge, 2011.

Gonzales, Laura. "Multimodality, Translingualism, and Rhetorical Genre Studies." *Composition Forum*, vol. 31, Spring 2015, http://compositionforum.com/issue/31/multimodality.php.

Grant, David M. "Writing Wakan: The Lakota Pipe as Rhetorical Object." *CCC*, vol. 69, no. 1, Sept. 2017, pp. 61–86.

Gregg, Melissa, and Gregory J. Seigworth. *The Affect Theory Reader*. Duke UP, 2012.

Gries, Laurie. *Still Life with Rhetoric: A New Materialist Approach for Visual Rhetorics*. Utah State UP, 2015.

Haas, Angela M. "Wampum as Hypertext: An American Indian Intellectual Tradition of Multimedia Theory and Practice." *Studies in American Indian Literatures*, vol. 19, No. 4, Winter 2007, pp. 77–100.

Haas, Christina. *Writing Technology: Studies on the Materiality of Literacy.* Lawrence Erlbaum Associates, 1996.

Haas, Christina, and Stephen Witte. "Writing as Embodied Practice: The Case of Engineering Standards." *Journal of Business and Technical Communications,* vol. 15, no. 4, Oct. 2001, pp 413–57.

Hairston, Maxine. "The Winds of Change: Thomas Kuhn and the Revolution in the Teaching of Writing." *CCC,* vol. 33, no. 1, Feb. 1982, pp. 76–88, https://doi.org /10.2307/357846.

Haraway, Donna. "Situated Knowledges: The Science Question in Feminism and the Privilege of Partial Perspective." *Feminist Studies,* vol. 14, no. 3, Autumn 1988, pp. 575–599, https://doi.org/10.2307/3178066.

Harris, Joseph. *A Teaching Subject: Composition Since 1966.* Prentice Hall, 1997.

Hawhee, Debra. *Bodily Arts: Rhetoric and Athletics in Ancient Greece.* University of Texas Press, 2004.

Hawk, Byron. "Reassembling Postprocess: Toward a Posthuman Theory of Public Rhetoric." *Beyond Postprocess,* edited by Sidney I. Dobrin, et al., Utah State UP, 2011, pp. 75–93.

Hayles, N. Katherine. "The Materiality of Informatics." *Configurations,* vol. 1, no. 1, 1993, pp. 147–70.

Heilker, Paul, and Peter Vandenberg, editors. *Keywords in Composition Studies.* Heinemann, 1996.

———. *Keywords in Writing Studies.* University Press of Colorado, 2015.

Honeycutt, Lee. "Review: Writing Technology: Studies on the Materiality of Literacy." *Kairos: A Journal for Teachers of Writing in Webbed Environments,* vol. 1, no. 2, Summer 1996, http://kairos.technorhetoric.net/1.2/binder.html?reviews/haas /haas.html.

hooks, bell. "Remembered Rapture: Dancing with Words." *JAC,* vol. 20, no. 1, 2000, pp. 1–8.

Jacobs, Dale, and Laura R. Micciche, editors. *A Way to Move: Rhetorics of Emotion and Composition Studies.* Boynton/Cook, 2003.

Jacobs, Debra. "Disrupting Understanding: The Critique of Writing as a Process." *JAC,* vol. 21, 2001, pp. 662–74.

Jensen, Kyle. *Reimagining Process: Online Writing Archives and the Future of Writing Studies.* Southern Illinois UP, 2015.

Kafer, Alison. *Feminist, Queer, Crip.* Indiana UP, 2013.

Kent, Thomas. "Paralogic Rhetoric: An Overview." *Rhetoric and Composition as Intellectual Work,* edited by Gary A. Olson, Southern Illinois UP, 2002, pp. 143–52.

———. *Paralogic Rhetoric: A Theory of Communicative Interaction.* Bucknell UP, 1993.

———., editor. *Post-Process Theory: Beyond the Writing Process Paradigm.* Southern Illinois UP, 1999.

———. "Preface: Righting Writing." *Beyond Postprocess,* edited by Sidney I. Dobrin, et al., Utah State UP, 2011, pp. xi–xxii.

———. "Principled Pedagogy: A Reply to Lee-Ann Kastman Breuch." *JAC,* vol. 22, no. 2, Spring 2002, pp. 428–33.

Killingsworth, M. Jimmie. "Reviewed Work: *The Wealth of Reality: An Ecology of Com-position* by Margaret A. Syverson." *CCC*, vol. 52, no. 2, Dec. 2000, pp. 308–11, https://doi.org/10.2307/358506.

Kirsch, Gesa, and Joy Ritchie. "Beyond the Personal: Theorizing a Politics of Location in Composition." *CCC*, vol. 46, no.1, Feb. 1995, pp. 7–29, https://doi.org/10.2307/358867.

Knoblauch, A. Abby. "Bodies of Knowledge: Definitions, Delineations, and Implica-tions of Embodied Writing in the Academy." *Composition Studies*, vol. 40, no. 2, 2012, pp. 50–65.

Kopelson, Karen. "Rhetoric on the Edge of Cunning; Or, the Performance of Neutral-ity (Re)Considered as a Composition Pedagogy for Student Resistance." *CCC*, vol. 55, no.1, Sep. 2003, pp. 115–46.

Kreiser, Chris. "'I'm Not Just Making This Up as I Go Along': Reclaiming Theories of Improvisation for Discussions of College Writing." *Pedagogy*, vol. 14, no. 1, 2014, pp. 81–106.

Lamott, Anne. *Bird by Bird: Some Instructions on Writing and Life.* Anchor Books, 1995.

Leander, Kevin, and Gail Boldt. "Rereading 'A Pedagogy of Multiliteracies: Bodies, Texts, and Emergence.'" *Journal of Literacy Research*, vol. 45, no. 1, 2012, pp. 22–46, https://doi.org/10.1177/1086296X12468587.

LeMesurier, Jennifer Lin. "Mobile Bodies: Triggering Bodily Uptake through Move-ment." *CCC*, vol. 68, no. 2, 2016, pp. 292–316.

Lindquist, Julie. "Class Affects, Classroom Affectations: Working through the Par-adoxes of Strategic Empathy." *College English*, vol. 67, no. 2, Nov. 2004, pp. 187–209, https://doi.org/10.2307/4140717.

Lopate, Phillip. "The Essay, an Exercise in Doubt." *The New York Times Opinionator*, 16 Feb. 2013, https://opinionator.blogs.nytimes.com/author/phillip-lopate/.

Lotier, Kristopher M. "Around 1986: The Externalization of Cognition and the Emer-gence of Postprocess Invention." *CCC*, vol. 67, no. 3, Feb. 2016, pp. 360–84.

Love, Meredith. "Composing Through the Performative Screen: Translating Perfor-mance Studies into Writing Pedagogy." *Composition Studies*, vol. 35, no. 2, Fall 2007, pp. 11–30.

Lu, Min-Zhan. "Writing as Repositioning." *Journal of Education*, vol. 172, no. 1, 1990, pp. 18–21.

Lu, Min-Zhan, and Bruce Horner. "Composing in a Global-Local Context: Careers, Mobility, Skills." *College English*, vol. 72, no. 2, Nov. 2009, pp. 113–33.

Lynch, Paul. *After Pedagogy: The Experience of Teaching.* NCTE, 2013.

Lynch, Paul, and Nathaniel Rivers. *Thinking with Bruno Latour in Rhetoric and Compo-sition.* Southern Illinois UP, 2015.

Macrorie, Ken. *Uptaught.* Boynton/Cook, 1970.

Mandel, Barrett J. "Losing One's Mind: Learning to Write and Edit." *CCC*, vol. 29, no. 4, Dec 1978, pp. 362–68, https://doi.org/10.2307/357021.

Mangen, Anne, and Jean-Luc Velay. "Digital Literacies: Reflections on the Haptics of Writing." *Advances in Haptics*, edited by Mehrdad Hosseini Zadeh. Intech, 2010.

https://www.intechopen.com/books/advances-in-haptics/digitizing-literacy -reflections-on-the-haptics-of-writing.

Marshall, James. "Of What Does Skill in Writing Really Consist? The Political Life of the Writing Process Movement." *Taking Stock: The Writing Process Movement in the 90s*, edited by Lad Tobin and Thomas Newkirk, Boynton/Cook, 1994.

Massumi, Brian. *Parables for the Virtual: Movement, Affect, Sensation.* Duke UP, 2002.

Matsuda, Paul Kei. "Process and Post-Process: A Discursive History." *Journal of Second Language Writing*, vol. 12, 2003, pp. 65–83.

Mauk, Johnathon. "Location, Location, Location: The 'Real' (E)states of Being, Writing, and Thinking in Composition." *College English*, vol. 65, no. 4, Mar. 2003, pp. 368–88.

McCarthy, Lucille Parkinson. "A Stranger in Strange Lands: A College Student Writing across the Curriculum." *Research in the Teaching of English*, vol. 21, no. 3, Oct. 1987, pp. 233–65.

McComiskey, Bruce. "Introduction." *Microhistories of Composition*, edited by Bruce McComiskey, Utah State UP, 2016, pp. 3–38.

———. "The Post-Process Movement in Composition Studies." *Reforming College Composition: Writing the Wrongs*, edited by Ray Wallace, et al., Greenwood Press, 2000, pp. 37–54.

McCurrie, Matthew Kilian. "When Shift Happens: Teaching Adaptive, Reflective, and Confident Writers." *Writers Who Care*, 17 Aug. 2005. https://writerswhocare .wordpress.com/2015/08/17/when-shift-happens-teaching-adaptive-reflective -and-confident-writers/.

McLeod, Susan. "The Affective Domain and the Writing Process: Working Definitions." *Journal of Advanced Composition*, vol. 11, no. 1, 1991, pp. 95–105.

———. "Some Thoughts about Feelings: The Affective Domain and the Writing Process." *CCC*, vol. 38, no. 4, 1987, pp. 426–35, https://doi.org/10.2307/357635.

McNely, Brian. "Taking Things Seriously with Visual Research." *Communication Design Quarterly*, vol. 3, no. 2, Feb. 2015, pp. 48–54.

McNely, Brian J., et al. "Spaces and Surfaces of Invention: A Visual Ethnography of Game Development." *Enculturation: a Journal of Rhetoric, Writing, and Culture*, vol. 15, 2013, http://enculturation.net/visual-ethnography.

Micciche, Laura R. *Acknowledging Writing Partners*. The WAC Clearinghouse and University Press of Colorado, 2017, https://wac.colostate.edu/books/perspectives /micciche/.

———. *Doing Emotion: Rhetoric, Writing, Teaching.* Boynton/Cook, 2007.

———. "Writing Material." *College English*, vol. 76, no. 6, July 2014, pp. 488–505.

Miller, Elisabeth L. "Literate Misfitting: Disability Theory and a Sociomaterial Approach to Literacy." *College English*, vol. 79, no. 1, 2016, pp. 34–56.

Mishler, Eliot. "Meaning in Context: Is There Any Other Kind?" *Harvard Educational Review*, vol. 49, no. 1, Apr. 1979, pp. 1–19.

Nelms, Gerald. "Reassessing Janet Emig's The Composing Processes of Twelfth Graders: A Historical Perspective." *Rhetoric Review*, vol. 13, no. 1, Autumn 1994, pp. 108–30.

North, Steven. *The Making of Knowledge in Composition: Portrait of an Emerging Field.* Boynton, 1987.

Nowacek, Rebecca S. *Agents of Integration: Understanding Transfer as a Rhetorical Act.* NCTE, 2011.

Nystrand, Martin. "Janet Emig, Frank Smith, and the New Discourse about Writing and Reading; Or, How Writing and Reading Came to be Cognitive Processes in 1971." *Towards a Rhetoric of Everyday Life: New Directions in Research on Writing, Text, and Discourse,* edited by Martin Nystrand and John Duffy, U of Wisconsin P, 2003, pp. 121–144.

Odell, Lee. "Beyond the Text: Relations between Writing and Social Context." *Writing in Nonacademic Settings,* edited by Lee Odell and Dixie Goswami, Guilford, 1985, pp. 249–280.

Olson, Gary A., editor. *Rhetoric and Composition as Intellectual Work.* Southern Illinois UP, 2002.

Paden, Frances Freeman. "Theatre Games and the Teaching of English." *The English Journal,* vol. 67, no. 2, Feb. 1978, pp. 46–50.

Pahl, Kate. *Materializing Literacies in Communities: The Uses of Literacy Revisited.* Bloomsbury, 2014.

Paraskevas, Cornelia. "Grammar Apprenticeship." *English Journal,* vol. 95, no. 5, May 2006, pp. 65–70.

Perl, Sondra. "The Composing Processes of Unskilled College Writers." *Research in the Teaching of English,* vol. 13, no. 4, 1979, pp. 317–336.

———. *Felt Sense: Writing with the Body.* Boynton/Cook, 2004.

———. "Research as a Recursive Process: Reconsidering 'The Composing Processes of Unskilled College Writers' 35 Years Later." *Composition Forum,* vol. 29, Spring 2014. http://compositionforum.com/issue/29/perl-retrospective.php.

———. "Understanding Composing." *CCC,* vol. 31, no. 4, Dec. 1980, pp. 363–69, https://doi.org/10.2307/356586.

———. "Watson Conference Oral History #2: Process Theory and the Shape of Composition Studies, October 1996." *History, Reflection, and Narrative: The Professionalization of Composition, 1963–1983,* edited by Mary Rosner, et al., Ablex, 1999, pp. 129–39.

———. "Writing Processes: A Shining Moment." *Landmark Essays on Writing Process,* edited by Sondra Perl, Hermagoras Press, 1994, pp. xi-xx.

Petraglia, Joseph. "Is there Life After Process? The Role of Social Scientism in a Changing Discipline." *Post-Process Theory: Beyond the Writing-Process Paradigm,* edited by Thomas Kent, Southern Illinois UP, 1999, 49–64.

———, editor. *Reconceiving Writing, Rethinking Writing Instruction.* Routledge, 1995.

Pigg, Stacey. "Emplacing Mobile Composing Habits: A Study of Academic Writing in Networked Social Spaces." *CCC,* vol. 66, no. 2, Dec. 2014, pp. 250–75.

Powell, Malea. "2012 CCCC Chair's Address: Stories Take Place: A Performance in One Act." *CCC,* vol. 64, no. 2, Dec. 2012, pp. 383–406.

Price, Margaret. *Mad at School: Rhetorics of Mental Disability and Academic Life.* University of Michigan Press, 2011.

Prior, Paul A. "Tracing Process: How Texts Come into Being." *What Writing Does and How It Does It: An Introduction to Analyzing Texts and Textual Practices*, edited by Charles Bazerman and Paul Prior, Lawrence Erlbaum, 2003, pp. 167–200.

———. *Writing/Disciplinarity: A Sociohistoric Account of Literate Activity in the Academy*. Lawrence Erlbaum, 1998.

Prior, Paul and Jody Shipka. "Chronotopic Lamination: Tracing the Contours of Literate Activity." *Writing Selves/Writing Societies*, edited by Charles Bazerman and David Russell, 2003, https://wac.colostate.edu/docs/books/selves_societies/prior /prior.pdf.

"Professional Knowledge for the Teaching of Writing." National Council of Teachers of English, Feb. 28, 2016, http://www2.ncte.org/statement/teaching-writing/.

Purcell-Gates, Victoria, et al. *Print Literacy Development: Uniting Cognitive and Social Practice Theories*. Harvard UP, 2006.

Reither, James A. "Writing and Knowing: Toward Redefining the Writing Process." *College English*, vol. 47, no. 6, Oct. 1985, pp. 620–28, https://doi.org/10.2307/377164.

Reyes, Maria de la Luz. "Challenging Venerable Assumptions: Literacy Instruction for Linguistically Different Students." *Harvard Educational Review*, vol. 62, no. 4, Winter 1992, pp. 427–46.

Reynolds, Nedra. "Ethos as Location: New Sites for Understanding Discursive Authority." *Rhetoric Review*, vol. 11, no. 2, Spring, 1993, pp. 325–38, https://doi.org/10 .1080/07350199309389009.

———. *Geographies of Writing: Inhabiting Places and Encountering Difference*. Southern Illinois UP, 2007.

Richmond, Kia Jane. "Repositioning Emotions in Composition Studies." *Composition Studies*, vol. 30, no. 1, 2002, pp. 67–82.

Rickert, Thomas. *Ambient Rhetoric: The Attunements of Rhetorical Being*. U of Pittsburgh P, 2013.

———. "'Hands Up, You're Free': Composition in a Post-Oedipal World." *JAC*, vol. 21, 2001, pp. 287–316, https://www.jstor.org/stable/20866406.

Rifenburg, J. Michael. *The Embodied Playbook: Writing Practices of Student-Athletes*. Utah State UP, 2018.

Roozen, Kevin. "Tracing Trajectories of Practice: Repurposing in one Student's Developing Disciplinary Writing Processes." *Written Communication* vol. 27, no. 3, 2010 pp. 318–354.

Rosenberger, Robert. "Siri, Take This Down: Will Voice Control Shape Our Writing?" *The Atlantic*, 01 Aug. 2002, https://www.theatlantic.com/technology /archive/2012/08/siri-take-this-down-will-voice-control-shape-our-writing/259624/.

Royster, Jacqueline Jones. "When the First Voice you Hear is not your Own." *CCC*, vol. 47, no. 1, Feb. 1996, pp. 29–40, https://doi.org/10.2307/358272.

Rule, Hannah J. "Writing's Rooms." *CCC*, vol. 69, no. 3, Feb. 2018, pp. 402–32.

Russell, David. "Activity Theory and its Implications for Writing Instruction." *Reconceiving Writing, Rethinking Writing Instruction*, edited by Joseph Petraglia, Routledge, 1995, pp. 51–78.

Samuels, Ellen. "Six Ways of Looking at Crip Time." *Disability Studies Quarterly,* vol. 37, no. 3, 2017, http://dsq-sds.org/article/view/5824/4684.

Sawyer, R. Keith. *Creating Conversations: Improvisation in Everyday Discourse.* Hampton Press, 2001.

———, editor. *Structure and Improvisation in Creative Teaching.* Cambridge UP, 2011.

Schell, Eileen. "Material Feminism and Composition Studies." *Fractured Feminisms: Rhetoric, Context, Contestation,* edited by Laura Gray-Rosendale and Gil Harootunian, SUNY P, 2003, pp. 31–43, http://www.sunypress.edu/pdf/60787.pdf.

Schreiner, Steven. "A Portrait of the Student as a Young Writer: Re-Evaluating Emig and the Process Movement." *CCC,* vol. 48, no. 1, Feb. 1997, pp. 86–104, https://doi.org/10.2307/358772.

Selzer, Jack. "Exploring Options in Composing." *CCC,* vol. 35, no. 3, Oct. 1984, pp. 276–84.

Selzer, Jack, and Sharon Crowley, editors. *Rhetorical Bodies.* University of Wisconsin Press, 1999.

Shipka, Jody. *Toward a Composition Made Whole.* U of Pittsburg P, 2011.

Shivers-McNair, Ann. "3D Interviewing with Researcher POV Videos: Bodies and Knowledge in the Making." PraxisWiki, *Kairos: Rhetoric, Technology, and Pedagogy,* vol. 21, no. 2, Spring 2017, http://praxis.technorhetoric.net/tiki-index.php?page=PraxisWiki%3A_%3A3D+Interviewing.

Siebers, Tobin. *Disability Theory.* University of Michigan Press, 2008.

Sirc, Geoffrey. "The Salon of 2010." *Beyond Postprocess,* edited by Sidney I. Dobrin et al., Utah State UP, 2011, pp. 195–18.

Smit, David. *The End of Composition Studies.* Southern Illinois UP, 2007.

Spolin, Viola. *Improvisation for the Theatre,* 3rd edition. Northwestern UP, 1999.

Stenberg, Sheri J. "Embodied Classrooms, Embodied Knowledges: Re-Thinking the Mind-Body Split." *Composition Studies,* vol. 30, no. 2, Fall 2002, pp. 43–60.

Stewart, Kathleen. "Atmospheric Attunements." *Environment and Planning D: Society and Space,* vol. 29, 2011, pp. 445–53.

"Students' Right to their Own Language." Committee on CCCC Language Statement. *College English,* vol. 36, no. 6, Feb. 1975, pp. 709–26.

Syverson, Margaret. *The Wealth of Reality: An Ecology of Composition.* Southern Illinois UP, 1999.

Takayoshi, Pamela. "Short-form Writing: Studying Process in the Context of Contemporary Composing Technologies." *Computers and Composition,* vol. 37, 2015, pp. 1–13.

———. "Writing in Social Worlds: An Argument for Researching Composing Processes." *College Composition and Communication,* vol. 69, no. 4, June 2018, pp. 550–80.

Talhelm, Melissa. "Second City Teacher Training: Applying Improvisational Theatre Techniques to the Classroom." *English Journal,* vol. 104, no. 5, 2015, pp. 15–20.

Thompson, Clive. "The Joy of Typing." *Medium,* 20 June 2014, https://medium.com/message/the-joy-of-typing-fd8d091ab8ef.

Tobin, Lad. "How the Writing Process was Born—And Other Conversion Narratives." *Taking Stock: The Writing Process Movement in the 90s*, edited by Lad Tobin and Thomas Newkirk, Boynton/Cook, 1994, pp.1–16.

Tobin, Lad and Thomas Newkirk, eds. *Taking Stock: The Writing Process Movement in the 90s*. Boynton/Cook, 1994.

Trimbur, John. "Changing the Question: Should Writing Be Studied?" *Composition Studies*, vol. 31, no.1, 2003, pp. 15–24.

———. "Delivering the Message: Typography and the Materiality of Writing." *Rhetoric and Composition as Intellectual Work*, edited by Gary A. Olson. Southern Illinois UP, 2002, pp. 188–202.

———. "Taking the Social Turn: Teaching Writing Post-Process." *College Composition and Communication*, vol. 45, no. 1, Feb. 1994, pp. 108–18.

Tung. "Reviewed Work(s)." *Film Quarterly*, vol. 17, no. 2, 1963–64, pp. 58–59.

Vandenberg, Peter, et al. *Relations, Locations, Positions: Composition Theory for Writing Teachers*. Urbana Free Library, 2006.

Van Ittersum, Derek, and Kory Lawson Ching. "Composing Text/Shaping Process: How Digital Environments Mediate Writing Activity." *Computers and Composition Online*, Fall 2013, http://www2.bgsu.edu/departments/english/cconline/composing_text/webtext/.

Van Ittersum, Derek, and Kim Hensley Owens. "Computing Injuries and the Role of the Body in Writing Activity." *Computers and Composition*, vol. 30, no. 2, 2013, pp. 87–100.

Vieira, Kate. *America by Paper: How Documents Matter in Immigrant Literacy*. University of Minnesota Press, 2016.

———. "Writing Remittances: Migration-Driven Literacy Learning in a Brazilian Homeland." *Research in the Teaching of English*, vol. 50, no. 4, 2016, pp. 442–49.

Villanueva, Victor. *Bootstraps: From an American Academic of Color*. NCTE, 1993.

Villanueva, Victor and Kristin L. Arola, eds. *Cross-Talk in Comp Theory: A Reader*. NCTE, 2011.

Vitanza, Victor J. "Three Countertheses: Critical In(ter)vention into Composition Theories and Pedagogies." *Contending with Words: Composition and Rhetoric in a Postmodern Age*, edited by Patricia Harkin and John Schlib, MLA, 1991, pp. 139–72.

Voss, Ralph F. "Janet Emig's The Composing Processes of Twelfth Graders: A Reassessment." *CCC*, vol. 34, no. 3, Oct. 1983, pp. 278–283.

Walker, Clay. "Composing Agency: Theorizing the Readiness Potentials of Literacy Practices." *Literacy in Composition Studies*, vol. 3, no. 2, 2015, http://licsjournal.org/OJS/index.php/LiCS/article/view/80/110.

Wallace, David L. *Compelled to Write: Alternative Rhetoric in Theory and Practice*. Utah State UP, 2011.

Wampole, Christy. "The Essayification of Everything." *New York Times Opinionator*, 26 May 2003, https://opinionator.blogs.nytimes.com/2013/05/26/the-essayification-of-everything/.

Wardle, Elizabeth. "Creative Repurposing for Expansive Learning: Considering 'Problem-Exploring' and 'Answer-Getting' Dispositions in Individuals and Fields."

Composition Forum, no. 26, 2012, http://compositionforum.com/issue/26/creative
-repurposing.php.

Warnock, John. "The Writing Process." *Rhetoric Review*, vol. 2, no. 1, Sept. 1983, pp. 4–27.

Weiss, Gail. *Body Images: Embodiment as Intercorporeality*. Routledge, 1999.

Wenger, Christy I. *Yoga Minds, Writing Bodies: Contemplative Writing Pedagogy*. WAC Clearinghouse and Parlor Press, 2015, https://wac.colostate.edu/books/perspectives/wenger/.

Whicker, John H. "Narratives, Metaphors, and Power-Moves: The History, Meanings, and Implications of 'Post-Process.'" *JAC*, vol. 31, no. 3–4, 2011, pp. 497–531.

Williams, Amy D. "Beyond Pedagogy: Theorizing without Teachers." *Composition Forum*, vol. 30, Fall 2014, http://compositionforum.com/issue/30/beyond
-pedagogy.php.

Wilson, James C., and Cynthia Lewiecki-Wilson, editors. *Embodied Rhetorics: Disability and Language in Culture*. Southern Illinois UP, 2001.

Wood, Tara. "Cripping Time in the College Composition Classroom." *CCC*, vol. 69, no. 2, Dec. 2017, pp. 260–86.

Worsham, Lynn. "Coming to Terms: Theory, Writing, Politics." *Rhetoric and Composition as Intellectual Work*, edited by Gary A. Olson, Southern Illinois UP, 2002, pp. 101–14.

"WPA Outcomes Statement for First-Year Composition 3.0." CWPA, July 17, 2014, http://wpacouncil.org/positions/outcomes.html.

Wyche, Susan. "Times, Tools, and Talismans." *Essays on Writing*, edited by Lizbeth A. Bryant and Heather M. Clark, Pearson, 2009, pp. 52–64.

Wysocki, Anne. "Introduction: Into Between—on Composition in Mediation." *Composing (Media) = Composing (Embodiment): Bodies, Technologies, Writing, The Teaching of Writing*, edited by Kristin L. Arola and Anne Wysocki, Utah State UP, 2012, pp. 110–26.

Yagelski, Robert P. *Writing as a Way of Being: Writing Instruction, Nonduality, and the Crisis of Sustainability*. Hampton Press, 2011.

Yancey, Kathleen Blake, et al. *Writing across Contexts: Transfer, Composition, and Sites of Writing*. Utah State UP, 2014.